MOSCOW CONVERSATIONS

MOSCOW CONVERSATIONS

by

SUSAN JACOBY

COWARD, McCANN & GEOGHEGAN, INC.

New York

First American Edition 1972

SBN: 698-10459-5
Library of Congress Catalog Card Number: 72-76675

PRINTED IN THE UNITED STATES OF AMERICA

11-28-72

FOR TONY
and all those who
stubbornly hang onto their inner freedom

Contents

MOSCOW CONVERSATIONS

To live life to the end is not a childish task.
                                    —Boris Pasternak
Fear and Muse stand watch by turn. . . .
                                    —Anna Akhmatova

Ghettos and Guards

MOSCOW IS ONE of the easiest places in the world for a journalist to become dishonest with himself and his readers. I arrived in the Soviet Union with the hope that I would come to know some Russians well enough to write about them in depth—their daily lives, personal dreams and fears, their view of the world and of their own country's past, present and future. My hope was neither entirely fulfilled nor entirely frustrated; Russia opens just enough doors to leave an outsider fascinated by what he has seen and angered by what has eluded him. Persistence and the ability to speak Russian did enable me to develop meaningful friendships with some Russians, but the inhibitions that govern all contact between foreigners and Soviet citizens prevented me from knowing my friends as well as I would have liked. The same constraints effectively ruled out sustained relationships with "common" people; foreigners in Moscow know only uncommon Russians.

Dishonesty becomes a part of journalism in Moscow when correspondents fail to tell their readers about these inhibitions and the profound effect they have on a reporter's perceptions of Russian life. The reluctance of the Moscow press corps to write about its working conditions is less a conspiracy of silence than a product of frustrated resignation; an abnormal situation begins to seem quite normal after only a few months of life in Russia. Moscow correspondents are not, of course, immune to the general vice of reluctance to admit that one's knowledge is anything less than complete. They are also bound by the hoary cliché, handed down by generations of city editors to generations of young reporters: "Never tell your readers how tough it was to get the story, kid." While such an admonition may be appropriate to coverage of fires or robberies, it is out of place in complicated situations where "getting the story" is a vital part of the story itself. A Moscow correspondent deceives his readers if he fails to tell them how difficult it is to acquire any real understanding of Russia and Russians; editors in home offices contribute to the deception by demanding impossible "man-in-the-street" reactions to events such as the death of former Premier Nikita Khrushchev. You cannot stand on a busy corner in Moscow and expect ordinary Russians to bubble over with opinions about a politically sensitive matter. On more than one of these occasions, the "Russian reaction" reported in American and British publications was handily supplied by a correspondent's ten-minute chat with his official Soviet translator.

Nearly all foreigners classified as "permanent residents" in Moscow—diplomats, journalists and a few businessmen—are required to live in ghettos of apartment buildings guarded by uniformed police who actually work for the KGB. The KGB carries out tasks that in the United States are the responsibility of both the Central Intelligence Agency and the Federal Bureau of Investigation. Its mandate to deal with alleged threats to internal security is broader than that of the FBI; one of its tasks is keeping close track of contacts between Soviet citizens and foreigners.

Several guard posts are located at the entrance to each foreign ghetto, its apartment buildings usually separated by a wire fence from any nearby buildings occupied by Russians.*

A few Soviet citizens, including maids, chauffeurs, translators and Russian-language teachers, are in effect "licensed" to

---

* I use the term "ghetto" in a figurative sense, although the reality is probably closer to the original meaning of the word. Residence in special apartment compounds is a requirement, not an option, for nearly all foreigners. There is no distinction by nationality; representatives from the Communist countries of Eastern Europe live in the same compounds with Americans and Western Europeans.

deal with foreigners. They must be hired through a special government agency that supplies such services to foreign residents of Moscow. Their faces are known to the guards and they are never bothered. Other Russians who attempt to enter the compound are stopped and usually ordered to produce identification.

Russians who are not carrying formal printed invitations from their foreign hosts are sometimes prevented from entering even after they have produced identification. One of our Russian acquaintances was taken to a police station and interrogated for three hours after he tried to enter the compound to have dinner with a friend. No pretext is needed for this type of harassment; the secret police look with suspicion upon any unofficial contact between a Russian and a citizen of another country.

Some foreigners evaded the system by picking up Soviet friends in their cars and driving past the guard posts to the doors of their apartment buildings. The guards seldom stop a Russian in the presence of his foreign host, in keeping with the official pretense that the purpose of the policemen is to prevent crime in the foreign compounds.

When one correspondent complained after a television set was stolen from his apartment, the guard bluntly replied, "Robberies aren't my job."

The ghettos and guards act as a powerful deterrent to Russians who might otherwise like to get to know people from other countries. Few Russians are willing to visit a foreigner's home; those who do are generally political dissenters already known to the KGB or, at the other end of the spectrum, officials whose contacts with the foreign community are an acknowledged part of their jobs. An ordinary citizen who does not want trouble with the authorities has a great deal to lose by trying to visit a friend in a foreign compound. When a Russian shows the required identification at the guard post, he assumes with good reason that the KGB will open a file on him, if one does not already exist. "The information might never be used against you," said an engineer. "But then again, it might. If you wanted to take a trip to the West, for example, it could really work against you to have the KGB know you had seen foreigners in Moscow. You never know, once you have attracted attention to yourself."

Russians also assume that all foreigners' telephones are tapped. They usually call foreign friends from public phones to avoid having their identity traced through a home phone. I do not know if every foreigner's phone was tapped, but I am certain ours was. The Soviet security apparatus does not, fortunately, have either the manpower or efficiency to follow every foreigner to every meeting with a Russian friend. On several occasions, however, my husband and I were conspicuously followed after Russians had phoned and made appointments to meet us. Sometimes the KGB agents would show up at the appointed meeting place instead of bothering to follow us all the way from the compound. The connection between the phone calls and our followers was obvious; they could not have learned about our meetings through any other channel.

Visitors to Moscow usually think resident foreigners are paranoid when they talk about bugged rooms, tapped phones and "tails." The visitors are half right; foreigners who live in Moscow are suspicion-prone, but the suspicion stems from real rather than imaginary causes.

On one occasion, I was unable to dial any numbers from our home phone for several hours. The line was alternately dead and filled with loud static. Picking up the receiver for the tenth time, I was astonished to hear a faint but distinct recording of a conversation with a Danish friend earlier in the day. She had, I recall, asked to borrow my maid. Such stories are handed down through generations of foreigners in Moscow, but I had always been inclined to believe they were apocryphal. A Russian friend summed up the situation: "So I'm paranoid and you're paranoid too. But since we are actually being persecuted, what else can we be?"

Russians outside of Moscow tend to be less fearful of contact with foreigners, possibly because they are not faced with the daily sight of special compounds with police guard posts. Soviet citizens tend to talk more freely to outsiders who are "just passing through"; an evening in a restaurant or a conversation on a train with someone you never expect to see again offers considerably less risk than continuing involvement with a foreign friend.

Anti-Russian feeling among some of the Soviet Union's national minority groups also loosens tongues in regions distant from Moscow. In the Estonian capital of Tallinn, we spent several hours in a bar with workers from a nearby collective farm who were only too happy to give us their opinions about why the Estonian economy was more productive than the Russian one.* Before the workers would talk freely, we had to prove we were Americans in good standing. They had been suspicious because we spoke Russian. "What kind of American is it who speaks Russian?" one asked. The same man came to see us off at the airport the next morning with a rose for me and a bottle of the local liqueur for Tony. Accustomed to the furtiveness of meetings in Russian cities, we were stunned by his open-hearted gesture.

Foreign correspondents do not travel as much as they would like to, partly because editors at home demand a steady flow of political news from the capital and partly because each trip involves endless bureaucratic snags. A correspondent must obtain special permission from the press department of the Soviet Foreign Ministry if he wishes to travel outside a twenty-five mile radius of Moscow and even for some points inside the circle. (A portion of Peredelkino, the site of Boris Pasternak's grave, is theoretically off limits to foreigners, but the rule is

---

* Estonia is one of the fifteen republics that make up the Soviet Union. The Russian Federation is the largest and most populous republic and, of course, has the highest percentage of Russians. Estonia has the highest per capita income in the Soviet Union; statistics also show its farms lead the nation in productivity.

regularly evaded by those who are enterprising enough to take an ordinary train instead of driving out in cars with foreigners' license plates. Pasternak's grave itself is not in the prohibited zone, but the main road to Peredelkino is.)

Permission to travel is sometimes granted routinely and sometimes refused if a correspondent's writing has displeased the authorities. Officials in the press department are far less apt to help correspondents travel by themselves than they are to promote large, official group tours. Although conversations on trips can provide valuable insights into certain aspects of Soviet life, they are no substitute for sustained contacts developed over months or years. Moscow, a journalist's home base in the Soviet Union, offers the only opportunity for continuing relationships with Russians.

There are basically five types of Russians who regularly associate with Moscow's foreign residents. The first and least important group consists of those whose jobs give them what amounts to official permission to deal with foreigners. This group not only includes maids and translators employed in foreign homes and offices but officials in the Foreign Ministry and related agencies who spin the complex web of bureaucratic regulations governing foreigners' lives. High-level Soviet journalists, especially those who specialize in international affairs, also fall into this category. "Official Russians," as they are referred to by the foreign community in Moscow, seldom provide genuine information about Soviet life. They speak guardedly and rarely venture even the mildest criticism of their society; the "license" does not permit relationships that go beyond narrowly defined contacts. Some official Russians gather information for the KGB; I particularly recall one writer for the Novosti Press Agency* who was always asking us questions transparently designed to identify the political

---

* Novosti prints foreign-language books intended basically for foreign consumption and performs a variety of tasks that have nothing to do with publishing. It is generally believed to be controlled and used for special purposes by the KGB.

dissenters we knew. At one lunch, he told us we were certainly wrong to think that the purpose of the guard posts was to keep Russians out of the foreign compounds. "I walked in with no trouble at all," he said soberly, as though we were all unaware of the special nature of his identification.

The second group encompasses a wide range of intellectuals basically loyal to the regime but "liberal" by Soviet standards. They all have a deep love of their country and some are committed Communists; at the same time, they see the need for change. They may be poets or painters, professors or scientists. They generally favor more freedom of expression in the arts, less repression of political dissent and an easing of dogmatism in all Soviet institutions. They try not to run too far afoul of the authorities who control their jobs, but their liberal tendencies sometimes get them into trouble anyway.

The intellectuals are interested in foreign contacts and ideas but sometimes avoid seeing Western friends when they feel it might create problems with the authorities. A well-known figure in the Soviet ballet world who was scheduled to go abroad on an official assignment once arranged to take English lessons from me. Our first lesson was abruptly canceled after the much publicized defection in London of Natalya Makarova, former prima ballerina of Leningrad's Kirov Ballet. A message conveyed through a friend informed me that the dancer had received a quasi-official warning: Anyone connected with the ballet who hoped to go abroad should avoid meeting foreigners in Moscow at such a "delicate" time. (The engineer had not, after all, been paranoid. The irony of denying foreign travel to people who have foreign friends is apparently lost on Soviet officialdom.)

Young people, mainly students, make up another group. They tend to be somewhat more open to foreign influences than their elders, although they often seem more interested in Western consumer goods than Western ideas. I was frequently approached by students because I looked young myself; most of the initial contacts never developed into friendships after

they learned I was a journalist and the wife of a correspondent. I always felt compelled to identify myself fully after an
initial meeting with a Russian, although I probably would
have kept some Russian acquaintances longer had I pretended
to be a casual tourist or even an exchange student. A young
visiting scholar with many Russian friends met my husband at
a dinner party and later asked her friends if they would like to
meet "an interesting American journalist." All the Russians responded negatively and one said with some regret, "We can
always explain our friendship with you by saying that you are
of our profession and we have scholarly interests in common.
We could not explain knowing a journalist so easily and we
know that journalists here are regularly followed by the KGB."

A fourth group consists of artists who paint in ways that are
frowned on by the Soviet authorities, usually because the re-
sults are too abstract. Since they refuse to follow the approved
line of "Socialist realism" in art, they are not allowed to exhibit
their work or sell through official channels. They are free to
paint privately, usually in miserably cramped apartments that
also serve as their living quarters, and sell to anyone who will
buy. Most of their customers are foreigners, plus a handful of
Russians—mainly scientists who seek a link between artistic and
scientific freedom. Relationships between foreigners and unofficial artists are usually based strictly on cold cash, but occasionally deals are replaced by genuine friendships.

Political dissidents make up the fifth and most unusual
group. The dissenters are a small, diverse collection of people
who disagree strongly on long-range goals for Russia; their
main area of agreement is their determination to make the
Soviet authorities observe their own laws. Their chief activity
is publicizing official actions against other dissenters; they
view the publicity as an important guarantee that no one will
quietly disappear into prison or exile, as in the Stalin years.
The dissenters naturally need foreign journalists to transmit
news of their activities to the outside world. Stories about Soviet political dissent published in foreign newspapers ensure

that many Russians also hear the news. The Voice of America and the British Broadcasting Corporation, which have large Russian audiences despite jamming, regularly broadcast facts about dissent that have reached the West through newspaper dispatches.

Some journalists are happy to consider dissidents friends as well as news sources; relationships with dissenters involve somewhat less strain and pretense than relationships with other Russians. The skepticism about absolute truth that is characteristic of most truly educated minds in the West is completely foreign to the majority of Russians; only with a few of the dissidents did I find a common approach to intellectual questions that had nothing to do with politics.

Khrushchev abolished formal censorship of correspondents' outgoing news dispatches in 1961. Foreign journalists are now free to transmit their articles by telephone, Telex or cable without prior approval of a Soviet official. The authorities now attempt to censor news dispatches indirectly, through post-publication warnings, KGB harassment and the ultimate sanction of expulsion from the country. Officials in the press department and in Soviet embassies throughout the world read articles that appear in newspapers and magazines with Moscow correspondents. If an article is both highly important and abrasive, a correspondent may receive an official warning from the press department in Moscow within two or three days of publication.

Soviet officials are clearly furious about being unable to prevent contacts between foreign correspondents and political dissidents. The press department has established a pattern of harassing and trying to get rid of correspondents who see dissidents frequently. Four foreign journalists were expelled from the Soviet Union during 1970; three of them had been particularly active in gathering news about political dissent and relaying it to other correspondents. Because it is difficult to arrange meetings and also because only the most urgent news is relayed over tapped phone lines, it is impractical for every correspondent to track down each piece of dissident news himself. One or two correspondents usually meet with a dissenter and pass the news on to the rest of the Moscow press corps. Unfortunately, many spineless Moscow correspondents are only too happy to acquire news of political dissent from their colleagues but are unwilling to incur official displeasure by meeting dissidents themselves. Such journalists disgrace their profession. Still more disgraceful is the behavior of some editors who are so afraid of losing their Moscow bureaus that they encourage correspondents to play by the rules the Soviets would like to lay down. Two conscientious journalists, one English and one American, were deeply depressed for months because they had been told, in effect, by their home offices: "We will consider it your own fault if you get expelled from Moscow and will have no sympathy for you."

During our two years in Moscow, the authorities intensified pressure against correspondents who wrote about dissent within the Soviet Union and about Jews who wanted to emigrate to Israel. As 1970 drew to a close, new journalists arriving in Moscow were given specific warnings by the press department not to associate with political dissidents like Pyotr Yakir, son of a well-known army commander who was executed in Stalin's purge of the military in 1937. The press department had previously contented itself with warning journalists against seeing "doubtful persons"; actual naming of names was regarded by Moscow correspondents as more direct intimidation.

In February and March, 1971, the KGB used thugs to make even more direct attempts at intimidation. An Associated Press correspondent's glasses were smashed and a beating was administered to Volodya Bukovsky, an important figure in the Moscow dissident community, when they tried to meet at a corner of one of the city's widest and most modern streets. (Arrested in April, 1971, Bukovsky was sentenced last January to seven years' imprisonment, followed by five years of exile and compulsory labor. He was charged under Article 70, a severe statute dealing with anti-Soviet activities. At least two correspondents were interrogated by the KGB in connection with Bukovsky's case.) Even more disconcerting were attempts to frighten correspondents out of seeing dissidents by serving notice that *all* meetings with Russians were under surveillance. At 7 P.M. in Pushkin Square, one of Moscow's busiest plazas, my husband had arranged (by telephone) to pick up a Russian friend and bring him back to our house for dinner. The friend was neither a political dissident nor a Jew who wanted to emigrate; he was simply a gentle and literate man with whom we would have shared many tastes in any country. As the Russian stepped forward to shake my husband's hand, five thugs surrounded them. Three grabbed my husband by the lapels and forced him back into his car, kicking out the right taillight for good measure. Our Russian friend was hauled away by the two other goons. My husband protested to the Foreign Ministry and received an answer in the form of an official reprimand from the number-two man in the press department. The spokesman expressed his department's outrage that my husband had implied the incident took place with official connivance.* All of the hoodlums had received their just punishment, the official said—including our friend. He then read off a statement allegedly signed by our Russian acquaintance to the effect that Tony should leave the Soviet Union. We never learned whether he really had signed the statement or, if he had, what pressures forced him to do it. He was sufficiently frightened so that we could not see him again.

In view of the abnormal circumstances surrounding the lives of resident foreigners in Moscow, it is not surprising that Russians who regularly associate with them cannot by any stretch of the imagination be classified as average citizens.

It can fairly be said that a journalist in Moscow is no more

* Despite this, private conversations between correspondents and some officials conveyed the impression that the press department was embarrassed by the rough KGB tactics. The press department and the KGB do not always work hand-in-hand in their treatment of foreign correspondents. After about two months, the physical harassment on the streets was discontinued. The KGB then shifted to dealing with the Russians when the correspondents were out of sight.

isolated from ordinary citizens who drive trucks, work in factories or shuffle papers than a foreign journalist in Washington. The difference is that a Washington correspondent can easily break the isolation if he chooses, especially if he is researching a story. A Moscow journalist has little opportunity to supplement his limited set of personal social contacts with the reporting that is ordinarily an important part of his profession. He cannot set foot inside a Soviet factory, school or any other institution without approval from the Foreign Ministry. Innocuous requests for visits are often shelved indefinitely by the press department—not always out of malice but because the complicated system of permissions makes it impossible for the bureaucrats to cope with every demand. One correspondent spent six months trying to obtain approval to visit a school and finally gave up in disgust.

Thus, a limited number of intellectuals in Moscow account for a disproportionate share of a journalist's information about the Soviet Union. Occasionally a foreigner makes contact by sheer accident with someone who does not fall into the usual categories. A pet gets sick and his owner makes friends with a veterinarian at the local clinic. A *babushka* (literally "grandmother," but the generic Russian term for "old woman") pours out her life story on a park bench. A steamstress who mends a ripped dress turns out to have relatives in the United States. A few of our most valued friends were acquired through such happy accidents.

"There is no such thing as a normal relationship between a Russian and a foreigner," one veteran correspondent told us shortly after we arrived in Moscow. Relationships between the two are fraught with mutual suspicion. A few of the Russians who are most accessible to foreigners—like some Novosti correspondents—unquestionably work for the KGB. Their existence leads foreigners to suspect many Russians, especially if they do not seem to be fearful. Suspicion even falls on dissidents, who are constantly followed and hounded by the secret police.

I eventually came to believe that suspicions about the dissenters were mostly unfounded. Nevertheless, the relationship between the KGB and some dissidents was not unlike the bond created between a jailer and his prisoners. In many little dramas involving dissidents and the KGB, the foreign audience was unequipped to tell the villain from the hero. A dissident would come in one door while a KGB operative went out the other—or perhaps the KGB man just came in and it was the dissident who just left? Americans, with a chronic innocence about the slimier manifestations of police power, were less able to deal with this quality of Moscow life than Europeans. Among Americans, there was a tendency either to laugh everything off because of its resemblance to a bad spy novel or to reject all meaningful contacts with Russians. "I don't understand how you can call any Russian a friend," one high-ranking American diplomat said to me. My reply was simply that I saw no purpose in spending two years in Moscow if I proposed to suspend all human and professional judgments for the duration.

There is another more common source of distortions in relations between Russians and the foreign community. A number of Russians who associate with foreigners are *kombinatori* (operators) whose only desire is to milk capitalist goodies out of their Western "friends." They understand and take advantage of the frustration—sometimes approaching desperation—of foreigners who find themselves unable to meet Russians. They play on it to acquire foreign products that cannot ordinarily be purchased in the Soviet Union.

The most frequent request is for foreign-currency coupons, which can be used in special hard-currency stores to buy imported and Russian goods that are not available in ordinary shops. The more seasoned operators also ask their "friends" to purchase a wide variety of objects for them in the West—clothes, records, books, radios. The bargain is understood: The Russian gets what he wants and the foreigner gets the satisfaction, for whatever it is worth, of contact with a Soviet citizen.

The relationship is often nothing more than that of a prostitute and a client, although one can legitimately ask who plays which role. Such Russians are privately contemptuous of foreigners who play their game; more than one of us had the painful experience of saying no to a request for the first time and being completely dropped by the so-called Soviet friend. Many foreigners never say no and continue to buy their Russian acquaintances, feeling anything is better than complete isolation. Such mercenary contacts can sadly distort an outsider's impressions of Soviet citizens.

Russians, on the other hand, often feel that foreigners regard them as zoological specimens rather than friends. Reporters in Moscow are never off duty; they tend to view relationships with Russians more as a part of their work than as a part of their normal social life. Russians realize they are grist for stories and sometimes suspect their foreign friends would not be so anxious to see them if Moscow offered more natural opportunities for strangers to bridge the culture gap. For the most part, foreigners in Moscow are not able to choose their Soviet friends as they would in another country but accept gratefully any opportunities for contact that arise.

Despite difficulties that at times seemed overwhelming, I never gave up the idea that a journalist's most important task in Moscow should be to establish communication with as many Russians as possible. As a free-lance writer not tied down by breaking political news, I devoted most of my time to placing myself in situations where it was possible to meet Russians and to cultivate friendships with those who showed a genuine interest in me. I arrived with the inadequate linguistic preparation of one year of college Russian; by the end of our first year, I was able to speak the language easily with an accent friends told me was more Polish than American.

With one exception, the people described in this book were true friends. I believe they would have been my friends anywhere else in the world. My husband and I met most of our Russian friends during our first nine months in Moscow, and we saw them regularly throughout the remainder of our two-year assignment. Henry Kamm, a former Moscow correspondent for the New York *Times*, described his feelings about his Russian friends in words that moved me only slightly when I first read them but later touched a deep, understanding chord:

They were intelligent men and women of various arts and professions, some young, some not so. I loved them not only because they dared to walk past the policemen posted at the entrance to the foreigners' ghetto where I was required to live, but also because they were all that made my two years in the Soviet Union bearable.

I also loved some of the Russians we knew who were not brave enough to walk past the guard but who were brave enough to invite us to their homes. I cannot say I respected them as much as our more courageous friends, but I came to feel compassion for intelligent Russians who compromised with their system of government either out of fear, ambition or a love of country that transcended politics. To protect them from their own fears as well as the real danger of official reprisals, I have changed most of the names in this book.

My friends were a diverse group, ranging from outspoken dissenters to committed Communists. They were all individuals who stood out from the mass of Russians who would never have opened their minds or their homes to a foreigner. They spoke for no one but themselves, but that meant a great deal in a society where individual voices were seldom raised. I owe these extraordinary men and women everything I learned during my stay in their country.

II
Galina

My aunt, whom I loved very much, was born many years before the revolution in a small village not far from Moscow. She never went to school; she knew nothing but hardship throughout her life. When she was fifteen, her father gave her away in marriage for the price of a cow and a few rubles. After the war began,* when she was already in her seventies, she looked after her grandchildren and nieces and nephews while their fathers were away at the front and their mothers worked in factories to boost war production. I was in my early twenties, but I very much needed someone to hang onto. She was that person for me.

Her one worry was that my uncle would be killed. "Like an old fool," she would say—but she was proud—he had volunteered for some kind of job as a medical assistant at the front. He came back from the war and did not die until several years later. My aunt was with him, and just before the end he looked at her and said, "I want you to know something because I am dying and must be honest. I have never loved you." My aunt died soon after that; she had no more will to live. That is what life before the revolution means to me—living fifty years with a man to whom you were sold and having him tell you on his deathbed that he never loved you.

GALINA WAS a fifty-two-year-old woman of considerable charm, gaiety and intelligence who seemed to be a thoroughly content citizen. Her life was a Soviet success story, and she regarded Soviet rule as a continuing process of liberation from a harsh past. The simple story of her aunt and uncle showed clearly how close Galina still felt to that past; in the United States and Western Europe, people of Galina's generation seldom voice such strong feelings about misery that originated in a bygone era.

* World War II.

33

Soviet propaganda constantly depicts an ideal citizen who personifies every virtue known to man before the Bolshevik Revolution and some that have been invented since 1917. He loves his country, works hard, lavishes devotion on his family, stays sober, drives carefully (if he is lucky enough to own a car), walks carefully (ever mindful of the official pedestrian safety campaign), adheres steadfastly to Marxist-Leninist ideals and believes in their eventual triumph throughout the world. Galina came closer to fulfilling this image than I would have thought possible, yet I eventually came to realize that she did not quite fit the mold. Her view of the world was conditioned by a Soviet education and her experience of war, but her thinking was not static; her willingness to accept propaganda at face value seemed to diminish as she grew older.

Galina was a person of many paradoxes: a believer in both Lenin and God, a worshiper of science and knowledge who thought folk charms could prevent miscarriages, a citizen who criticized banned Russian writers for publishing in the West but was eager to read their books. In one breath, she would decry the low level of popular culture in capitalist countries and sermonize about cultural advances made by the Russian masses under Communism. The next moment, she would complain because it was nearly impossible to find a good Russian dictionary in Soviet bookstores. "You can't find a dictionary," she once said, "but there are stacks of unsold books about the heroic feats of tractor drivers." In a country with real elections,* she would probably have been the unpredictable voter who confounds pollsters. The contradictions within her character ultimately symbolized for me the contradictions within Russia itself that no foreigner ever fully understands.

Galya (the Russian diminutive for Galina) had been a

---

* Government legislative bodies and some judges are elected in the Soviet Union, but there is only one slate of Communist Party-approved candidates. A citizen can vote "yes" or "no" but may not write in any other names. The elections always produce a "yes" vote of 97 to 99.9 percent. The important choices of leaders are made within Party councils.

French teacher for twenty years; she was a member of the foreign languages faculty at one of Moscow's most highly regarded institutions of higher education. I met her at a going-away party for a French diplomat's wife who was a gifted linguist and had acquired many Russian friends during her husband's tour of duty in the Soviet Union. Galya and I enjoyed each other's conversation and made a date to meet the following week at an ice-cream café.

Our meetings always occurred in public places. We talked as we rode the city buses together, strolled in parks or drank watery coffee in stand-up cafés with high tables and no chairs. Occasionally we went to the movies or the theater, where she would explain complicated nineteenth-century language or modern slang for me in conventional phrases I could understand. Her husband, who was a middle-level official in a government ministry, sometimes joined us on these excursions after Galya and I had known each other for several months.

During the entire time we knew each other, I was never invited to Galya's home. Most Soviet citizens prefer to see their foreign friends in public places; invitations to Russian homes are rare and highly prized by foreigners. Apartment complexes in Moscow do not provide the anonymity that is both a curse and blessing of urban life in the West. Neighbors, especially old men and women who receive pensions and have nothing better to do all day, are always minding each other's business. It is an old Russian tradition that predates the revolution and took on a sinister aspect during the Stalin years when citizens were officially encouraged to spy on each other. The hangover from the Stalin era is such that Soviet newspapers find it necessary to run articles criticizing officials who pay attention to anonymous denunciations of citizens by co-workers or neighbors.

Galya never offered any explanation of why she had not invited me to her home, and I never asked for one. She had an obvious professional motive for seeing French-speaking foreigners, but there was no official excuse for her relationship with me because I spoke no French and she spoke no English.

Educated, loyally orthodox Soviet citizens, loath to concede that their society is capable of such unreasonable restrictions of personal freedom, are embarrassed to admit they cannot openly associate with foreign friends. There are many facts about Soviet life that Russians find too painful to admit to themselves, much less to a foreign visitor. Only a foolish outsider would press for such admissions.

Some Russians are also reluctant to display their relatively poor material standard of living to American and European friends. This was not true of Galya; she talked quite freely about her own living conditions in terms that did not paint an overly rosy figure of a Soviet citizen's everyday existence.

Galina considered herself an extremely lucky woman. She earned 300 rubles a month or more, depending on the number of classes she chose to teach. She seldom taught more than eighteen hours a week, and her lessons required less preparation than courses in most other subjects because the syllabus varied only slightly from year to year. Salaries for university-level instructors are high by Soviet standards, especially after twenty years of service. The average Soviet worker makes approximately 133 rubles a month for a forty-hour week. Galya's husband earned 250 rubles a month at his government job. He was not disturbed because his wife made more money than he did; by Soviet standards, the difference between 250 and 300 rubles a month is not particularly significant. Also, he had been the main wage earner at various points in their married life.

A ruble is worth approximately $1.11 at the official rate of exchange. On the Russian black market and in the handful of neutral countries that will exchange rubles for hard currency, it is worth only one-fourth that amount. The most meaningful measure of the ruble's value for Russians is, of course, its relationship to the cost of living and the kinds of products it can buy. Rent is cheap—between 5 and 12 rubles a month for an average apartment—but food and clothing are expensive. Most Russians spend over half their monthly salaries on food; chicken costs several rubles a pound when it is available in farm markets, while most fruits and vegetables are beyond the means of an ordinary worker during the winter. The cheapest winter coat for a man or woman costs 125 to 150 rubles; a pair of women's shoes sells for between 40 and 75 rubles. Prices charged by technically illegal private entrepreneurs who meet consumer needs when the state economy fails are much higher.

Like many members of the Soviet intelligentsia who make above-average salaries, Galya and her husband had more money than they were able to spend; desirable consumer goods are so scarce that extra rubles become superfluous beyond a certain income level. Galya paid only 9 rubles a month rent. But money could not buy the kind of apartment she and her husband wanted. With their fifteen-year-old son and Galya's seventy-nine-year-old father, they occupied three rooms of a communal apartment in an old building. Three other families shared their kitchen and bathroom. Even so, they were more fortunate than many Muscovites in that their apartment had three rooms for four people. Galya said her family had been on the waiting list for a separate apartment with its own kitchen and bath for ten years. The family had been offered a two-room apartment in a new building, but Galya and her husband felt the kitchen and bath would not make up for the loss of a room.

According to official Soviet figures, about 25 percent of Moscow families live in communal apartments like Galina's. Fifteen years ago, the figure was 70 percent. Galya was impressed by the housing progress of the past decade and never complained about her own cramped quarters; she was sure her family would receive a new apartment big enough for its needs within the next few years. I once complained because the hot water had been turned off in our apartment for a month, and she laughingly answered, "But we never have any hot water in ours. I just heat it when I need to wash my hair and take quick showers instead of baths. It's not a real inconvenience. You Americans are spoiled." (In fairness, it must be noted that a majority of Moscow residents do have hot water in their apart-

ments. Only the oldest, most decrepit buildings are without it
and in some cases adequate plumbing. The hot water is turned
off in every Moscow apartment house for two weeks to a month
during the summer while the water system is purified.)

The necessity of living in a three-generation household—a
problem shared by millions of Russians—was the major source
of daily tension in Galya's life. Her father and her son had not
gotten along well together for at least three years. "Our house is
filled with arguments," she said. "My father was born in 1891.
He is not illiterate, which gives him an advantage over many
people his age, but he does not understand complicated modern
ideas. He does not understand a boy in 1970 who already knows
more about some things than he has learned in his entire life.
And my son does not understand him and is very impatient,
although I have tried to explain. But it's no easier for the young
to be patient with the old than for the old to be patient with the
young."

The normal tensions between a teen-age boy and an aging
grandfather were aggravated by the limited living space. Galya's father had suffered two strokes and was growing senile, yet
she could not bear to put him in a state home. "My friends have
told me this is very common in America and some parts of
Europe, and we also have such facilities. But I cannot bury my
father alive there. No one would care about him the way we do;
what interest would he have in life? Even the fights with my
son give him something to live for. I think we Russians still
have too much devotion to our families to accept the idea of
putting parents away when they become difficult to care for. I
know it is hard for my son, but he will understand when he is
older. Although I would rather die in full possession of my
health than be a burden on my son the way my father is on us."
When Galya and her husband were first married, her mother
and his parents were still alive. During the first seven years of
their marriage, they lived with both sets of parents.

If Galya and her husband had been less scrupulous, they
might have used their money to grease their way into a new

apartment ahead of their turn on the waiting list; other Russian acquaintances spoke matter-of-factly about having paid under-the-counter money to do just that. Galya, however, was shocked by even small instances of what Russians call *vzyatka* (graft). She became extremely upset when I spoke with some irritation about the need to ply customs officials with bottles of vodka so that they would not charge excessive duty on the dog food we imported for our terrier. (Dog food is one of the many consumer items the Soviet Union lacks.) "It is very unpleasant for us to hear that such things happen," she said. "It is wrong to let such an official go on cheating the public." She was morally right, of course, but more cynical Russian acquaintances hooted at the idea of lodging a formal complaint. "You'd only have to pay three times as much the next time," one said. Unlike Galya, most of the Russians I knew were quite happy to grease palms if they thought it would do any good.

Galya's money, the nature of her work and the respect her job commanded gave her some significant advantages over the ordinary Soviet citizen. Her ability to read and speak French, combined with her faculty position, opened a cultural world to her that was closed to most Russians. She saw foreign films—not only French ones—that were shown regularly for select groups of scholars and figures in the entertainment world. Since they were not destined for public viewing, the films were neither dubbed nor subtitled but were shown uncut in the original language with a simultaneous Russian translation. While I was in Moscow, Galya's favorite was the French *A Man and a Woman*—her least favorite, *Bonnie and Clyde*, because of what she considered its excessive violence. She also borrowed French books from her foreign acquaintances, including translations of banned Russian writers like Aleksandr Solzhenitsyn. (Diplomats and journalists are generally free to bring any books they like into the Soviet Union, as long as they are not printed in Russian.)

Galya had not settled into dowdy, premature old age like many Russian women in their forties; her hair was still black, with some effective aid from a dye packet, and her figure trim. "My husband is not like most Russian men," she explained. "He hates plump women." Her appearance was greatly enhanced by occasional presents her French friends brought back for her from holidays in Paris. Galya's pride in the Soviet Union's achievements did not extend to its frumpish fashion industry. Decisions about styles are made not by designers but by clothing factory managers, most of them middle-aged men with conservative tastes. One young designer told me ruefully that he had sketched a whole line of pantsuits, but the factory managers only wanted to buy the jacket patterns without the pants.

Galya's teaching schedule frequently enabled her to take time off in the middle of the day, and this was one of the greatest advantages of her job. It is difficult for someone who has never been in the Soviet Union to comprehend the amount of time wasted by Russians in completing daily errands and chores. Shopping consumes an hour or more a day because of a system requiring customers in most stores to stand in three lines to make a purchase—one to choose what they want, a second to pay and a third to pick up their packages. (The three lines grow to six or nine because the procedure is repeated for different products—*i.e.*, one set of lines for meat, another for vegetables, another for daily foods.) Galya owned a refrigerator—she had been on a waiting list four years to buy it—but she still had to shop every day because the freezer was too small to hold large quantities of meat. She saved countless hours each week because she could avoid the heaviest shopping crowds at lunchtime and in the early evening.

Her working hours also enabled her to arrive home before her son on most days. Working mothers worry constantly about the lack of proper supervision for their children in after-school hours; Galya was afraid her teen-age son would "hang around on the streets" instead of doing his homework. The official press has recognized lack of supervision for young people as a major problem in a society where 80 percent of all women between the ages of twenty and fifty-five hold full-time jobs. A normal school day ends at three or four o'clock, and only a few have extended programs that keep children busy until the end of the adult working day. There are extracurricular activities for children of all ages but, as Galya said, "kids in their teens are likely to get sidetracked if no one at home is paying attention to what they're doing." She believed the government would eventually decree shorter working hours for women than for men. She approved of the idea because "despite the fact that so many Russian women work outside the home, the men have not taken over their share of chores inside the home. So we all have two jobs, and it can be very difficult. I cannot understand how an American housewife could just sit at home all day, even after her children had gone off to school, but I am glad that my working hours are not completely rigid. I think it would be better for our society if all women had more flexible schedules. We have a growing juvenile delinquency problem, and I think it's mainly because teen-agers are allowed to run wild at certain hours of the day. However, we don't have any trouble with our young people that approaches what you have in the West."

Many Americans would not consider Galya's life an easy one despite her relatively privileged position in Soviet society, but it was not difficult for me to understand why she thought herself fortunate. She was born in Moscow four years after the revolution. Lenin was still alive; it was a time of political ferment, experiment and hope for people like her parents. Her mother was an uneducated woman who worked as a seamstress. Her father, an ardent Bolshevik, was a factory foreman who had finished four grades of school; by the standards of his day he was by no means an uneducated man. Galya said she seldom saw him without a book in his hands during his free hours. Her mother later told her that her father had become deeply depressed after Lenin's death in 1924 and had begun to drink heavily. Galya said her father "mistrusted" Stalin and told his children so. He must have possessed a certain amount of courage, because Soviet schools and youth groups urged children to spy on their parents during the late 1920's and 1930's.

Galya did not describe her childhood in any detail and, after receiving several vague, meaningless answers, I stopped asking questions. I have no idea what the Stalin years were like for her family or whether any of her close relatives ever disappeared into a camp. Her reticence here, when she talked freely about so many other subjects, made me suspect her family had experienced something of the arbitrary terror of Stalin's rule. However, she may simply have been exhibiting the response of many Soviet citizens to anything concerned with the Stalin era. The reluctance to talk about Stalin today is deep and widespread, even among people who recognize the dimensions of the tragedy that befell their country under his dictatorship. Admissions of Stalin's evil, which meant the death and imprisonment of millions of Russians,* are not forthcoming from most Soviet citizens who grew up during that period. To acknowledge the full extent of the tragedy would be to admit complicity in horrors too great for most people even to think about: The refusal of many middle-aged Germans to admit they knew about the Nazi concentration camps is a similar reaction.

Stalin was never fully toppled from his pedestal, even when Khrushchev's de-Stalinization campaign was at its height. Too many officials still in power had been the executors of Stalin's policies; indeed, many Western analysts believe Khrushchev's seriousness about de-Stalinization was the major factor that led to his loss of support within the Party Central Committee. After Khrushchev's partial cleansing operation, the new Brezhnev-Kosygin leadership said in effect, "Enough is enough," and clamped the lid back on the sewer.

---

* Robert Conquest, in what is the most detailed Western scholarly work on the great purges of the 1930's, estimates on the basis of Soviet sources and reports of camp survivors that some 20,000,000 died during the twenty-three years when Stalin held absolute power. The figure does not include World War II casualties. (Conquest, *The Great Terror,* London and New York, Macmillan and Co., Ltd., 1968.) The first attempt at an honest history of the period by a Soviet scholar, Roy A. Medvedev's *Let History Judge,* was published by Macmillan in late 1971. Medvedev does not emphasize statistics as much as Conquest, but his figures would tend to support Conquest's estimate. Medvedev suggests that 4,000,000 to 5,000,000 were executed or received long camp sentences tantamount to death in the period between 1936 and 1939 alone.

Unlike some Russians her age, Galya made no attempt to justify Stalin's crimes. She vigorously denied that the present Soviet leaders want to cover up the memory of what Stalin did but, at the same time, she was clearly disturbed by the regime's refusal to publish Solzhenitsyn. Solzhenitsyn troubles many Russians who are otherwise loyal supporters of whatever policy their government happens to be following; they remember that he was published during the Khrushchev years and find it difficult to swallow the official explanation that he has somehow turned anti-Soviet. Galya's comments showed that she was deeply worried lest there be some truth in accusations from abroad and from dissenters at home of a "return to Stalinism."

"We know very well what Stalin did," she said. "That he unjustly accused all his opponents of being anti-Communist, that he made many of our people live in total fear—we know that. When his personality cult was at its height, our country was in a very bad state. My parents thought so, and they spoke to us about it when we were children. The Soviet-German treaty was obviously another of his worst mistakes." (Signed on August 21, 1939, the pact allowed the Soviets to take over the Baltic states and some eastern Polish territories in return for Stalin's noninterference with the Nazi conquest of Poland.)

"There are times when I don't know what to think. I have no answer, at least no answer I can accept, to the question of why Solzhenitsyn is not published. But I do not think a country can flagellate itself forever over what happened in the past. Sometimes it seems to me that people from the West want us to go on doing this endlessly. You talk only about Stalin, never about things that happened in your own country. Like the McCarthy period, when many Communists and what you call liberals were put in jail."

The "cult of personality" is the prevailing Soviet euphemism for Stalin's policies. Galya's equation of the McCarthy era, which lasted about four years, with Stalinism, which lasted twenty-five years—nearly half of the Soviet Union's life as a nation—is an example of the distorted view even relatively sophisticated Russians have of their own history. I challenged the comparison, pointing out that while McCarthy was responsible for the harassment of thousands, Stalin was responsible for the death of millions; that Joseph McCarthy was a Senator, not an absolute dictator; and that he was eventually defeated by strong forces inside and outside of the government. I told Galya I could cite any number of distinguished Americans—from Senator Margaret Chase Smith to the journalist I. F. Stone—who spoke out against McCarthyism, survived and prospered. "Some of what you say is right," she admitted. "I am sorry I cannot point to anyone honored today who fought Stalin openly. Those who did fight are dead." With me, Galya was never willing to carry the discussion further and to consider what it was both in the character of the Russian people and in their system of government that allowed opposition to be so thoroughly suppressed. (This does not, of course, mean she refused to think about it herself or discuss it with other Russians.)

One subject Galya was willing to discuss at length was World War II—unquestionably the second formative experience for her generation. Both Stalin and the war invariably come up in any frank conversations with Russians over forty. The latter is known to Soviet citizens simply as the Great Patriotic War.

Galya was a second-year student at the Institute of Foreign Languages in Moscow when the Germans invaded her country. She was shocked at the news, having swallowed all the propaganda about eternal peace and friendship between Germany and the Soviet Union. Like all young women of her age, she immediately went to work in a factory to take the place of men who were leaving for the front. Higher education was virtually suspended as the comparatively underdeveloped Soviet economy struggled to resist the onslaught of a highly industrialized nation. Everyone above the age of fourteen worked.

Galya spent the entire war in Moscow, but she tells the story of a cousin who went to visit relatives in a village while the German armies were advancing toward the capital. Soviet news

about the progress of the war was so divorced from reality that
no one had any idea the Germans were within one hundred,
much less ten, miles of Moscow until they actually saw soldiers
taking up positions for the defense of the city. Galya's unsus-
pecting cousin was caught by the swift advance of the German
troops and spent more than a year in occupied territory. "It was
only by accident that I didn't leave Moscow myself," Galya
said. "I had planned to join my family in the village two weeks
later, because we thought the food situation would be better in
the country than in the city. By then, everyone knew the countryside around Moscow was occupied and I didn't leave." Moscow was surrounded on three sides but never occupied. The
advance of the German troops was stopped not far from the
present site of Sheremetevo International Airport, about eight
miles from Moscow.

Galya was engaged when the war began. "My fiancé was sent
to the defense of Leningrad. In Moscow we were cold and half
starving, but when he came home on leave after the so-called
'starvation winter' in Leningrad, he told us that hundreds of
thousands of people were dying there of starvation. They said
people were actually eating human flesh—we had no idea. We
were married during the two weeks he was home. He died in a
minor battle just three months before the war ended, having
survived much bigger fights. To be killed at the end, when
victory was so near—it seemed almost more terrible than death
itself. We lost twenty million men, did you know that? Most
foreigners don't know. You Americans never had a war on your
own soil; you do not know what war is really like.

"All along we kept wondering, hoping, 'When will the Americans open the second front?' And it didn't come until 1944,
long after Stalingrad, long after we had already shed more
blood than all the other countries put together. I don't blame the
Americans anymore; we are aware that economic aid from
America was very important in our winning the war. We also
know that you were attacked at Pearl Harbor and it took time
to recover from that. But I cannot feel your country experi-

enced what we did during the war. I know no one—no one—
who did not lose a lover or husband or son."

It is impossible to state precisely how many people died in
the two-and-a-half-year blockade of Leningrad that began in
September, 1941. Soviet and Western sources suggest that approximately 1,000,000 died of starvation, with an additional
300,000 to 500,000 military and civilian casualties. Estimates of
total Soviet war casualties vary, but most Western scholars
agree that a minimum of 15,000,000 Russians died. Soviet
sources set the minimum figure at 20,000,000.

Galya's memories of the war strongly influenced her feelings
about current political events. Like many Russians, she felt the
Soviet invasion of Czechoslovakia in 1968 was at least partially
justified because the Czechs had a common border with West
Germany. She accepted the official Soviet contention that the
liberalization of the "Prague spring" would lead to more German influence, and not simply more Western influence, in Eastern Europe. She saw the potential German influence as a direct
threat to the Soviet Union's security, and she was unable to
swallow the official line two years later when the historic Soviet-
West German friendship treaty was signed in Moscow. "I suppose all wars must end some time," she said in a skeptical voice
that made her distrust plainer than any explicit statement. (Interestingly, the Russian men I knew who had served in the
army during the war were generally less bitter toward Germany than middle-aged women. I asked one friend why this
was so, and he said, "because we who survived had our women
to come back to but most of the women didn't have any men
who came back.")

After the war, Galya returned to the institute and completed
her studies. She was one of the top graduates in her field, and
her high academic rank enabled her to obtain a college rather
than a secondary school teaching job. She began her career at a
second-rate institute and moved after five years to the outstanding one where she teaches today.

The shortage of men after the war gave an extra push to

competent women in many professions, although it also meant that women had to take over a disproportionate share of heavy manual labor.

Galya remarried in 1950 and her son was born five years later; she was thirty-four at the time. She would have liked another child but felt it impossible because of cramped housing conditions. When the baby was born, she and her husband were lodged in a two-room apartment with both sets of their parents. The housing shortage had eased somewhat by the early 1960's, but Galya felt she was too old to try having another baby. The one-child family is still the rule rather than the exception in large Russian cities, and nearly all Russians attribute their small families to the housing squeeze. Newly married couples today have little trouble obtaining a single room with its own kitchen and bath—which would have been luxury to Galya's generation—but they hunger for more privacy. Families with children are usually allotted only two rooms, and most young couples are unwilling to live in that space with more than one child.

Galya was extremely proud of her son, who was an outstanding student at a special school where he received intensive English instruction every day. (Members of the intelligentsia are able to get their children into such schools more easily than ordinary citizens.) She wanted her son to study English rather than French, because English is now the most important second language in the Soviet Union and the key to many desirable jobs. She hoped her son would one day have a post that would take him abroad; travel outside the Soviet Union is her chief unsatisfied desire. It is shared by much of the intelligentsia.

Only a handful of carefully screened Soviet citizens are allowed to visit the West each year, most of them in tightly supervised groups. Galya had not yet been able to work her way into one, although her job gave her a perfect reason for visiting France and she could easily have afforded the price of a foreign tour. She did have hopes of being able to join a group tour for foreign language teachers in the not-too-distant future. "My

real dream is to visit America," she confessed but acknowledged that it was unlikely to come true. Meanwhile, she tried
to satisfy her curiosity about the rest of the world through her
few foreign acquaintances in Moscow. (Galya was not part of
the regular "circuit" of Russians who see foreigners. The
French diplomat's wife who attended a class at Galya's institute
met her quite by accident. Galya told me I was her only foreign
friend who did not speak French.)

Like many Russians, Galya liked Americans and admired
many aspects of American life despite her belief in the superi-
ority of the Soviet system. Whatever the subject, America is
always the standard of comparison for Russians; they seem to
regard the United States as the only country important enough
to qualify as a worthy rival. (China is feared by many Russians
but also scorned because of its technological backwardness.
The comparisons with America might become less obsessive if
the Common Market developed into a united Europe.) I believe there is another reason for the Russian interest in the
United States: On an unofficial basis, Russians and Americans
get along very well together. When it is possible to peel away
the layers of mutual suspicion, there is a rough open-hearted-
ness that makes understanding possible, particularly on an
emotional level. "Americans have a *shiroky kharakter*, just as
we do," Galya said. Loosely translated, the expression means
"broad spirit."

Galya told me several times how "stricken" she was after the
assassinations of President Kennedy and his brother Robert. "I
was lying on the beach at Sochi when we heard the news that
Robert Kennedy had been killed. I remember no one could
believe that such a thing had happened a second time, and
people were crying all around me. President Kennedy was identified with peace in the minds of many of our people, because
when he was President it seemed to us there was the first real
improvement in relations between our countries since the war.
We too liked the image of a young man with small children as
the leader of a great country, although our own leaders have

always been much older. My mother used to say that a man with children like that could only want peace. Robert Kennedy was identified with his brother in the minds of Russians, although from what I read about him he seemed in his own right to be a man with great sympathy for the problems and sufferings of other people."

Galya asked me several times if I thought Richard Nixon would have become President had Robert Kennedy lived. To her, Nixon was a shadowy, rather unpleasant figure, remembered more as an opponent of John Kennedy's in 1960 than as Khrushchev's antagonist in the famous "kitchen debate."* (Nixon made a poor impression on Russians during his visit as Vice President in 1959. Among other blunders, he tried to press an overly large sum of money on a farmer selling fruits and vegetables in Moscow's central market. The gesture was regarded as condescending and ignorant, since the seedy-looking farmers make large profits by flying their produce in suitcases from the south and selling them in the citrus-hungry northern Soviet cities. While there are Soviet citizens who could use charitable contributions, the fruit sellers in the farm markets are not among them.)

Although Galya sometimes criticized the American government—especially its policies in Vietnam—she never criticized Nixon personally. She was profoundly shocked when I volunteered my low opinion of his performance as President. Despite some previous experience of Western irreverence toward political leaders, Galya was unable to understand how an American could sharply, even bitterly, criticize his country's leaders and their policies and still consider himself a patriotic citizen. The day after Nixon sent American troops into Cambodia in the spring of 1970, she was aghast when I said, only half facetiously, that it was the first time I had ever agreed with a *Pravda* editorial.

"I can understand how you would say such things among yourselves," she said, "but I cannot understand how you can

* This was, of course, before Nixon's Presidential visit in May, 1972.

say them to someone from another country. A foreigner would think that you do not love your country, and I am sure you do not mean to give that impression. Sometimes Americans carry individualism too far."

There were many Americans in Moscow who agreed with Galya and refused to make even mildly critical comments about the United States in the presence of Russians. I felt very strongly that they were failing to convey the most important idea they might have offered their Soviet acquaintances: the meaning of free expression in an open society.

The Soviet spectrum of thought on freedom of expression ranges from arch-conservatives who would like to reimpose the monolithic censorship of the Stalin years to dissidents who call for an end to all restrictions on freedom of speech and of the press. The latter are outcasts; the Soviet system has no place for them except in labor camps or exile. The conservatives, on the other hand, wield enormous influence within the government's censorship apparatus despite the fact that they are opposed by "liberals" within the Soviet establishment who advocate somewhat looser controls.

Within the Soviet context, Galya belonged on the liberal rather than the conservative side. She believed the easing of restrictions on artists under Khrushchev was a good thing because she felt Soviet society was strong enough to tolerate more than one point of view. However, she was unable to grasp, much less accept, the Western idea that freedom of expression is inherently valuable, apart from whatever social utility it may possess. Her ideas on free speech were governed entirely by her belief that wider latitude in the arts was good for Soviet society. She would never have agreed that an idea should be allowed to circulate freely even if it was bad for Soviet society or, in the official jargon, "anti-Soviet." She simply defined the range of acceptable ideas more broadly than the conservatives. I asked her why, if it was wrong to put American Communists in jail during the McCarthy era, it was right to put Soviet dissenters in camps today. "Communism is a progressive force," she replied. "Only the most reactionary people go to jail in our country." Her statement shows the influence of political jargon on thought. Progressive = Good. Reactionary = Bad. No country should punish what is good, but every country should punish what is bad.

Galya's definitions led her to the conclusion that the Soviet government had made a mistake in not allowing Solzhenitsyn's novels to be published. She had read *Cancer Ward* in French, and she told me with a certain bewilderment that she did not see how it could be regarded as anti-Soviet. Her position was that everything Solzhenitsyn said in literary form had already been set forth in documentary form during the Khrushchev period, so there was no reason to suppress it now. In many instances, she confused news that had reached Russian intellectuals by word of mouth with what was actually published in the press. Khrushchev's "secret speech" at the Twentieth Party Congress, in which he denounced many abuses of the Stalin era, was never officially published in the Soviet Union although its substance was leaked by delegates, printed in the West and widely discussed by Russians. Galya often talked as though every Russian had been able to read the speech when in fact she herself had never seen the text. "Still," she said, "we know about these things even if they weren't all in print."

Galya never questioned the government's right to make decisions about literary matters, and she felt it was wrong for a Soviet writer to allow his works to be published in the West if they had not been printed in the Soviet Union. "They should wait," she said, "and obey the laws of their country. There were many writers who could not be published in Stalin's day but who are published now." She had no concept of a right to free speech that did not depend on a particular government's decision. At the same time, she was capable of admitting that her government did not always make the right decisions. Consciously or unconsciously, she continually exposed herself to information that contradicted orthodox Soviet thought. Outside influences from foreign friends and radio broadcasts and, more importantly, Solzhenitsyn's flame from inside her own country contributed to a growing awareness of universes that did not coincide with the official version of reality.

The last time I saw Galya, I gave her a French translation of *The First Circle*, Solzhenitsyn's novel about life in a special camp for scientists and intellectuals. She wrapped it in a copy of *Pravda* and stuffed it into her shopping bag. As she walked away, I wondered how many other ordinary-looking men and women were going about their daily errands with real books hidden in the folds of *Pravda*.

III

Boris Alekseivich

BORIS ALEKSEIVICH IS a huge, bull-necked man with startlingly bright green eyes, a soft voice and an ironic smile. He is sixty-seven. In his youth, he was a dedicated Bolshevik. Like many old revolutionaries, he later spent twenty years in Stalin's prison camps. Unlike many of his former comrades, he survived the camps and was "rehabilitated" after the Twentieth Party Congress in 1956. He now lives quietly in a new suburb on the outskirts of Moscow, viewing his country and the world with the detachment of a True Believer who has lost his faith.

Boris Alekseivich is an exception among the Russians in this book. I only met him once and he did not know I was a journalist. We were introduced by a trusted Russian friend who felt I should not return to America before talking personally with someone who had seen and endured what Boris Alekseivich has seen and endured. The band of survivors who remember both the heady aura of the revolution and the crushing terror of Stalin's rule dwindles each year; it is generally impossible for a foreigner to make contact with them. I was the only foreigner Boris Alekseivich had spoken to since he was arrested for the first time in 1935—with the exception of a few Western Communists who had come to Russia during the 1920's and early 1930's and had later been sent to camps. "My international comrades became comrades in fear," he said.

He was nervous about meeting me and apologized, saying, "the fear is in your blood and your bones, and you cannot overcome it with your mind. But those of us who were there have an obligation to tell our stories, if we cannot summon up the courage to do anything more. So that the record of what happened can never be wiped out, just as the record of what the Nazis did can never be destroyed. So now you and I will speak *dusha-dushi* [soul to soul], and you will understand something of what it was to be a Russian and a Communist in this century."

We talked late into the night, he admonishing me repeatedly to stop him if his Russian became too fast or filled with prison camp slang for me to understand. The *dusha-dushi* conversation is a uniquely Russian experience in which near strangers will speak of matters so intimate that even old friends in the West might shy away from them.

Boris Alekseivich pulled out a faded snapshot, dated 1922, of thirty earnest-looking young men and women who all seemed to be in their late teens. "My first Komsomol cadre," he explained. "Ten girls, twenty boys. Only five of us are alive today —all camp survivors. We have reunions sometimes, but I don't enjoy them very much. All we do is argue endlessly about what went wrong. It's usual for old people to live in their memories —but for us, what memories! But enough . . . I am getting ahead of my story."

He poured us scalding tea, and we sat at his kitchen table. His narrative, while not strictly chronological, seldom needs interpretation.

"I was born in Odessa—the most cosmopolitan, sophisticated city in Russia. It was the most important port in czarist times, just as it is now—a magnificent city—brawling, bawdy and cultured, all at the same time. It seemed to me when I was a child that you could hear ten different languages being spoken at once as you walked down the street. There were Germans and French and British and Poles and Czechs and Japanese. We didn't get very many Americans, although there were a few from time to time."

I told him one of my husband's grandparents emigrated to the United States from Odessa before the revolution. "Well, naturally, my dear, at least half of the talented people everywhere in the world have some Odessa blood in them. Are you sure one of your own long lost relatives didn't come from Odessa too? Never mind, I'm sure one did even if you say you are Irish." (An aura of sophistication clings to Odessa even today, embodied in the slang expression "Odessa mama." A Russian will say "Odessa mama" if he considers something particularly up-to-date, perhaps somewhat Westernized. It is also pronounced in sarcastic tones to describe anything backward or shoddy. I once saw a young Russian girl staring at women emerging from the foreigners' compound in stylish thigh-high boots. She peered at her own red vinyl Soviet-made boots, shook her head and said, "Odessa mama" in a disgusted voice.)

After the digression on Odessa, Boris Alekseivich picked up the thread of his narrative.

"I came from a family that had belonged to the upper-middle-class intelligentsia for several generations. My father owned various kinds of real estate and was a provincial school superintendent—exactly the sort of job Lenin's father had in Kazan. My mother was a concert violinist—not a great one but a good one—and a music teacher. We spoke Russian in our home, although everyone in the family was bilingual in French. My father detested those members of the intelligentsia who thought Russian was too crude to use, that it was somehow a mark of status to speak only French. I also spoke German from the time I was ten years old. That was useful later on in camp, where there were a lot of unfortunate German Communists who had fled east from Hitler only to get caught up in Stalin's net. My French used to be pure Parisian, but I didn't get much chance to practice it in camp. Now it's pure Moscow. I can still read French, but only with considerable difficulty and the help of a dictionary.

"There were six children in our family and I was the youngest. It's surprising that our roof never caved in, considering all the political arguments that went on beneath it. We were a very politically minded family. All of us, including my father, thought the czarist form of monarchy was doomed. Not that my father ever talked about his ideas outside the house. But there was a great difference between that time and what came later —it would never have occurred to my father not to voice his opinions inside his own home, that there might be spies in his own family. We revolutionaries brought that wonderful progressive change to our country—parents not being able to trust their children. My father thought the Romanovs would never survive because they had been too stupid to give up some of their powers, unlike the more intelligent English monarchs.

"Two of my brothers sympathized with the Bolsheviks and one with the Mensheviks—they had the bitterest arguments. My one sister believed in a mystical idea of the Russian peasantry, though she had hardly spoken to a peasant in her life. She thought the peasants were the personification of everything good in Russia. My brothers just laughed at her.

"My mother used to say that all of our fighting turned whatever she was cooking sour. She tended to sympathize with the Bolsheviks herself."

In 1917, the revolution changed the family's talk into action.

"I was thirteen years old then, and from that time on politics became my whole world. Two of my older brothers, who had immediately joined the Bolshevik Party, decided I could be useful because of my gift for languages. We were in Sevastopol [another Crimean port] at the time of the revolution; my father had been promoted in 1916, and we had left Odessa so he could take over his new job. From your own study of Russian history, you know that the years between 1918 and 1920 were a time of constant civil war and foreign intervention. It seemed that we had one government on one side of the street and one on the other, with a third on the rooftops. The English occupied Sevastopol, the French were in Odessa and the coastline was blockaded. We managed to get back to Odessa, and I would go hang around the port and talk with the sailors, trying to get information about what their next move would be. The French sailors were overjoyed to meet a small boy talking their own language—I was very small for my age then, not the over-size monster I am now.

"They would show me pictures of their mistresses or wives or children, whichever were appropriate—sometimes all three— and I would find things out. That's how I learned about a mutiny of French sailors in the Black Sea and how much all of them wanted to go home and not be entangled in the politics of a strange land. They had no idea what they were doing in Russia.

"In 1920 the French took off and the rule of the Soviets was established in Odessa. I immediately joined a Komsomol training course. I was sixteen then. From that point on, the revolution became my life. My parents had their doubts and emigrated to France with my sister. They said they might return when things settled down, but they feared there would be no place for the old intelligentsia in the new Soviet state. I said very sarcastic things to them about getting out with their money after all the talking they had done about revolutionary politics. I laughed at their fears; I was utterly convinced of the rightness of our cause."

Boris Alekseivich paused and refilled our tea glasses. His voice grew more distant.

"What did we believe then? How often I have asked myself that question, and sometimes I can recapture a glimmer of the beautiful faith I had in man at that time. How can I explain to you the glory of believing absolutely in the justice and inevitability of an idea? As Communists, we believed that man and his physical surroundings would be brought into greater harmony. The resources of the earth would be used not to make a few men rich but to make life better for everyone. We truly believed we were building a new world, not just in Russia but everywhere. A world in which there would be no prisons and no police, no hunger and poverty, no war, no national borders. One world. Not a capitalist camp or a Socialist camp, but the human race. Of course it didn't turn out the way we expected, here or in any other country. We were naïve. Power and naïveté are a fatal combination.

"We were uninterested in objective analysis, although Communism was supposed to be based on an objective analysis of human affairs. My father, who knew more about the rest of the world than I did, tried to talk to me about the modifications being made in industrial capitalism in England and America. I didn't listen. We believed that world revolution was inevitable, that the old order was dying everywhere. I, with my language skills, was to go to France or Germany where I could talk with the workers and promote revolution there. If anyone had told me that a citizen of the new Soviet state would soon be forbidden to go abroad for any reason, I would have thought him mad. But again, I am getting ahead of my story. . . .

"When our Komsomol group finished its training and was to be dispersed throughout the country to train other cadres, we were received in Moscow by Lenin for fifteen minutes. I am sure that for all of us it was the crowning moment of our lives to that point. But I refuse to play the game of wondering whether the course of our lives would have been different if Lenin had lived. People my age are always letting themselves think that nothing bad would have happened if Lenin hadn't died before the work of the revolution was finished. Why? The only reasonable society is one that doesn't depend on the personality of one man. The apparatus of the terror was set up in the twenties; everything was already being justified 'for the good of the cause.'* No, I don't believe everything was fine until Stalin perverted Communism. The warnings were there, but we refused to see them.

"So. I was a Komsomol organizer for fifteen years. I traveled to all of the Soviet republics, setting up loyal Komsomol organizations. I was particularly careful to look out for unorthodox political tendencies in the republics that had hoped for independence from Russia at the time of the revolution. Those were my instructions, and I carried them out. Of course, weeding out the unorthodox didn't mean sending them to camp, not at that

---

* *For the Good of the Cause* is the title of a Solzhenitsyn short story printed during the Khrushchev years in the monthly magazine *Novy Mir*. It deals with a group of enthusiastic students who build a new school for themselves with their own hands, only to find it commandeered by another more influential institution.

point. I believed in persuasion; I talked myself hoarse with people who didn't agree with me. Only a blockhead could fail to see the rightness of my arguments. . . . I never thought it was only one short step from prohibiting individual voices in public life to the horror of the camps.

"About the rest of my life before camp, there is little else to say. It was happy, normal. There isn't much to say about a normal life, except when your world becomes such a crazy house that it becomes abnormal to be normal. I married. My wife was also a dedicated party member. We had two daughters. We named them Maya and Nadezhda—Maya because the First of May is an international workers' holiday, Nadezhda after Lenin's wife. And because we were filled with hope at that time. [*Nadezhda* means "hope" in Russian.] My wife and I loved each other, our children and our work.

"We became aware, especially in the early 1930's, that more people were being sent to prison and that my kind of 'persuasion' was going out of style. We justified it on the grounds that the people arrested must have been actively pursuing counter-revolutionary activity. People couldn't be arrested for what they thought, after all. . . ."

Boris Alekseivich's life, like the lives of many party members, was changed irrevocably by the murder of Sergei Kirov, boss of the Leningrad Party apparatus, on December 1, 1934. The story given out at the time was that Kirov had been shot by a disgruntled Trotskyist. His murder served as the excuse for the first wave of arrests that were only a prelude to the great purges of the late 1930's. It is now generally thought that Stalin engineered Kirov's murder.

"I was arrested a few months after Kirov's murder, in early 1935," said Boris Alekseivich. "The official grounds were that I had been a friend of someone in Leningrad who was accused of being a conspirator in the Kirov murder and a secret Trotskyite. I had known the man only slightly, when I was based in Leningrad for two years. I was in Kiev when they [the secret police] came to take me away.

"Why was I really arrested? Who knows—there were never

any reasons for arrests in those days. I suppose my basic mistake was that all my life, if someone called me *ty* I called him *ty* right back without stopping to ask about his political background." (In Russian, *ty* is the familiar form of "you" and *vy* is the impersonal form. People generally call each other *vy* unless they are well acquainted.)

"Anyway, whatever the reason, I was arrested. My wife and I had worked together very closely; she was arrested a few weeks after they took me away. She died in camp shortly after the war, although I wasn't able to establish that definitely until after I was released in 1956. Our daughters had been given into the care of friends for safekeeping, but they [the friends] were also arrested eventually. I have never been able to trace what happened to my girls; these things happened in our progressive state. Children of prisoners would be sent to institutions by the state and given new names. I had no family left when I finally came out of the camps. The brother who was once a Menshevik must have been summarily executed at some point; there is no record of his having been in a camp. My three other brothers all died in camp. It's possible to establish these things both by official records and by talking to other camp survivors who may have known your relatives. We all recognize each other; how, I couldn't tell you—but we do. The only blessing is that my parents and sister never returned to Russia, unlike some other emigrés who were fooled by the good face Stalin put on for the rest of the world. But I don't blame the rest of the world for being fooled; we ourselves didn't realize what was happening until it was too late.

"I must tell you I signed a confession that I had been a Trotskyite. And I was not tortured excessively; I was only on the conveyer for a few days and nights. [On the conveyer prisoners were kept without sleep for days while they were interrogated by successive investigators.] I was lucky in that I was arrested before the mass use of terrible physical torture became standard. It seemed to me in the madness overtaking our country there was no point in not confessing. I was asked to implicate my wife in the confession, but I wouldn't do that. The investigators didn't push it with me, although of course she was arrested anyway. If I had been taken in 1937, I probably would have been tortured until I betrayed my wife and other comrades. I was not a hero; I admired those who died rather than confess. But I wanted to survive. Today I don't feel any particular regret about the confession, because it implicated only me. Everyone knows now that the confessions were phony, induced by fear or torture. But I would be haunted if they had wanted me to betray other people to the point of torturing me. I probably would have broken; that guilt would never have left me. The guilt I feel now is for my silence during the twenties, when screams might have changed the course of our history."

Boris Alekseivich brought out a bottle of Georgian wine and poured us each a small glass. He sat in silence for what seemed a long time, as if he were trying to force his most painful memories to the surface.

"What can I tell you of the camps that has not been told by Solzhenitsyn and other writers in *samizdat*?* Nothing in general, only the personal experiences that were most meaningful to me. I never wanted to talk about it during the early years after my release. But when I was in the hospital with heart trouble in the late 1950's, the doctor told me I must think and talk about my experiences or I would never be whole again. She said emotional pain could be a weight pressing on my heart just as physical pain was. She was right, of course. If only our country would realize that it will never be whole again as long as we pretend not to remember.

"I had one session with the doctor in which she took an electrocardiogram while I talked. She asked me to describe what I remembered as the worst experience of my life. You might think it was the loss of my wife and daughters, but those

---

* *Samizdat* literally means "self-published." It refers to typed copies of books and verse that cannot be officially published but are passed from hand to hand. *Samizdat* first became a significant vehicle for circulating forbidden manuscripts during the Khrushchev years and continues under his successors.

were such great catastrophes that I could hardly take them in. They seemed to come with inevitability, over a long period of time. I always assumed they were dead, at least dead to me, while I was in camp. The chief feature of Russian life in this century was our almost calm acceptance of the unthinkable.

"For me, the worst thing was something much more simple. It was having to go to the toilet in a Stolypin car in front of the guards." (Stolypin cars are used for the railway transport of prisoners. They are unofficially but universally named after Czar Nicholas II's Prime Minister, who introduced them after the revolt of 1905. They are railroad cars with cages for prisoners instead of ordinary compartments, a long corridor for armed guards on one side and only one small barred window at the entrance. The construction of the Stolypin cars, still in use today, is basically unchanged since 1905.)

"We were being taken from Moscow to an unknown destination in Siberia. I had already taken two rides in Stolypin cars, one from Kiev to Leningrad and one from Leningrad to Moscow, so I knew what to expect. We received a cup of water twice a day and were allowed to use the toilet twice a day. The only food we received on the trip was heavily salted canned herring.

"The new prisoners, the ones who weren't wise in the ways of survival in prison, ate the herring because they were starving. The older ones like me knew we couldn't touch the herring because it was so salty we'd be dying of thirst before our next cup of water. The new ones would cry, 'Comrades, give us water. We are dying.' 'Comrades'—what a joke. Those guards, except for a rare exception, didn't know the meaning of the word. If a guard seemed to be sympathetic to the prisoners, he would be reported by the other guards.

"The toilet was at the end of the corridor, and the guards refused to allow the prisoners to close the door when they went. I suppose they thought we might escape through the plumbing —no, that wasn't it—they just wanted to break down our sense of being men. Most people didn't worry about it, with the hunger and thirst and lack of air in the windless cages seeming more important, but for me it was the worst indignity of all. I begged to be allowed to close the door, and they wouldn't let me. The thing was, for weeks and weeks I was literally unable to urinate while the guards were watching me. They knew how I felt and would watch especially closely while I was in the toilet. They would joke about it, saying I was the only prisoner they'd ever seen who wasn't overflowing with shit and piss.

"Then I would be in terrible pain and sometimes would go in my bunk in spite of myself, which made the living conditions even worse for the other prisoners. I was so ashamed—I, a revolutionary, an intellectual, a cultured man, pissing in my bed. I had nightmares for years about this after I was let out of camp. To this day, I can't even bring myself to use a public toilet.

"I told the doctor in the hospital this story, and she showed me on the electrocardiogram how my heart had begun to beat six times as fast when I began talking about the toilet with the open door. Even today, it is difficult for me to think about it. I tell you, a young woman, only to give you an idea of what it is like when men try to reduce other men to animals.

"Every prisoner in camp had a terrible feeling of helplessness, knowing at all times that his fate depended on mean, little people. There was a pretty nurse in a camp infirmary—I don't remember what was wrong with me, only that I was happy to be lying in bed instead of working at hard labor—and she followed me to the entrance of a shower room and rubbed her breasts against me. I kissed her, and she immediately turned me in to the administrator. So I wound up in a punishment cell for five days instead of in a bed. She was playing me like an insect."

Boris Alekseivich's voice trembled slightly, and then he continued in a more even tone.

"In general, I think the worst single aspect of life in the camps for everyone was the constant hunger for women. It was never far from our minds. Those of us who were from the old intelligentsia were at least able to fall back on our memories of books and poetry. We had some inner intellectual life to help us master our physical longings. Sometimes I would get a chance to practice my French or German with foreign Communists who had come to our 'promised land' during the twenties. They wanted to build a new world too. . . .

"The situation in regard to women became far worse after the war, when there was a flood of new prisoners who had never belonged to any intelligentsia, even the new Communist intelligentsia, if one could call it that. I was let out of camp for two years during the war to fight in the army—quite a few people got out that way if they had held onto their health. Then in 1943 after Stalingrad, when the situation was no longer so desperate, I was rearrested. It's a common enough story. Told someone what I really thought of Stalin. That's what happened to Solzhenitsyn—the power of his writing is that it reflects the experience of millions of people. But I would have been arrested again even if I hadn't said anything; most people who had been released were sent back to camp after the war.

"At this point, a crush of new people came to the camps because they had been on occupied territory and that was regarded as sufficient evidence of collaboration with the Germans. They were mostly young men between the ages of eighteen and twenty-five, charged with bourgeois nationalism—Ukrainian, Latvian, Lithuanian, whatever. Most of them were just peasant boys, completely illiterate, without politics of any kind. A few had fought with nationalist partisan bands because it seemed like an adventure. A lot of them had just been swept up in deportations of entire villages suspected of having aided partisans who wanted independence from Russia. These boys were like young bulls—all they had cared about in life was chasing girls and drinking vodka. In camp, a good percentage of them went completely mad without women. It wasn't just the sex, but the longing for some reminder of softness and tenderness.

"Even those of us who had some kind of intellectual life also felt we were going crazy. We lived for the rare occasions when we were able to buy a woman for a few minutes. Yes, that was possible, thanks to the fact that there were some free workers in the camps.

"This is how the system worked: There were some jobs in camp, like construction projects involving dynamite, which the prisoners were not trusted to perform. They might blow up the camp, after all. Free workers were brought in to do these jobs, at very high salaries because the work was dangerous and the surroundings unpleasant, to say the least. Actually, the free workers just sat around and drank all day and parceled out their jobs to the prisoners. When the free worker received his salary, a tiny percentage would go to the prisoner who had really done the job as a payoff. There were also some women who were free workers. Sometimes, you could buy one of these women for five or ten minutes with the money you had made.

"It was strictly against the rules—you could receive days in the punishment cell without food or water for it—but we took the chance. If someone had said to me, 'If you take this woman, you will be shot,' I would have said, 'Then go ahead and shoot.' The sex was animal sex—no, something lower, because there was no animal warmth. There was nothing womanly about these women, wrapped in layers of felt and rags, their faces covered with black grease against the Arctic wind. If you looked at them from more than a few meters away, you would never have known they were women. But we risked everything just to have them for a few minutes."

Boris Alekseivich said he could not offer me an explanation of why he had survived in camp while so many others died or went insane. "Partly luck, partly a strong physical constitution. I never got tuberculosis, for example. I certainly had no noble source of strength that the others didn't have. Some truly great spirits, like Mandelstam, died simply because they had no physical strength.* I think I survived not out of nobility but out of

---

* Osip Mandelstam, believed to have died in camp in 1938, is regarded by many Russian intellectuals as the greatest twentieth-century Russian poet. His widow, Nadezhda Yakovlevna, has written a book about her life with Man-

sheer orneriness; I wanted to be around when those mean little people got what was coming to them. Strangely, I never doubted that there would be an eventual reckoning."

Boris Alekseivich was in the first group of prisoners released from camps after the Twentieth Party Congress. The trickle of returning prisoners became a flood between 1956 and 1960; Boris Alekseivich, like many former Party members, applied for "rehabilitation"—an official admission that he should never have been imprisoned. He showed me a creased document from the Supreme Court of the Russian Republic stating that his case had been closed because there was never any proof of the original charges against him. Many posthumous rehabilitations were also issued upon the application of relatives; such was the case with Mandelstam.

"Our lives are governed by documents," Boris Alekseivich said. "I used to wonder whether the person who signed mine ever thought about the man who would receive it and about the fact that this piece of paper meant the end of a whole life and the beginning of another. I think not; the same person may cheerfully have signed whatever papers were needed to send people to camp in the first place.

"I did try to begin a new life when I was released, quickly, very quickly, because there was so little time left to me. I married again within a few months. I was able to talk to someone who had known my first wife in camp; she had simply collapsed one day as she was working with another woman trying to cut down a tree. As I told you, I could not find out what happened to my daughters. The people we left them with had also died in camp. They probably have no idea now who their real parents were. They were only babies when we were taken away. Still, sometimes I dream that they might find me. I wonder what

---

delstam and her efforts to save his verse from destruction; it is required reading for anyone who wishes to understand what happened to the intelligentsia under Stalin. It first appeared in Russia in *samizdat* and has been published in the United States under the title *Hope Against Hope*.

kind of people they are, whether they have the true picture of the revolution and what followed that I could give them. But I know I will never have the chance.

"I had a son by my second wife. You see, I thought I could build another family to replace the one I had lost. But you can never really begin a new life after you have been through what I went through—not really. Can the survivors of the Nazi concentration camps ever put it all behind them? I can't believe it is possible. I was unfit for normal family life with a woman; the years in camp, with the never-ending, elemental threat to survival, had destroyed whatever it is in a person that makes him able to share a life with someone else. You may think this was only my personality. I can only tell you that everyone I know who lived through the camps is unbalanced in some way, even if it doesn't show on the surface. My wife was a good woman, but she became deeply depressed and angry because of my constant self-absorption, my unending memories. And she was much younger than I—my memories didn't mean anything to her. She kept saying, 'Can't we just forget about it and go on living.' But I can't forget. She divorced me after five years. I don't blame her. I see my son often, and she never criticized me to him.

"I have also spent a good deal of time in hospitals since I was released. I have serious heart trouble, like the vast majority of prisoners who had 'hard physical labor' written on their documents in camp. I have had two heart attacks—one in 1959 and the second in 1965, after Khrushchev was thrown out.

"I had hopes for the renewal of our country during the Khrushchev years, especially after *One Day in the Life of Ivan Denisovich* was published. What a sensation it made—saying the unsayable for all of us. I still have the copy of *Novy Mir** in

* The monthly magazine *Novy Mir* and its editor, Alexsandr Tvardovsky, championed Solzhenitsyn and other anti-Stalinist and liberal writers. In 1970, Tvardovsky was removed from his job as editor of the magazine as the culmination of a campaign waged against him for many years by literary and political conservatives. When Tvardovsky died last December after a long

which it first came out. I no longer hoped for a new world or a perfect world—my experiences had stripped me of that illusion —but I did hope for a society that was a little more decent, a little more just. At that time, there seemed to be some reason to hope. I have no such hopes now. When they refused to publish *Cancer Ward*, I knew the process of trying to uproot Stalinism had ended.* They could only go so far and no further—there were too many people still in the government whose hands were filthy and bloody from what they had done during the Stalin years. I should have known this would happen and not have allowed myself to hope. Now I have no hope and my mind is at peace. Hope can drive a man madder than despair.

"I am not a revolutionary anymore. I no longer believe in the perfectability of man; if I weren't an atheist I would believe in original sin. I suppose you might say I believe in original evil. We were wrong to be dazzled by one idea, to believe that it and it alone could save the world. I know now that no single idea can explain everything and solve everything; human life is too complex. Fanaticism destroys more than it creates."

Boris Alekseivich cited the death of the old Russian intelligentsia as an example of what he meant by the destructive power of fanaticism.

"The intelligentsia of my youth in Russia was an extraordinary phenomenon. In my home there were always visitors from other countries—French, Czechs, Germans. But I believe to this day that the Russian intellectuals had broader minds than all the others. I hope you do not think I am just an old man rambling about my youth to no point; I am trying desperately to convey to you the importance of what was lost.

"We of the old intelligentsia were interested in both eastern

---

struggle with cancer, Solzhenitsyn made his first public appearance in years at the funeral. Some orthodox literary figures were also present, and they were reportedly stunned when Solzhenitsyn appeared at the graveside.

* Plans for publishing Solzhenitsyn's *Cancer Ward* were ended in 1966 after the fall of Khrushchev as a logical step in the new leaders' policy of preventing any further public discussion of Stalin's crimes.

and western civilization, because Russia was the meeting point of East and West. We all spoke several languages. The world in which we lived is perfectly re-created in Nadezhda Mandelstam's memoir. I often think of Mandelstam, our supreme poet in this century, reading Dante in the original Italian. He felt that reading poetry was engaging in conversation with another poet across the centuries, as his wife has written. This was the world we lived in, we intellectuals who became irrelevant. The Russian tragedy was that we never had a middle culture between the illiterate masses and the men who had conversations with Dante.

"We could have built upon the old intelligentsia, but instead we destroyed it with our intense belief that all art must directly further the aims of the revolution. I say 'we' advisedly and with shame; I was both a member of the old intelligentsia and one of its destroyers, although I didn't realize what was happening at the time.

"Only a tiny minority of the young know anything about their intellectual heritage from before the revolution. Some of the young writers who emerged during the Khrushchev years were trying to re-create links with the past, but they can never succeed completely. Censorship and fear have destroyed too much. I know it is a popular view in the West that Russian cultural life only went underground during the Stalin era; that is true to some extent but not entirely. Much of it was simply torn up by the roots. You may know a poem by Andrei Voznesensky about Pasternak. . . ."

He then recited a poem written after Boris Pasternak's death by Voznesensky, one of the new generation of writers who have not only attempted to re-create links with the past but who have tried to restore the Russian language after its long debasement by political jargon.

"Leaves and Roots"

They bore him to no entombment,
They bore him to enthronement.

Greyer than a monument's
Granite, a roan tint
Like its bronze, who living
Had been a locomotive in
Full steam,
   the poet, unkempt
Found spades more divine
Than any votive lamp.

Thirst parched his lilac . . .
Like a starstream
     sweat
Was steaming from his back,
An oven full of bread.

His house gaped, empty from
Attic down to hall;
No one in the dining-room.
In Russia—not a soul.

The artists depart, hats
Off
  as to a church,
Far echoing estates,
The oak tree and the birch.

Burgeoning, they vanquish,
Vanish to a new beginning
For the plains and planets,
Away from false guilding.
Above, the forests loose
Their leaves, but out of sight
In the soil fivefold roots
Are twisting, tough and tight.

       —translated by Robert Conquest

Said Boris Alekseivich:

"I recite this poem only to tell you I disagree with it. Pasternak, it is true, lived through both the old world and the new.
And he did leave roots. But how many? And will they be pre-

served? Most of the old intelligentsia died. In some cases their work has been preserved, but the vast majority of even our best-educated young people do not have access to it. Mandelstam isn't published. Other great poets of the same era, like Anna Akhmatova, are published in truncated form; the censor slices away the most meaningful lines. Young people today have no idea what it meant to be an intellectual before the revolution; they have no accurate sense of their own country's history, much less the rest of the world. Today learning means a diploma, the possibility of a new apartment, maybe now a car. We destroyed the idea that learning and truth and beauty were worth pursuing for their own sake."

He stared into his now-empty wine glass. "Sometimes I look into the history of other countries for a clue of what happened in ours. Your own history is not without fanatics, but they were never able to acquire enough power to do what we did. You are blessed in America; you never had any revolutionaries who wanted to destroy everything that had gone before. I am particularly interested in the young radicals today in America and Western Europe. Of course, the Soviet press has nothing worth reading about them, but I have been able to acquire some information from foreign publications that fall into the hands of my friends.

"They are not revolutionaries in the sense that we were, because they seem to have no real plan for the construction of a new world. But they do resemble us in one respect—the belief that all old values must go to make way for the new, whatever the new is. How well I recognize that arrogant assumption that it is possible to construct a just new society without any regard to past human experience.

"But despite the fact that I have said I believe in original evil, I cannot honestly say I have no belief in progress. These are two contradictory ideas inside one head, of course, but I now believe that sanity has something to do with being able to live with contradictory ideas. The fanatic must have everything wrapped up in one glittering explanation.

"I admire the young men in our country who are going to prison for the right to speak and write what they think. Just as I admire young men who are willing to go to prison in your country to protest what they regard as an unjust war in Vietnam.

"The political dissenters in Russia today are not going into the camps helplessly, as we did, without any idea of why these things were happening. They go knowing what they believe in, and they are willing to take the consequences. I do not really believe their dissent can change this system under which we live, but I salute them anyway. They have chosen their own fate, and this is already a basic difference and a hopeful improvement over my generation. When I think of the people my age who went to their deaths believing that if only Stalin knew what was going on, he would put a stop to it. Only we could have stopped it, and we were too silent and confused to do anything. My heart pounds when I hear on the Voice of America or the BBC that a Russian has gone to prison for writing a book about Russia. We went to prison for doing nothing; that is the real tragedy. I love these young people so much for what they are doing.

"Ach, now you will go away thinking that deep down in my heart, I am still an old revolutionary."

IV

Tanya

At nineteen Tanya seemed younger than she was in every respect except her seriousness of purpose. Compared to most of the young people I met in Moscow, she was both socially and intellectually unsophisticated. Foreigners generally see only the surface of provincial life during their travels inside the Soviet Union; the limited amount of time available for touring any given city—determined partly by visa regulations—usually permits only passing contacts with local residents. Because Soviet citizens do tend to speak more freely outside of Moscow, my conversations on trips were tantalizing in that they raised issues which could not be fully explored due to lack of time. With Tanya I was able to explore them at greater length. Her attitudes convinced me that I had vastly underestimated the specialness of Moscow. It is the center of Soviet intellectual as well as political life, and the presence of a large resident foreign community gives Moscow links to the rest of the world that do not exist elsewhere in the Soviet Union. One example of this is the amount of foreign-language-literature in circulation. Moscow has a heavier concentration than any other city of Soviet citizens whose special jobs give them the right to order books and magazines from abroad. They may be high-level scholars or journalists, scientists, Party leaders or KGB officials. In addition, foreigners who live in Moscow are free to receive any publications they want and often pass them on to Russian friends. I sometimes noticed old copies of *Time* or *Newsweek* in Russian homes. "I beg, borrow or steal them from any foreigner I meet," a cheerful student admitted. In Tanya's hometown, there was no comparable seepage of foreign literary influences. On her trips to Moscow, she was thrilled at being able to buy *Moscow News*, a turgid English-language paper published by the Soviets that consists mainly of reprints from speeches by Party leaders. In Moscow it is read primarily by desperate American tourists who are foolish enough to come to the Soviet Union without an adequate supply of their own reading matter. But *Moscow News* was unavailable in Kustanai. Tanya, who was studying to become an English teacher, was delighted to practice her reading on some new material. Compared to Tanya, most of my Moscow friends were the equivalent of Vice President Agnew's elite snobs. From time to time, Party leaders make statements about Moscow intellectuals that are comparable to Agnew's views on the eastern intellectual establishment.

I first saw Tanya in the Tretyakov Gallery, which houses a conglomeration of old Russian masterpieces and contemporary monstrosities. The museum-goer wanders dazedly through room after room of Lenin in myriad postures but is dazzled in the basement upon encountering icons painted by the fourteenth-century master Andrei Rublyov. (Rublyov, who introduced a new flow of motion into the previously static icon, would be the Russian equivalent of Giotto had Russian history produced a Renaissance. Instead, he is an isolated master whose breakthroughs represent the highest point of old Russian art rather than the beginning of a new era.)

Tanya was sight-seeing with a Bulgarian engineering student who was also a tourist in Moscow. Overhearing my husband's conversation with a friend, she commented on a painting in halting classroom English. She gestured excitedly, trying at once to remember her English verb forms, tuck in a pink-and-white-checked blouse that had slipped out of her turquoise skirt and push a long mop of reddish-blond hair out of her eyes. She peered at the paintings with an earnestness accentuated by the rimless glasses she wore to correct severe myopia. The icons were Tanya's favorite works of art, and she nodded in vigorous agreement when my husband commented on Rublyov's use of motion. "I love the icons so much," she said. "It is very pleasant for us that a foreigner is interested in our art."

Many Russian young people share an interest in prerevolutionary art. It is part of their search for links with the past—a search whose importance Boris Alekseivich may have underestimated. For many years, the old art—like old literature—was disparaged, neglected and sometimes destroyed because of its religious character. Since Stalin's death, the Soviet government has come to recognize that its pre-1917 art treasury is both a tourist attraction and an important part of Russian cultural history. The government spends considerable sums on restoration of old art objects, and young people are now encouraged to take a cultural and aesthetic, though not religious, interest in the icons and churches. "I am an atheist," Tanya once said, expressing her feelings in an odd formulation that was probably due to her shaky grasp of English negatives. "I cannot but doubt that god does not exist. This is the way I have been brought up and taught all my life. I was baptized in the Orthodox Church to please my grandmother, because she is old and it gave her happiness. But it meant nothing to my parents. I love the churches and icons because they are part of our history. The Kremlin is filled with beautiful old churches, and it is the center of our government. I don't find this strange."

Walking through the museum, Tanya told us she was a second-year English student at a teacher-training institute in Kustanai and that we were the first people she had ever met who spoke English as their native language. She would be in Moscow only two weeks, and then her classes would resume after the summer break. Would I meet her the next day? I could practice my Russian on her, and she would practice her English on me. We agreed to meet at the Lenin Library, a building of Babylonian proportions that houses the second-largest collection of books in the world (after the Library of Congress in Washington). Tanya was impressed that I had acquired a library card there, a privilege usually reserved for students and faculty of the more prestigious Moscow universities. Unlike my Moscow friends, she did not yet realize that foreigners in Russia enjoy privileges denied ordinary Soviet citizens.

A cold September rain was pouring at our appointed meeting time, but that did not deter Tanya's enthusiasm for a walk around Moscow. She continually pointed to large red-and-white signs with the usual political slogans—LONG LIVE THE SOVIET PEOPLE, PEACE AND FRIENDSHIP or LONG LIVE THE COMMUNIST PARTY OF THE SOVIET UNION.

"Are you able to translate the signs?" she asked. At first I thought she was joking, since Soviet political slogans carry messages with all the subtlety of DRINK COCA-COLA. Also, my Moscow friends were either bored speechless by Party slogans or tended to look for the occasional obscenities that resulted when an illuminated letter short-circuited, creating a change in the meaning of a word. It took me several minutes to realize that my new friend from Kazakhstan was entirely serious in her desire that I take in the meaning of the slogans.

She saw everything in Moscow with a fresh and delighted eye. Her Bulgarian friend had taken her to dinner the previous night at a restaurant with a spectacular view of the Kremlin from the twenty-first floor of the Rossia Hotel, Moscow's equivalent of a Hilton. They had drunk Georgian champagne and enjoyed service and food which more closely approximates Western standards than at any other restaurant in Moscow. "You have been to London and Paris," she said, "and I suppose such places are usual there. But to me this is all new and wonderful." Another Moscow amenity that pleased Tanya was the chance to buy Polish fashion magazines, which were not on sale in Kustanai. (Magazines from the Socialist countries of Eastern Europe are livelier than Soviet publications and disappear quickly from newsstands. They are generally available only in the larger cities and are harder to find the farther east you go in the Soviet Union.) Despite her seriousness, Tanya was a young girl very much interested in fun and romance. She would not, and indeed could not when I tried to explain to her, understand the rejection of material middle-class pleasures by radical youths in the United States and western Europe.

Tanya's city in Kazakhstan had swelled in population during the past ten years as Russians emigrated—some lured by higher salaries and others by the promise of adventure—to help develop the Soviet "virgin lands." Her father was a construction engineer, one of a growing class of mobile military and civilian technocrats who are responsible for the physical development and administration of new projects ranging from dairies to

dams. Like employees of large American corporations, the Soviet technocrats are on the move continually, from one far-flung
province to another. They are usually Russian or Ukrainian, and
they work in areas that are still educationally backward in
comparison to the western part of the Soviet Union. In twelve
years, Tanya's family had lived in five different towns. Her best
friend, Irina, whose father was an army major, had moved to
Kustanai from Tashkent, capital of the Central Asian republic
of Uzbekistan. Before Tashkent, Irina's family had lived in a
small settlement near the Arctic Circle.

The presence of a large Russian upper middle class in areas
heavily populated by members of other nationality groups is
one manifestation of a serious domestic problem—relations between the various nationalities that make up the Soviet Union.
Every Soviet citizen has a nationality stamped on his internal
passport, a document required for everyone over age sixteen.
Nationality can mean ethnic origin, language, skin color or all
three. Russian, Ukrainian, Armenian, Uzbek, Kazakh, Jewish—
all are regarded as nationalities by official Soviet standards. If a
youngster has parents of different nationalities, he can choose
between them when he receives his first passport. In the non-
Russian republics, many Russians are also placed in strategic
Party and government jobs because they are considered essen-
tial to the central government's control. Although they rule the
country, ethnic Russians are expected to be in a minority by the
end of the 1970's. While the housing shortage helps bring about
an extremely low birth rate in the cities of European Russia, the
opposite is true in Soviet Central Asia and the Far East.

As in other developing areas of the world, the tradition of
having large families has continued while medical advances
have cut both infant mortality and the adult death rate. The
birth rate soars in Soviet Asia, while in some areas of Russia
deaths exceed live births. Whether the Russians can maintain
their present degree of control and power when they become a
minority within the total Soviet population is an unanswered
question but a vital one for the nation's future. Having grown

up inside the Russian management class in the provinces, Tanya seemed to have given little thought to relations between nationalities. Her unconscious observations, particularly those related to her life as a student, provided some incidental insights into the working of the nationalities hierarchy in everyday life.

Tanya had chosen her teacher-training institute in Kustanai in order to remain near her family. On the basis of her academic performance, she could have been admitted to the larger and more prestigious University of Kazakhstan in Alma-Ata. In size and academic quality, the difference between the two is comparable to the gap between a small Midwestern teachers' college and a Big Ten university. "Alma-Ata is a city of over one million," Tanya explained. "I don't know how it would be, living there without my family. I have never been away from home for a long period of time. I really prefer to be surrounded by loving people." Her desire to stay at home was atypical, judging from the students I met both in Moscow and other cities. Most of them complained bitterly because it was nearly impossible for young unmarried men and women to obtain apartments of their own. The housing shortage is such that marriage is usually a requirement for receiving separate apartments from one's parents.

To enter her institute, Tanya was required to pass four examinations in Russian language, Russian literature, English, and Soviet history. There were seven applicants for every place in the foreign-language department* and four for each place in the institute as a whole.

There are some eight hundred institutions of higher education in the Soviet Union known as VUZ (the initials stand for *vyshee uchebnoe zavedenie*, literally "institution of higher education"). Only about fifty of these are full-fledged universities with a wide variety of departments. The rest train students for

---

* A university department is translated as *fakultet* in Russian. Sometimes, though, a *fakultet* is the equivalent of colleges that exist within large American universities.

jobs in specific fields such as teaching, engineering or medicine. Some are as prestigious as universities in their own academic fields. A foreign-language student, for example, would probably get a better education in his area of interest at the Moscow Institute of Foreign Languages than at Moscow State University, generally regarded as the best comprehensive university in the Soviet Union.

Competition for admission to universities is fierce; at the most prestigious in Moscow and Leningrad there may be fifteen or twenty applicants for every place. Only one out of seven high school graduates is now able to enter an institution of higher education; the proportion is expected to drop to one in ten by 1975. According to the 1970 Soviet Census, 5.5 percent of the adult population had some education beyond high school; 4.2 percent had completed their higher education.

Tanya was keenly aware that Soviet students constitute a privileged minority and at the same time defensive about any suggestion that they are a recognizable elite. "I realize I am fortunate to be a student," she said. "That is one reason I feel such an obligation to work diligently. But in our country, everyone has the right to a higher education, and it is free. In my opinion, that is one of the main advantages our system has over yours."

Tuition is free at Soviet universities and dormitory fees range from five to eight rubles a month. If a student eats in the college dining hall, food costs an extra ruble a day. Because she lived at home, Tanya's education cost her virtually nothing. When I told her that about half of all American high school graduates go on to college despite steep fees, she was at first disbelieving and then confused. "But it is not written in your constitution that you have a right to an education," she finally said. "It is written in our constitution for everyone to see."

Tanya also echoed the official Soviet rationale for strictly limiting access to higher education. "We need workers in the factories as much as we need people trained in universities. It would not do to have everyone become a professor, so what would be the point of admitting everyone to a university?" Since 1951, the number of high school graduates has increased 700 percent, while the number of university places has only doubled. Soviet sociologists are beginning to worry about whether their society may be creating a class of frustrated young people whose aspirations have been raised by a high school education only to find the door to further upward mobility shut at the university level. At this stage of economic development, the Soviet Union's greatest need is for more skilled blue-collar workers. Soviet economic planners would apparently rather have dissatisfied high school graduates working in factories than college graduates with no jobs at all. For Tanya, the only important fact about the Soviet educational system was that there are no theoretical barriers to entering a university. The reality of a university structure that is closed to between 85 and 90 percent of all high school graduates did not concern her. She was absolutely convinced that the Soviet Union offered its citizens greater educational opportunity than any other country in the world.

Tanya shared the common Soviet misconception engendered by official propaganda that there is no free public education in the United States or Western Europe. "Only the rich can afford to go to school in your country," she said. "What happens to the children whose parents cannot pay?" I explained to her that no one in the United States has to pay tuition for elementary or high schools but that parents who wish to do so can enroll their children in private schools. She was unable to grasp the concept of state-supported and private schools existing side by side. "How can your government permit this?" she asked. "These private schools must be in competition with the state." Tanya also believed that blacks were forbidden to enter American universities. That idea undoubtedly stemmed from Soviet newspaper articles about racial segregation in the United States. It was harder to trace the source of some of her other notions about the rest of the world. She told me solemnly that it was so difficult to enter a high school in England that even the queen's son was not admitted. When I asked her why she believed that, she said she had heard it from a professor who lived in England many years ago. In none of my conversations with Moscow residents—educated or uneducated, liberal or conservative—did I encounter such farfetched concepts about life in foreign countries.

Tanya's views added up to the conviction that she was a very lucky young woman. She was particularly enthusiastic about her future career as an English teacher; despite her belief in the weakness of capitalism, she too hoped that knowing a foreign language would enable her to travel abroad someday. She was determined to prepare diligently in order to succeed in her chosen field.

Tanya was genuinely shocked when I told her that class attendance is not compulsory at American universities. "If a student missed more than one class at my institute," she said, "he would be called before a meeting of the Komsomol and would receive a reprimand. If he continued to miss class, there would be much stronger discipline—he might be accompanied to class every day by a Komsomol member and required to spend his free Sunday preparing for class. A student who was absent regularly would not be allowed to remain at the institute."

Tanya attended classes five hours a day, Monday through Saturday. (The six-day week is standard both in universities and lower schools, although factories and offices have switched to a five-day week.) During her sophomore year, she spent three or four hours a day in English courses and one to two hours in a political course on the philosophy of Marxism-Leninism. All students are required to take political classes, but otherwise they are not allowed to take any classes outside their specialized field of study. A future English teacher does not take science; a future scientist does not study history or philosophy. There is no equivalent of the "basic college" courses that require most American university students to do some work in humanities, physical science and sociology. A Soviet student does not have any say in planning his own curriculum, other than the initial choice of a department. During the latter half of her sophomore year, Tanya's program was expanded to include the history of the English language and Kazakh.

Tanya and her Russian friends spoke Kazakh poorly or not at all, although most of them were likely to begin their teaching careers in Kazakhstan on a government assignment. All Soviet college graduates, with the exception of a few outstanding students who receive special "free diplomas," are required to spend two or three years wherever the state sends them. It is one way of meeting the need for trained personnel in rural areas where few people want to live or work, although most college graduates return to the cities as soon as their period of compulsory service ends. Kazakh-language schools exist, as do schools in nearly every language spoken by national minorities in the Soviet Union. (Yiddish is an exception, and this has fueled accusations that the Soviet government's policy is the suppression of Jewish culture.) But parents who want their children to get ahead in Soviet society generally send them to Russian-language schools. Tanya expected to teach in a high school, where she would have little need for Kazakh in her work. "It is a very difficult language," she told me, "and all of the high school students who are studying English will already speak Russian. Kazakh is my third language, so it would be much too difficult for me to teach English to students who did not speak Russian."

In areas like Kazakhstan, a large percentage of the schoolteachers are Russian. Tanya showed me a picture of her class at the institute and proudly pointed out the one Kazakh and two Tatars in the group; most of the other students were Russian or Ukrainian. Yet Kazakhs or other non-European minorities, like the Tatars, make up over half the population of Kazakhstan. Tanya was completely unaware that her pride in the presence of three Asians in the class was a small but perfect illustration of the Soviet version of unequal opportunity.

The reasons are complex and have some resemblance to the factor operating against blacks, Puerto Ricans and Mexican-

Americans in the United States. Many members of Asian minorities live in rural areas where educational attainment was lowest before the Bolshevik Revolution; nationality and geography reinforce each other. Despite massive Soviet educational efforts that have turned a largely illiterate population into a largely literate one, a rural child is three or four times more likely than a city child to become a high school dropout.

There is seldom deliberate discrimination against children from national minorities; educational inequities stem from a cycle of culture deprivation that is familiar in every other part of the world. Parents who are poorly educated themselves are seldom equipped to provide their children with adequate incentives to succeed in school; in the Soviet Union, as in the United States, public efforts have not been able to compensate for this deficiency. Many young people from rural areas and/or national minority groups who do manage to obtain a higher education use it to escape to the cities. Tanya said she would probably return to a city as soon as she had completed her compulsory service in a rural Kazakh school. Educated Kazakhs and Tatars desire the amenities of city life as much as Russians.

Tanya realized there were some inequalities in Soviet society, but she believed a Communist version of the Puritan work ethic would solve all such problems. "Anyone who works hard can have any kind of life he wants in our country," she asserted. "There are no limits to what anyone can achieve here."

Tanya's belief in hard work was more than rhetoric; she practiced what she preached. "I'm trying to get a better command of the language and to get profound knowledge in order to put it into practice," she wrote me. "To tell the truth, I'm thirsting for knowledge . . . I'm disappointed at twenty-four hours [in a day]. Why so little? Why?"

Soviet universities require an extraordinary amount of daily written work. They resemble secondary schools in this respect —a fact noted unfavorably by some prominent Soviet scientists who feel the universities do not give students enough scope for independent work and creative thinking.

Tanya said she spent three to five hours a day on English homework and one or two hours preparing for her course in the philosophy of Marxism-Leninism. "So, it is true, I spend between nine and thirteen hours every day either attending classes or getting ready for them. The work is difficult, but it is necessary."

Tanya also took on extra work beyond her course requirements. She listened intently to English-Polish records that were a present from a boyfriend stationed with the Red Army in Poland. Such records are widely available in Eastern Europe but are difficult to find in Soviet stores—especially outside of Moscow, Leningrad and Kiev. Tanya said the models of English pronunciation on the records had been extremely helpful to her. "It didn't matter that I couldn't understand Polish. What mattered was the speakers on the records were Englishmen, and I could see where I was going wrong in my pronunciation." The limited supply of English-Russian records sells out quickly in Moscow stores, but Tanya was able to find several and bring them back to Kustanai. "All of my friends use them too," she said. "Everyone was very excited."

On the basis of Tanya's descriptions, I concluded that foreign-language teaching at her institute must be old-fashioned by Western standards. English lessons began every day with phonetic exercises based on some reading—usually a memorized proverb or poem. She gave me three examples of poems used in her lessons: Byron's "She Walks in Beauty," Longfellow's "The Slave's Dream," and Coleridge's "She Is Not Fair." After the phonetic exercises, students were required to retell several pages in their own words from the passages they had read at home. They made up short stories based on the new English expressions they had learned and either recited or handed them to the teacher in written form. I asked Tanya, "Do you ever try to have ordinary English conversation in class?" She replied, "That isn't part of the curriculum."

Tanya said the students often had to remain after class to copy portions of the text they were to study at home because "unfortunately, many of us have no textbooks." Irate letters about textbook shortages in the provinces appear frequently in Soviet newspapers. The complaints come from teachers, parents and students in widely scattered areas of the country. The less prestigious institutions in small cities like Kustanai receive short shrift when new books are distributed; sometimes texts do not arrive until weeks or months after the academic year has begun. The same problem occurs in elementary and secondary schools. Educators blame publishers, publishers blame truckers and the railroads and everyone blames the general shortage of paper in the Soviet Union.

Tanya's teacher-training institute was not even in the second rank of Soviet higher education establishments; it would be a mistake to conclude on the basis of her descriptions that foreign language teaching in all Soviet universities is equally out of date. In the Republic of Georgia, I met students at Tbilisi State University who were well grounded in important English and American literature through the 1940's. They had just finished Faulkner and, to my surprise, were beginning D. H. Lawrence. Their teacher was a sophisticated man who had spent considerable time in England, and he would certainly never have told his students that the queen's son could not get into high school. However, Tanya's institute is probably more typical of the general level of instruction—particularly for future teachers. Most of the English teachers I met in ordinary Soviet high schools were as atrociously prepared to teach a foreign language as the average high school French or Spanish teacher in the United States. They had more excuse than Americans, of course, because their opportunities for foreign contacts and travel were severely limited. There are special language institutes and programs where the level of instruction is high, but they are geared toward students being trained for special jobs—usually in the Foreign Ministry or KGB. Tanya was a potential exception to the general mediocre run of high school English teachers, because she was so serious about trying to supplement her training. She displayed that earnestness during her acquaintance with me by constantly using her English in conversations, even though communication would have been easier in Russian.

She had only been studying English seriously for a year when I met her, but her pronunciation and vocabulary were both quite advanced. Her accomplishments contrasted with those of some high school English teachers I met who were unable to put together more than one sentence outside their classroom drills.

While Tanya's life beyond the classroom was placid and uneventful by Moscow standards, she did not seem to find it dull. Trips to Moscow were the high points of her vacations, but she enjoyed traveling almost anywhere in the Soviet Union. When I met her in August, she told me how sorry she was that she could not join her friends who were helping bring in the harvest on a collective farm. Soviet universities remain closed until October 1 so that students can help with the harvesting. "I had a stomach operation last winter," she said, "and the doctor said farm work was forbidden for a year. I had such a wonderful time when I worked on the farm last summer that I am very unhappy. We were paid 100 rubles, and there were students from all over. There were also lots of soldiers, and it was all very gay. I want to go again next year." Tanya's positive attitude toward compulsory summer work was not shared by the young Muscovites I met; many of them tried fake excuses to free them from their duty to the state.

Tanya did not spend all of her time worrying about her English lessons and pining away for work on the *kolkhoz*. She was interested in boyfriends and ultimately in marriage, but like most young Soviet women, she could not imagine marriage and a family without a career. She half believed in many romantic folk legends and told me she intended to look into a mirror on New Year's Eve in hopes of seeing the image of her future husband. The partial nature of her belief was evidence of a generation gap; Galya—thirty years older than Tanya—believed in the New Year's Eve legend absolutely and told me it had helped her find her husband. Despite her romanticism, Tanya was determined not to marry until several years after graduation from the institute.

"I want to be free and independent for some time," she said. "After I finish school, I will go away to work somewhere in the country and be of service to my society. Then I will probably return to a city. I don't expect to get married until I'm sure of what I want in life. Children are a great responsibility, for one thing, and I don't want them until I am sure of myself." Tanya's girlfriends were equally emphatic about the undesirability of early marriage.

I asked Tanya what she did in her spare time. "As I only get 'good' and 'excellent' marks, I do have some extra time," she said. "Although I must admit it's not as often as I would like. I go to the movies, read English books, watch television or knit and crochet. I knit myself a scarf and am crocheting a white jacket for my mother's birthday. I love to dance too. But I don't know many boys who are good dancers."

Tanya said she personally knew no one who took drugs but added, "I have heard it happens." Hashish grows freely in many parts of Soviet Central Asia, where it is often a part of the traditional culture. It is illegal but nevertheless makes its way to the cities of European Russia. We met many students in Moscow, Kiev, Leningrad and Tbilisi who said openly that they and their friends smoked hashish. A student in Leningrad invited us to a pot party, but we were not about to take part in an activity prohibited by Soviet law. Most students agreed that heroin and other hard drugs had not penetrated the hashish-smoking subculture to any significant extent. "Things like heroin are strictly for criminals," Tanya said. "In any case, no drug could ever be as exciting as a book to me."

The books Tanya meant were, again, quite different from the literature that captivated young people in Moscow. Her favorite American author was—probably inevitably—Jack London. London is one of the few American authors widely available in translation in the Soviet Union. Also predictably, her favorite

English author was Galsworthy. (The BBC version of the *Forsythe Saga*, dubbed in Russian, was shown on Soviet television beginning in the fall of 1971. Russian viewers, long fascinated by the book, were as enthralled as American audiences had been by the endless TV serialization of *Peyton Place*.)

Of the classical Russian authors, Tanya preferred Mikhail Lermontov and Tolstoy. The Soviet authorities take a more positive view of Tolstoy than of any other classical Russian writer, mainly because he wrote about the harsh life of peasants. Dostoevsky was virtually banned during the Stalin years and is just beginning to be reintroduced in high school literature courses. The newest Soviet edition of *The Brothers Karamazov* is much shorter than the original because the censors have deleted most of the religious portions.

Boris Alekseivich would not have been surprised to find that Tanya was almost totally ignorant about the great writers and poets who were murdered or muzzled during the Stalin years and whose works have not yet been restored to their rightful place in Soviet literature. She had read virtually nothing by Mandelstam, Boris Pasternak, Isaak Babel, Anna Akhmatova, Velimir Khlebnikov or Marina Tsvetayeva and in some cases did not even recognize their names. To draw a proper analogy, one would have to find an American university student specializing in foreign languages who had not read Yeats, Hemingway, Eliot, Auden or E. E. Cummings.

In contrast to most young people I met in Moscow, Tanya had not read any *samizdat* manuscripts. Her preferences in modern Soviet writers were completely different from those of my Moscow friends. She did not care for the poems of Voznesensky or Yevtushenko, both of whom are especially popular among young people. She had not read any Solzhenitsyn; she was only ten years old when Khrushchev allowed *One Day in the Life of Ivan Denisovich* to be published. By the time she was in her teens and old enough to take an interest in such matters, Solzhenitsyn was already in political disgrace and copies of his officially published works were being removed from library shelves. "I do not need to read these things to know that Stalin's time was bad for our country and how wrong it is for one man to rule everything," she said. Tanya believed Stalinism was dead in the Soviet Union; she said one of the main reasons she did not like the Chinese was that they approved of Stalinist methods. "And," she said smiling, "there are so many of them." I felt her attitudes justified much of Boris Alekseivich's pessimism about youth; if Stalinism did return, she would have no standards by which to recognize it.

Oddly, Anatoly Kuznetsov had been one of her favorite authors before his defection in London. She was old enough to have read his *Babi Yar*, first published in the Soviet Union in heavily censored form in 1966. "It is a pity he abandoned his country," she said in a tone like that of a pre-Vatican II Roman Catholic mother whose daughter had married out of the church.

Tanya and her friends all wished for free travel, both in Eastern Europe and the West. "It's a pity," said one of her girlfriends. "I have the money for a trip to England but I could not possibly hope to be picked for a tour at my age. There should be more tourism for anyone who wants to travel and can pay for it." Tanya wrote me that her class was studying the subject of "London" and asked for my impressions of the city to supplement what she and her friends had been able to find in books.

Because she was interested both in music and in improving her English, Tanya listened regularly to the English-language broadcasts of the Voice of America. I never met a student in any part of the Soviet Union who did not listen to the VOA. Although reception is hampered by jamming, Russians patiently persevere. For obvious reasons, English-language broadcasts are interfered with less than Russian-language ones. Many students also listened to the BBC, saying they preferred its news broadcasts because the reports were less slanted by American government propaganda. (I preferred the BBC for the same reason in Moscow.) The student consensus, however, was that the VOA offered better music than the BBC. Tanya loved jazz and rock records. "The classical music we can hear on our own [Soviet] records," she said. "But, to tell the truth, much of the music I like is on the foreign radio stations."

Tanya's view of the world did not appear to have been significantly affected by the news she heard on Western radio. When she visited Moscow in the winter of 1971, the much-publicized campaign of Soviet Jews who wanted to emigrate to Israel and the official counterattack were at their height. Tanya told me the vast majority of Russian Jews who had already been permitted to leave for Israel wanted to return to the Soviet Union. I asked her why she thought that, and she said because she had read an article about Jewish emigration in the newspaper *Vechernaya Moskva* (*Evening Moscow*). Tanya's attitudes toward what she read in the official press were far less critical than those of anyone I knew in Moscow. It was instructive to learn this, because I had incorrectly concluded after six months in Moscow that no one believed anything he read in the official press. I told Tanya it was true that many Soviet Jews encountered serious problems adjusting to life in Israel but that all available evidence suggested only a tiny minority actually wanted to return to Russia. She said very politely that I was wrong and had been brainwashed by American and Zionist propaganda. At that point, her friend interrupted with the observation that there should be more tourism. I replied that emigration should be a right in any country. "That," Tanya's friend said firmly, "is of course a completely different matter." Said Tanya: "The state has the right to control its citizens."

The girls said they did not believe everything in Soviet newspapers "any more than you believe everything in yours." Tanya's favorite paper was *Komsomolskaya Pravda*, the organ of the Komsomol Central Committee. Tanya and her friends were members of the Komsomol, as are virtually all Soviet high school and university students. *Komsomol'ka*, as the paper is popularly abbreviated, prints many youth-oriented stories and and also runs more articles than many other papers about needed reforms in Soviet society. During the 1970 centennial year commemorating Lenin's birth, *Komsomol'ka* chided various groups for going overboard by organizing dance contests in honor of Lenin and producing a chocolate medallion imprinted with an outline of Lenin's head. "We like stories of that kind," Tanya said. "I really object more to what is left out of our newspapers than to what is printed. When the Americans landed on the moon, young people were very disappointed that so little appeared in our papers and on television about it. An event like this is important for the whole world, not for just one country. I wanted to see those men walking on the moon myself."

Tanya was astonished to learn that neither television nor newspapers in the United States are government-owned. Interestingly, she believed that American newspapers print only what advertisers want at the same time she believed the papers are owned by the government. "But the businesses and the government want all the same things, is that not true?" she asked.

Tanya had read an article by a Soviet correspondent who questioned students at the University of Michigan about World War II. Not one of the students, according to Tanya, knew that 20,000,000 Soviet citizens had died in the war. (On the basis of my own experiences as an education reporter in the United States, I found the Soviet correspondent's assertion plausible.) It was a strange coincidence that Tanya should have mentioned the article to me at that time, because another Soviet acquaintance who worked for a well-known magazine had just told me his journal surveyed a sampling of Russian high school students and found that more than half had no idea the United States had participated in the war. An additional 25 percent thought the Americans had fought on the Nazi side. (The poll was never published.)

Tanya herself spouted an astonishing amount of historical misinformation, reflecting an uncritical acceptance of Soviet textbooks. She said the U.S. Army never really saw hard fighting during the war because the Germans were so weak in the West that it was no chore at all to liberate France. President

Truman had dropped the atomic bomb on Japan simply to frighten Russia with America's nuclear strength. As Tanya outlined her version of recent history, I was reminded of something Boris Alekseivich had said: "Only those with memories of the truth can challenge a lie."

Despite her belief in various historical iniquities of the West, Tanya was not suspicious of foreigners. She longed for an expansion of student exchanges and was regretful that so few foreigners lived in her town. The only ones she had seen in Kustanai were African students, whom she originally thought were black Americans because their clothes looked so expensive to her. "We like to meet people from other countries so much," she said. "I have dreamed of talking to Americans, to English people, to students from all over the world. We would argue about our differences, the way you and I do, but we would always be friendly. We all must live together on this earth and respect different ways of living and thinking."

Tanya wanted me to visit her in Kazakhstan and was surprised when I told her I probably could not stay in her town because it is closed to foreigners, with the exception of a few students. Large areas of the Soviet Union are off limits both to foreign tourists and foreign residents of Moscow. Many towns —Kustanai was probably one of them—are closed not because they harbor any state secrets but because they lack hotel facilities deemed suitable for Western tourists. Tanya said it didn't matter if I could not come to Kustanai. "I will come to Alma-Ata to meet you and bring all my friends. They are all very much in envy that I should know an American."

Unfortunately, the visit to Kazakhstan failed to materialize for a variety of reasons. Heavy KGB harassment, plus a severe arthritic attack that put my husband on crutches for a month, made traveling nearly impossible during the last six months of our stay in the Soviet Union. At about the same time, Tanya's innocent view of foreigners—and the Soviet government's attitude toward Russians who associate with foreigners—was shattered.

Tanya had written me that she would be coming to Moscow for several weeks during her February class break. The possibility that her letters to me might be opened by someone else had obviously never occurred to her. I was certain from the ragged appearance of the envelope flaps that her letters had been opened by the KGB before they reached me. It was hardly surprising that an envelope with a Soviet citizen's return address would have been inspected before it arrived at an American correspondent's house in Moscow. Tanya's visit came in the midst of the heaviest harassment we had encountered, when the KGB was physically breaking up meetings on the street between foreigners and Soviet citizens. I was afraid to warn her directly by mail for fear that her letters from me were now being opened in Kustanai. The warning itself might have caused her trouble, and she probably would not have believed me anyway. So I simply wrote her that it would be best if we met at the Lenin Library without setting a meeting place over the phone; the meaning of my sentence would not have escaped any Moscow acquaintance. However, Tanya did phone me and mentioned the library, so the meaning escaped her.

After we met, we walked and talked for hours, stopping for coffee and cakes in a café on one of Moscow's newest shopping streets. Tanya wanted to see an exhibit of French impressionist drawings that had just opened at the Pushkin Gallery, but we were unable to get in due to the crush of people who were eager to view a newly arrived exhibit from aboard. All the universities were on vacation, and it seemed every student in Moscow was standing outside the Pushkin that day. Tanya brought a friend along, and we had a lively discussion about the situation in the Middle East. I remember that she asked me about American racial problems; she said she thought intermarriage was a good idea because the children were so beautiful. At the end of the day, we agreed that my husband and I would meet Tanya and two friends for dinner on Saturday night at the Aragvi, an excellent Georgian restaurant. No one seemed to be following us; I thought the completely innocent contents of

Tanya's letters had made the KGB decide it wasn't worth the trouble to frighten her away from me.

On Friday morning, Tanya phoned and asked if we could meet again before our dinner date. I said it was impossible because I already had two other appointments. She was disappointed, because she had two other friends who wanted to meet me and would only be in Moscow for one day. But she said gaily, "Then I'll see you tomorrow at the Aragvi." Groaning inwardly at the unnecessary repetition of a meeting place on the phone, I said good-bye.

A few hours later, Tanya phoned again but her gay voice had changed. She seemed to be crying and said she would be unable to have dinner with us Saturday night because her parents had just phoned and asked her to meet them in a town 300 kilometers from Moscow. I asked if she would return to Moscow before her vacation ended. She said she would be back next week and would phone me then. I never heard from her again.

The conclusion that the KGB had chosen that day to warn her away from me was inescapable. They could have learned about our friendship from phone taps, the letters or by following me to our appointed meeting places. There was no other logical explanation. I spent many sleepless hours wondering whether I should have done anything differently. Should I have warned her directly? Had I justified my failure to do so on grounds that the warning would have been dangerous to her only because I wanted to go on seeing her?

Inquiring about my husband, she had once written me, "Isn't it happiness to be a journalist of such a famous newspaper?"

I wondered what the KGB had suggested to her. Did they tell her that one or both of us were spies? Or perhaps Zionist agents, because of the conversation about Israel?

I also wondered if her faith in the Soviet system—and the death of Stalinism—had been shaken by what was undoubtedly her first encounter with the KGB. Or had it been reinforced by whatever lies the secret police may have told her about us?

The one question I can answer is why the KGB bothered to frighten Tanya away from me. She was so innocent that she could not conceive of getting into any trouble over our conversations and letters. Anything I told her only interested her—it did not affect her fundamental faith in Communism or in her country. Part of the answer is that the KGB wanted to harass and upset Tony and me still further by breaking up still another friendship with a Russian. The rest of the answer is that *any* contacts between Russians and foreigners can attract KGB scrutiny at any time. A Russian who is involved with a foreigner automatically earns a black mark of suspicion. Moscow residents, schooled by the KGB guards at the entrance to foreign compounds, know this. Tanya did not.

V

Gyusel Amalrik

For your sole sake—that all heart's ache have known,
And given to others all heart's ache,
From meagre girlhood's putting on
Burdensome beauty—for your sole sake
Heaven has put away the stroke of her doom,
So great her portion in that peace you make
By merely walking in a room.

—W. B. YEATS
from "Broken Dreams"

GYUSEL AMALRIK IS best described by a Russian word which has no exact English equivalent. *Zhizneradostny* means a person is filled with the joy of living—not a superficial gaiety but an affirmation of life capable of transcending pain and despair. It literally means "life-glad." In my most vivid memory of Gyusel, I see her walking into our living room a few days after her husband, Andrei, had been sentenced to three years in a Soviet labor camp. She was dressed in a floor-length sweep of maroon velvet, her grace and bright beauty contrasting sharply with the November sleet outside the windows and with the bleak outlook for her immediate future. "I felt like being beautiful for just the three of us," she explained, replacing her heavy winter boots with silver sandals. "I will not wear black while Andrei is in prison. I will put on my best clothes. He would want me proud and beautiful, not ugly and despairing."

Gyusel is married to Andrei Amalrik, a thirty-three-year-old historian and writer now serving the third and final year of the camp sentence he received for writing and publishing his unorthodox opinions of Soviet society. His books *Involuntary Journey to Siberia* and *Will the Soviet Union Survive Until 1984?* have been published in the West* and are circulated in *samizdat* in his own country. The largest proportion of *samizdat* is devoted to works that are unacceptable to the authorities on political rather than purely literary grounds.

Many foreign correspondents, a few diplomats and occasional tourists have met Andrei and Gyusel during the past five years: The Amalriks did not observe the unwritten rules that discourage such contacts. Because I never met Andrei, my picture of their life differs from that of most foreigners who knew them. I saw Gyusel for the first time on May 21, 1970, a few hours after her husband's arrest. I felt that I came to know Andrei through his books and Gyusel's descriptions, but my view of their existence inevitably became a portrait of Gyusel.

Andrei is both an acute political thinker and a moral opponent of "the Soviet way of life." By all accounts, he is a thorny personality who cannot be classified with any of the other small groups of political dissidents in the Soviet Union. Yet he is unquestionably a dissident, and although his dissent is entirely personal, it is perhaps all the more significant in a society where most endeavors are collective. Gyusel is not an overtly political person. Her only dissent is that her way of life, with its grace and taste and stress on small details that can exalt the spirit, seems out of place in a society where such inclinations are considered at best socially unproductive. Gyusel is a painter, but painting is not her greatest talent. Her most precious gift is her ability to inspire those around her with a sense of beauty—a rare ability in any country.

She often seemed to me to belong not merely in another place but in another dimension; she might have been either a

* *Will the Soviet Union Survive Until 1984?*, published by Harper & Row, was a Book-of-the-Month Club selection in 1970. *Involuntary Journey* was published by Harcourt Brace Jovanovich.

Muse or a Good Witch. She was a little of both for the friends who came to see her in her cramped room at the back of a communal apartment. It was a poorly placed room for an artist, because the sunlight never quite reached it.

Gyusel was born on January 11, 1942, in a small village on the Volga River. Her parents were Tatars, and she inherited most of the distinctive physical characteristics that have given Tatar women a reputation for beauty. Her hair is a glossy blue-black, her eyes so dark that they seem black although they are actually the deepest imaginable shade of brown. The expressiveness of Gyusel's eyes, with their slight upward tilt at the corners, makes it possible for a Westerner to imagine how alluring such a woman's face might be if it were veiled in the traditional Moslem fashion.

Gyusel's pale skin, with a slight tint of pink that owes nothing to cosmetics, contrasts strikingly with the deep shades of her hair and eyes. She is tall and slim, with gracefully molded arms and shoulders and an elongated neck. A flowing combination of solidity and fragility, she imposes her own elegance of bearing on her Tatar inheritance. The total effect brings a Modigliani portrait to mind. Not by coincidence, many of the female figures Gyusel paints are also reminiscent of Modigliani women. Gyusel's ideal of feminine beauty and her image of herself coincide far more closely than is the case with most women. She is not a narcissist; on the contrary, she is so at peace with the way she looks that much of her grace is totally unconscious.

Gyusel's family originally came from Kazan, an ancient center of Moslem culture. (Kazan is now more celebrated in Soviet guidebooks as the seat of a university that expelled Lenin for rebellious activities when he was a student there.) Gyusel describes some of her nineteenth-century ancestors as men of considerable learning and culture. Her great-grandfather on her father's side wrote religious books in Arabic. Gyusel says he was also regarded as a *znakhar*—a combination of wise man and sorcerer, with special skill at healing by folk methods. But he seems to have been a man of virtually no education, formal or informal. Gyusel was unable to adequately explain why the family's nineteenth-century learning did not survive into the twentieth century. She knew even less about her maternal ancestors, because her mother maintained that she knew nothing about the family history. "But you must have known something about your own grandparents," Gyusel said to her mother in a conversation that had obviously been repeated many times. "Children always ask their parents, 'How was it when you were little?'" Her mother, a work-roughened woman who nevertheless carried herself as though she had been trained by a governess to sit without touching the back of a chair, replied: "I was one of nineteen children, Gyusel. You know that. How did my mother have time to tell us stories about when she was a little girl, to pay attention to silly, childish questions? I remember the collectivization of the land.* The adults never got more than three hours' sleep a night during the early years. I remember, the call to work would come when it was still completely dark outside. At harvest time the children went into the fields too. When was there time for fairy tales about what life was like in the old days?"

It seems likely that the culture represented by Gyusel's grandfather was intimately linked with religion and a traditional way of life and could not survive the chaos of revolution and wars. By the time Gyusel was old enough to think about such matters, all that remained of that cultural heritage was a bigoted chauvinism. When Gyusel married Andrei, her parents objected less because he had already been exiled to Siberia as a "parasite" than because he was not a Tatar. (Andrei's passport registers him as a Russian. One of his great-grandfathers came to Russia from Avignon in the mid-nineteenth century.)

Gyusel has no memories of the village where she was born,

---

* She was referring to the process that took place during the late 1920's and early 1930's when all private farms, both large and small, were abolished. Land-owning peasants, called *kulaks*, who refused to go along with the collectivization were shot.

because her family moved to Moscow when she was a year old. "There was a famine in the countryside and my parents told us they moved to Moscow because they believed there would be more food. There was a little more, but not as much as my parents expected. But people weren't starving in Moscow— they were only hungry. My parents used to talk about the canned meat the Americans had sent to Russia during the war. I think I remember eating it, but maybe that's only because I was told about it." (She is probably referring to Spam, which was shipped to the Soviet Union along with other nonperishable food products during the war.)

Life in Moscow was never easy for Gyusel's family. In many respects their problems paralleled those of people throughout the world who emigrated from the countryside to the city in search of a better life but lacked the skills to succeed in an urban environment. Gyusel's parents were no better prepared to make good in a large city than the rural Southern immigrants who have become welfare statistics in Northern American cities. The flood of rural immigrants to Soviet cities, both during and immediately after the war, was an important factor in the authorities' decision to impose strict limits on population mobility within the country. Most of the large cities of European Russia, including Moscow, are now closed to anyone without residence and work permits—permits difficult to obtain unless a worker possesses skills that are in great demand in the city where he wants to live. A veteran construction worker would find it easier to acquire a Moscow residence permit than a bakery clerk, because the construction industry is short of skilled labor. No one can legally move from the countryside to the city in search of work, as Gyusel's parents did during the war. Nevertheless, Russians do find semilegal and illegal ways of evading the regulations, and the general migration to urban areas has continued, although at a slower rate.

"My parents were lost people," Gyusel says. "They left the village and its culture behind, and there was no new culture to replace it in their lives. They lived in the city, but they were always strangers. They did not have the strength, or the education, or whatever was needed to really adapt to the new life." Gyusel usually speaks of her parents in the past tense, probably because she has been so far removed from their world for so many years. She sees her mother and sister occasionally, but they are not close. I heard Gyusel and her mother call each other *vy*, although it is almost unheard of for family members to use the formal Russian "you" in addressing each other. Gyusel's mother is a simple woman who is disturbed, as any parent in any part of the world would be, that her daughter is married to a social outcast. At the same time, she does not understand the laws that govern Andrei's and Gyusel's lives. When Andrei nearly died of cerebral meningitis in a prison hospital, Gyusel's mother said, "But, of course, he will be coming home. You don't keep a sick man in a prison." Gyusel was unable to explain why Andrei would not, of course, be coming home.

Gyusel's mother and father spoke only Tatar when they arrived in Moscow. They learned to "get along" in Russian only over a long period of years. Her father's limited education and language difficulties barred him from all but unskilled, poorly paying jobs. Her mother bore eight children, four of whom died in infancy. Gyusel was the oldest of those who survived.

The material want of Gyusel's childhood was not unusual in a country impoverished by war. Life was harsh for nearly all Soviet citizens during the postwar period; the first significant improvements in the standard of living for ordinary people began only after Stalin's death. Other aspects of Gyusel's childhood were unusual; all the occupants of her communal apartment were poor but the Russian neighbors looked down on the Tatars. She remembers the communal toilet vividly, because other children would pick the times she went there to taunt her about being a Tatar. "Tatarka, tatarka," they would cry. Used in an insulting tone, the word has the same force as spic, yid, or hunky. "Once a bigger girl was waiting for me in there," Gyusel recalled. "It wasn't a toilet like you have today, but a hole that you stood over. She pushed me into the hole, held my head underneath. I came up covered with filth and ran crying to our apartment, but no one was home. My mama and papa were both out working. I had to wash my dress myself—I was eight years old, and it was the only one I had. I remember sitting and shivering, waiting for it to dry. I wanted to get it clean before anyone came home, so no one else would know about my shame."

Gyusel had rickets, which prevented her from walking until she was six years old. "I crawled around until I was six," she said. "My father especially distrusted doctors and hospitals—this was common among peasants transplanted to the city. But my mother finally stood up to him and took me to the clinic in our neighborhood. She didn't think it was normal that I should be crawling around or that I would just grow out of it. They helped me there—I don't remember much about how, except they gave me a lot of vitamins. I was walking by the time I started school, when I was seven."

Gyusel spoke only Tatar then, but she was able to learn Russian quickly. But the school had the same effect on her that public schools have had on minority group immigrants in many nations: She became ashamed of her family and cultural background as she became assimilated into the larger society.

"My parents would speak to me in Tatar and I would answer them in Russian. There were days when I wouldn't speak to them at all. I would cry with shame over my home. When I was eight, I ran away from home to find some new parents who were intelligent and cultured. I remember it was the middle of winter and I had a spring coat on. I cried and cried. I even hated the way I looked sometimes, because I didn't look like the Russian children. It was not until many years later that I began to think about why I had been so ashamed and to wonder whether a school should have made me feel that way. I know the school did some good things for me. I had to learn Russian; I would never have learned it at home. And the medical checkups and food made me healthy when I had been a sick child before. But couldn't they have done it without making me ashamed of my Tatar blood? I don't know."

Gyusel was surprised when I told her that her experiences might have occurred anywhere else in the world and that dominant power groups often display disrespect for minorities in public institutions. I described the self-hatred instilled in many black American children by their experiences in white school systems, and she was keenly interested in my comments on assimilation and cultural pluralism in the United States. Her surprise that such problems could occur elsewhere reminded me that the vast majority of Soviet citizens—even those with questioning minds like Gyusel's—simply have no access to information that would enable them to make meaningful comparisons between the Soviet Union and other societies.

Gyusel's early interest in art, only one expression of her yearning for beauty, was one of the first traits that set her apart from her family and her immediate environment. "I was always drawing from the time I was five or six years old. I used up every scrap of paper in the house—there weren't many extra scraps of paper in those days. When the paper was gone, I drew in the dirt in the courtyard. All of the drawing was one of the first things my parents couldn't understand about me. It seemed like such a waste of time to them." Gyusel received encouragement and praise for her drawings in school, but she says the idea of continuing her interest in art at a higher education institution never occurred to her. "None of my teachers ever suggested it, and my family would never have dreamed of sending a child to a university, especially a girl. There wasn't much value placed on education at all, but especially not for women."

I thought Gyusel might already have begun to chafe in high school at the restrictions on creativity imposed by the official philosophy of "Socialist realism," which frowns on abstraction and insists that all art must serve the purposes of the state. With characteristic honesty, she disabused me. "I just didn't have any ambitions, and I came from a world in which no one suggested that I should have any. I did have dreams but no concrete idea of what forms they would take."

When she was sixteen, Gyusel's life was changed by a chance meeting with a stranger in the courtyard of her apartment building. "I was gossiping with two girlfriends and I saw a strange-looking man with a beard walking into the courtyard. I was very much attracted by his appearance and I found out he was visiting a girl I knew. I stopped by her apartment. The girl told him I was always drawing, and he asked me to do one for him. After I had finished, he said, 'You will come and be my student.' "

The man was Vasily Yakovlevich Sitnikov, one of Moscow's best-known unofficial artists.* In Sitnikov's studio Gyusel began to learn to paint in a way that went beyond the rudimentary techniques she had learned in school. She also received her first real exposure to art that was not Socialist realism.

Sitnikov is a man of bizarre character and undisputed talent; no foreigners and, I suspect, few Russians know the real story of his past. He was arrested for an unknown reason—during the period when no reason was needed for an arrest—at some point during the early war years. He spent much of the war in a mental institution. His paintings reflect strong elements of fantasy and eroticism; his use of eroticism is more important and explicit than that of other known unofficial Russian artists. (Official artists, whose work is shown publicly, must avoid eroticism entirely. It does not coincide with Socialist realism.) Sitnikov's favorite painting technique is difficult to explain; it can perhaps best be described as "micro-pointillist." In many of his best paintings the figures seem to emerge from a haze in much the same manner that sculpture emerges from stone. There is also some resemblance to the effect produced by spray painting.

The influence of Sitnikov's technique is evident in Gyusel's paintings, especially in her early work. While she was studying at his studio, she earned enough money to live by scrubbing floors at the Bolshoi Theater, where she also painted portraits

---

* Sitnikov's work is also known in the West. Two of his paintings are included in the collection of the Museum of Modern Art in New York.

of the dancers. She hated the work and was ashamed of it, but she declined an opportunity to help paint sets for the Bolshoi productions. After two years of working with Sitnikov, Gyusel had begun to feel the constrictions of official Soviet art. The Bolshoi sets at the time were extremely old-fashioned and un-imaginative, though rich in color and excessive ornamentation. Nineteenth-century *Kitsch* and Socialist realism are perfectly compatible. Gyusel decided she would rather scrub floors and continue to paint her own way.

(The Bolshoi backdrops, it should be noted, have improved considerably in recent years. Gyusel was pleasantly astonished by the modernity of the sets when we went to see a perform-ance of *Carmen Suite*, a sensual ballet created by a Cuban choreographer for the great Soviet ballerina Maya Plisetskaya. "Ten years ago that production would have been unthinkable," Gyusel remarked.)

Gyusel eventually met Andrei as a result of their mutual in-volvement in the world of unofficial art. Andrei owned a small collection of unofficial paintings—an activity that was con-nected with his exile to Siberia in 1965—and he had seen one of Gyusel's portraits during a visit to Sitnikov's studio. He was intrigued and asked the name and address of the artist. "He liked my painting first, and when he met me he liked me."

Gyusel and Andrei had seen each other only three times be-fore he was arrested and exiled to Siberia as a "parasite." The decree on parasites was issued under Khrushchev in 1961 and was designed to clear the cities of vagrants and chronically absent workers by exiling them to harsh areas like Siberia. All persons without regular employment were liable to prosecution under the parasite law, and it was soon applied to unorthodox intellectuals who insisted on using their time to write or other-wise express themselves in a manner not approved by the state. Because of their nonconformist ideas many such intellectuals cannot obtain jobs commensurate with their abilities and are reduced to sporadic unskilled employment that interferes with what they regard as their real work.

Andrei had been expelled from Moscow State University in 1963 after he wrote a dissertation suggesting that the twelfth- and thirteenth-century Russian state in Kiev owed many of its cultural achievements to the Normans and the Byzantines. The civilization of Kievan Rus is correctly regarded as a vital stage in the development of Russian culture, but Andrei's conclusion was unacceptable to the university authorities. Official Soviet historians hold that Russian civilization was created entirely by Slavs, who then made a gift of their superior culture to the barbarous Asiatic hordes. Andrei refused to change his conclusions, although the research itself was apparently acceptable. The quarrel over what seems to be an obscure and safely distant historical point is, of course, directly related to the official view of modern Soviet history: The approved line is that non-Russian peoples were extremely lucky to have their lands incorporated into the Soviet Union after the revolution. (The kind of history Gyusel learned in school may have some relation to the shame she learned to feel because she was not from a "cultured" Russian family.)

At the time of Andrei's exile, he was desperately needed at home to care for his father, an invalid who could speak and walk only with great difficulty after three strokes and a heart attack. His health had been irreparably damaged years before by battle injuries during the war and starvation in a prison camp. Also a historian, the elder Amalrik was sentenced to camp after being indiscreet enough to remark in the presence of other soldiers that Stalin was at fault for Soviet defeats during the opening months of the war. (At this point, it may seem to the reader that I deliberately sought out Russians whose lives were mangled during the Stalin era. I did not have to seek out the victims of Stalinism; it was simply impossible to avoid them. No foreigner can enter even partway into Russian life without meeting people who were in camps, whose relatives were in camps or who were affected by the Stalin terror in other ways. For every Russian who told me his true story, I believe many others held back.)

Andrei's father died shortly after his son's exile to Siberia. Implicit in Andrei's description of his father's death in *Involuntary Journey to Siberia* is the bitter belief that the Soviet authorities were at least partly responsible because they disregarded his need for constant care. While working on the collective farm where he had been assigned, Andrei received a cable from Moscow informing him that his father was seriously ill. He was able to obtain a temporary permit from the local police allowing him to return to Moscow, but when Andrei arrived after a long boat and train trip his father was already dead. (He did not have the money to buy a plane ticket.) Andrei saw Gyusel again during the two weeks he was permitted to remain in Moscow. All his belongings had to be stored, because the combination of his exile and his father's death meant that their one room in a communal apartment would now be occupied by someone else. A few days before Andrei was due to return to Siberia, he asked Gyusel to marry him.

I asked Gyusel how it happened that she, an essentially non-political person who was interested mainly in beauty and art, had chosen a man whose views were bound to bring him into direct conflict with his society.

"I did not think of him as political then," she answered. "He had been in trouble as a student—but that happened to a great many intelligent students. He was interested in art, and most of the people in the unofficial art world seem odd by the standards of orthodox Soviet society. I only thought that Andrei was an extremely intelligent, sensitive man. And he understood me very well, better than I did him at the time. You understand, I always wanted to create a home with someone who appreciated all of the beauty that was lacking in my own family background. Did I think of myself as the wife of a Decembrist? Of course not—not when I went off with Andrei." (The Decembrists, a group of noble young officers, made a doomed attempt in 1825 to replace the czarist autocracy with some form of European parliamentary government. They were all shot or exiled to Siberia. Most of their young wives followed them into exile; many of them had been deeply committed to the political ideas that motivated their husbands.)

The impulsive nature of Gyusel's departure for Siberia with Andrei was undoubtedly connected with the fact that she had been deeply in love for several years with a man who did not return her feelings. Andrei, according to Gyusel's account, represented a chance for a new life—a life not based solely on a one-sided infatuation. Gyusel would not like me to write about such personal matters; she is far more reticent about discussing love and sex than most women her age. (Russians tend to shy away from frank talk about sex in mixed company, but the reserve does not ordinarily prevail in conversations between members of the same sex.) Yet it seems to me important to say that she was a young, confused girl who chose a man out of a complex of reasons that would not become entirely clear to her for many years. The choice was neither extraordinary nor heroic. What *is* extraordinary about Gyusel is the grace with which she was able to bear its unforseen consequences.

In *Involuntary Journey* Andrei describes the night before he and Gyusel set out for Siberia:

On the evening of the 9th, helped by a woman acquaintance, I began to sort out my papers. Many of them I tore up, shouting, "To hell with it!" and threw them all over the room, so that the floor was soon white with scraps of paper. Later Gyusel and the husband of my friend arrived and the four of us drank to our melancholy marriage and the end of my life in Suvorov Boulevard. We put on some records and I remember how my wife, slightly tipsy, danced Spanish dances in her red boots, kicking up scraps of white paper and making them swirl around the devastated room.

Gyusel and Andrei's marriage was officially registered in Siberia, where their main concern was how to keep from starving on an impoverished collective farm. The exiles were only slightly worse off than the ordinary farmers. "What I remember most about Siberia is potatoes, morning, noon and night,"

Gyusel says. "Never anything else. Fried potatoes and mashed potatoes, rotten or not—we ate them. Or we would have starved."

In the daytime, Gyusel occupied herself by trying to paint while Andrei fulfilled the compulsory farm labor required of exiles. Gyusel had brought her paints and some paper with her, correctly suspecting that art materials would not be available anywhere near a Siberian farm. She did not accomplish a great deal in the shack where they were allowed to live, but she did complete what I considered to be one of her best paintings of the period between 1964 and 1970.

She is standing in a mirror, naked from the waist up, and Andrei is a few steps behind her, bearded and bundled up in a sweater. Both figures were painted from images in a mirror; Gyusel had started to do a self-portrait but decided to include Andrei because he often came close to watch her work. The painting took several months to complete because Gyusel, shivering in the Siberian wind which cut through the cracks despite attempts to stuff them with paste, straw and newspaper, could not bear to stand without her sweater for longer than half an hour at a time. They both look cold in the picture; Gyusel's shoulders seem to tremble. Her eyes are sad, as though she has begun to realize the price of the life she has chosen.

Gyusel eventually returned to Moscow months before Andrei, primarily because the local authorities were insisting she give up her Moscow residence and register in Siberia. Had Gyusel turned in her permit to live in Moscow, it might have been impossible for either her or Andrei to return because Andrei had already lost his "living space" with his father's death. One of the regulations governing internal population movement is that no citizen can be registered to live in two places at the same time.

As it turned out, Andrei's sentence was eventually reversed by the Supreme Court of the Russian Republic—a highly unusual occurrence that came about largely as a result of the unremitting efforts of a lawyer working on his behalf. In the summer of 1966, Andrei was permitted to return to Moscow.

Since 1966 Gyusel and Andrei had lived in one room at the back of a communal apartment they share with six other families. Thirteen people live in the apartment's seven rooms; they share the same toilet, bathtub, kitchen and telephone. Because it does have a tub and phone, the apartment is more comfortable than many communal dwelling places. People with Andrei's political record are not likely to be given high priority on the waiting lists for new separate apartments.

Gyusel lives on Vakhtangov Street, which connects a row of rundown stores known as the Old Arbat with Prospekt Kalinina, a new showcase shopping street with high-rise office buildings and glass-fronted stores that Soviet guides always show off to tourists. Old names die hard, and Prospekt Kalinina is known simply as the New Arbat to most Muscovites. The Old Arbat was a wealthy mercantile-residential district before the revolution; many still prefer shopping there despite its present shabby appearance. Old reputations also die hard.

Many of the buildings on Gyusel's street predate the revolution: Her building seems no older or shabbier than the adjoining dwellings. The one exception is a fine old house in beautiful condition. It houses only one family, because it is the residence of the British Minister. Like other foreigners' dwellings, it comes complete with its own police guard post. The façade of Gyusel's building is crumbling, and the inside is even more poorly maintained. It is easy to trip on the stairs because the edges are so worn down by tramping feet that each step slants dangerously forward. Lights in the hallways often burn out, making the climb down from Gyusel's third-floor apartment especially annoying at night. Beside the door are seven nameplates, one for each family, and a communal bell that rings throughout the apartment.

"The communal apartment is our country in miniature," Gyusel says. "You can find out everything about Russian life from listening to the neighbors right here."

Predictably, all of Gyusel's neighbors are cold and distant. Apparently no one wishes to be friendly with the wife of a man who is known to have been arrested, particularly since one resident of the apartment is a small-time police informer. The informer always took care to step out and take a good look at my face when I was walking down the long communal hall to Gyusel's room. Several times I observed her busily writing something down on a piece of paper as I passed. She took an equal interest in all Gyusel's visitors, whether they were Russians or foreigners. The same neighbor would spit into the receiver when I telephoned Gyusel and she was not at home to answer. Police informers do not serve the same function they did in Stalin's day, when their denunciations could send someone to a camp or death. They are used mainly to annoy and keep tabs on people who have attracted special KGB attention, and they may be paid or unpaid. In a communal apartment, the tendency of old women to poke their noses into their neighbors' business usually serves the police well enough without any need to plant a professional informer. The modern Soviet informer is usually a busybody whose natural tendencies are encouraged by the government.

Gyusel's other neighbors showed their distaste for her in many ways. On International Women's Day, an official Soviet holiday on which men are supposed to treat women with special consideration, someone had wrapped small packages of candy and left them in the communal kitchen for every woman in the apartment except Gyusel. One woman turned off the hall light every night, making it impossible to see on the way to the phone or the toilet. When Gyusel politely asked her to leave the light on, she replied spitefully, "I'm just a poor pensioner. I have no money for luxuries. I don't get my money the way you do, by being anti-Soviet. I'm just an honest woman and proud of it. My hands are clean." A Russian friend of Gyusel's was terrified one day when she rang the communal bell and was informed by a neighbor that Gyusel had "gone to live in a whorehouse, where she belongs." The friend was afraid Gyusel might have been taken away by the police.

The attitude of the neighbors does not affect Gyusel as deeply as one might expect; the sniping causes her more annoyance than pain. "It's like a drip-drip-drip. But you don't have much inner strength if you can be broken down by crudity like that. But I dream of having an apartment of our own, where we could really have a private life. Maybe when Andrei comes back from camp we can find one."

The crudity ends when Gyusel closes the door of her room. When I first began to visit her, I thought of the bedroom above the antique shop in George Orwell's *1984*, where Winston and Julia made love under the illusion that they were beyond the reach of the Thought Police. In Gyusel's room, a suspension of disbelief was possible; you could forget the ugliness and tension of the world beyond the door. The knowledge that KGB microphones planted in the room were picking up every fragment of our conversation did nothing to diminish the sense of sanity and integrity within those four walls.

Gyusel disliked bright light, except when she was painting. (A fortunate preference, since the natural light in the room was so poor that it was dim even during the brightest hours of the day.) The room was usually lit by soft colored lights from a wrought-iron copy of a nineteenth-century lamppost made for her by a friend. The walls were covered with paintings by some of the best unofficial artists in Moscow, as well as Gyusel's own work. Furnishings included a double bed, a wardrobe, a piano that had belonged to Andrei's father, a desk Gyusel used as a dining table when she entertained friends, and a bookcase. The library consisted mainly of nineteenth-century literature, historical works and art books; some of their most valued books had been carried off in successive KGB searches connected with Andrei's case.

We would sit at the desk and drink tea, covering a wide range of topics in our conversations. We spoke of Andrei, of course—I came to know Gyusel best during the year of his arrest and trial. We seldom talked about politics as such, although we often discussed Russian and American history, art and literature—subjects that invariably intercepted with politics. And we spoke of the more mundane subjects friends discuss everywhere—old loves, marital problems, a woman's difficulties in combining marriage and a career, sometimes religion. The relaxed conversations were a rare gift in Moscow, where so many encounters between Russians and foreigners are verbal fencing matches with the participants intent on scoring points and concealing their real thoughts.

I came to look forward to our meetings with an eagerness that I hope was not an imposition on Gyusel's hospitality. I always knew I was welcome; the importance of that knowledge can be fully understood only by one who has been a stranger in a land where most people fear him. We took strength from each other—she from me while Andrei was awaiting trial, I from her when my husband was sick and the KGB was hounding us at every turn.

We would listen to Handel or Bach or Ella Fitzgerald as the mood struck us. The records were prized possessions, gifts from foreign friends over a period of years. I could gauge Gyusel's mood both from the music she chose and the tea she made. If she were in an optimistic frame of mind, the tea would be strong and fragrant after brewing in a pot for at least an hour. When she was nervous and depressed, the tea was weak and tasteless because she had simply poured boiling water over leaves tossed in a cup. She was ashamed of the watery tea, because Andrei liked it carefully brewed. "You begin to live like a bachelor," she noted, "and that's bad."

The period immediately following Andrei's arrest actually provided Gyusel with a brief span of emotional relief; the expected blow had fallen and the reality was not as terrible as waiting. "Each of us was afraid when the other would leave the house alone. We were terrified that Andrei would be taken when I wasn't there with him and I wouldn't know what had happened."

Gyusel's relief was partly attributed to earlier rumors circulated in Washington and London that Andrei was really a KGB agent because he had not been arrested immediately after his books were published. The rumors were based on flimsy bits of "evidence," such as the fact that some Western correspondents had been present on a few of the many occasions when the Amalriks' apartment had been searched by the KGB. It was suggested that Andrei had really been used as an instrument to trap Westerners into compromising situations. In fact, any foreigner, or Russian, is likely to encounter the Soviet secret police face-to-face if he associates with Soviet citizens who are constantly under surveillance. Most of the rumors about Andrei began after he wrote an open letter to Anatoly Kuznetsov suggesting that Russians like Solzhenitsyn (and Amalrik) are on sounder moral ground than Kuznetsov because they have chosen to stay in the Soviet Union and fight the system openly despite the possible consequences. The letter was viewed in some Russian emigré circles—possibly connected with the CIA —as a subtle attempt to discredit Kuznetsov that might well be part of a KGB plot. The letter was one of the documents upon which the Soviets based their case against Andrei at his trial.

The arrest took place not in Moscow but in Akulovo, a tiny village about 105 miles southeast of the capital. The Amalriks had scraped up enough money to buy a shabby peasant cabin in order to escape the tension of KGB surveillance in Moscow. It was their version of "going to the *dacha*," a phrase Russians use when they are leaving the capital for a time because their lives had become politically uncomfortable. Political dissidents go to the *dacha*, and so do official writers who have fallen into temporary disfavor. In ordinary usage, a *dacha* is simply a summer or country home; it can be applied to a tiny cabin or a mansion.

After the formal arrest, Andrei was taken under guard to their room in Moscow, where a search was conducted. The police brought Gyusel in another car—they stopped to pick lilacs along the way—and she arrived at the apartment just before Andrei was taken away to the Butyrki prison, weher political dissenters were also held in czarist times and under Stalin. Gyusel had kind words for the police who drove her to Moscow, because they were not required to provide her with any transportation. "I wouldn't have been able to say good-bye to Andrei or give him a sweater otherwise. Some of the police really meant to be kind to me."

A few weeks later, Gyusel returned to the cabin to collect her belongings and board it up. Someone had already broken the windows. By that time Andrei had been taken to Sverdlovsk, about 900 miles from Moscow, where his case was officially linked with that of a young man who had been picked up in that city with a *samizdat* copy of the open letter to Kuznetsov. Most Moscow observers believed the case had been arranged so it would be tried in a city closed to foreigners. The authorities did not want to attract the kind of world attention aroused by the trial of Andrei Sinyavsky and Yuli Daniel in 1966, and a quiet trial was easier to manage without foreign correspondents hanging around outside the courtroom doors.

Throughout the summer, Gyusel made fruitless trips to Sverdlovsk with parcels of food for Andrei, always hoping against hope that she would be allowed to see him for a few minutes. Under Soviet law, prisoners are not permitted to receive visitors and are usually without legal counsel until a pretrial investigation is completed. In Andrei's case, the investigation dragged on for more than five months before formal charges were filed. Once Gyusel stood on a nearby hill with a small telescope, trying to see into the prison windows. A policeman ordered her to leave.

As time passed and no charges were filed, she grew increasingly nervous. She began smoking for the first time in her life, and her lustrous hair began to fall out. Unable to sleep, she would fall into a restless doze in the early morning hours only to force herself out of bed by ten o'clock to begin another round of visits to official agencies in Moscow concerned with Andrei's case.

In August Gyusel went to the country with a friend to rest for a few days. A man came riding on horseback from the nearest village, which had the only telephone for miles, and said a call had been received from Moscow informing Gyusel that

Andrei's trial would take place the next day. Terrified of missing the trial, she set out on foot through a forest for the nearest railway station—she would have to return to Moscow to catch a plane for Sverdlovsk. She lost her way but was lucky enough to spot a truck on a road where vehicles only seemed to pass every few hours. For a small wad of rubles, she was able to hire the truck to take her to the station. When she arrived in Moscow, she was informed that the man who took the telephone call at the village post office had misunderstood. The Moscow branch of the prosecutor's office only wanted to ask her some further questions about Andrei's case.

In November, 1970, Andrei was finally charged with violating Article 190-1 of the Russian Republic criminal code, which deals with the spreading of "falsehoods derogatory to the Soviet state and social system." The trial was held in Sverdlovsk on November 11. (In the Soviet legal system, decisions are made by judges, not juries.) After Andrei was sentenced and the guards started to lead him away from the courtroom, Gyusel ran after him and threw flowers. She reported with glee that Andrei managed to catch one. "One of the guards stamped on a flower as it fell to the ground," she said. "I felt like crying. But as I turned around, I saw an old cleaning woman pick up a flower and try to smooth it out."

Gyusel was able to see Andrei shortly after the sentencing, as provided for in Soviet law. The trial over, her health gave way as a result of the prolonged nervous strain. She made a futile second trip to Sverdlovsk, hoping for another meeting, only to find that Andrei had been moved to a prison 150 miles away. She returned to Moscow with a chronic cough that developed into severe bronchitis. She was unable to leave her room for several weeks; friends brought her food and medicine. I believed she had pneumonia, but she stubbornly refused to visit a clinic. (This was before I knew about her childhood case of rickets, or I would have reminded her of her father's stubbornness.) When I came to see her, she was huddled on the bed, trembling under an ancient moth-eaten fur coat. I began to wonder if she would ever pull out of her deep mental and physical depression.

One day I arrived to find her laughing and spooning up honey out of a honeycomb. An unknown young man had presented himself at her door several weeks before and said he had decided to bring Gyusel a gift from the countryside after he heard about Andrei's case on a foreign radio broadcast. Fresh honey, he said, was filled with energy and vitamins, and she should take it to her husband in camp. At first she was afraid to touch it, fearing the man might either be a maniac who had poisoned the honey or a KGB agent who had concealed something illegal in it that would get Andrei into further trouble. Taking it to Andrei in camp was obviously impossible anyway, because the prison officials could not make a proper search for concealed objects. (Gyusel could not take Andrei toothpaste for the same reason. The guards would have had to squeeze all the paste out of the tube to make sure it contained no contraband.) To an American, Gyusel's fears might seem paranoid, but that is because most Americans do not understand the full implications of secret police power. When people are constantly harassed by the police, it becomes difficult for them to tell an agent from a friend unless the person in question is an old acquaintance. (In Stalin's day, old acquaintances were also suspect; that is one of the differences between the Soviet Union today and thirty years ago.)

Gyusel finally decided to take the plunge because honey—especially fresh country honey—is highly regarded as a folk remedy for respiratory ailments. The honeycomb, it turned out, was just what it appeared to be—delicious. The incident helped Gyusel's cough and raised her spirits. "There comes a point where you have to take a chance and say, 'Enough, I will trust someone.' Sometimes we think it is impossible to trust anyone. But it is also impossible not to trust, or you become less than a human being."

Gyusel recovered so thoroughly that she was not merely frightened but fighting mad when she received a letter from

Andrei in the spring informing her that he had been unconscious for ten days and had nearly died of cerebral meningitis. He had been en route from prison to a labor camp when he fell ill with the disease, which flourishes in crowded, unsanitary conditions. Andrei was convalescing in a special camp hospital for tubercular patients near the Siberian city of Novosibirsk. Gyusel flew there, hoping to see Andrei or find out about his condition from the doctors. She had anticipated difficulties and tried to find a Moscow doctor to accompany her, but none were willing to become involved in a political case. In Siberia, the hospital director refused to answer her questions about Andrei's condition or the medication he was receiving and would only tell her his temperature was "about normal." "What are you, a doctor?" he asked.

Gyusel also talked with camp officials, who were sympathetic but who also treated her to a tirade about Solzhenitsyn. One of the officials said, "Such people should leave the country because they only look for the bad things in Soviet life." Gyusel replied that she and Andrei did not know Solzhenitsyn personally. "But how can you build Communism if you ignore the bad things?" she asked. "If you have a boil and you cut it open, it gets better. If you just cover it up with a bandage, the pus spreads and the whole organism becomes diseased." The official said, "You haven't studied your Marxism-Leninism very well." Gyusel answered, "I think Marx and Lenin would have spoken just as I do." Gyusel came home to Moscow feeling that she had accomplished very little, but Andrei was eventually categorized as a Class II invalid, which released him for a year from hard physical labor. He knew she had tried to visit him before she wrote him about it, because she had shouted her name to prisoners who were well enough to look out the barred hospital windows and enchanted to see a pretty *Moskvitchka*. Andrei's sentence permits him and Gyusel to write an unlimited number of letters to each other, subject to inspection by the prison censor. In one she told him that she was going to a beauty parlor once a week for treatments to restore her thinning hair.

He wrote back, "One lock of your hair is dearer to me than thirty cubes of beef bouillon." Camp officials had refused to pass on a package from Gyusel containing thirty bouillon cubes. Andrei and Gyusel never seem to lose their sense of the absurd.

I hope Gyusel is bearing up as well now as she was when I left Moscow. After the bout of meningitis, Andrei was sent to Kolyma, a camp in one of the Soviet Union's coldest and most desolate regions. The camp was a particularly dreaded one during the Stalin years, and many Russians and foreigners assumed it had been closed under Khrushchev, when millions of prisoners were released. Andrei was the first well-known political prisoner to have been sent there in many years, and his transfer prompted many observers to question their assumptions about how many Stalin camps *had* been permanently closed.

Before I left Moscow, Gyusel began to paint again; she had almost stopped working during the year after Andrei's arrest. My friendship undoubtedly disqualifies me as an objective critic of her art; emotional responses to the work of a loved friend can overwhelm one's critical judgment. Other foreigners in Moscow provided little help in forming a more detached view; Gyusel's foreign visitors dropped off sharply after Andrei was arrested. Most of the correspondents in Moscow are men, and they tended to lose interest in Gyusel when Andrei was no longer accessible to them. They viewed her mainly as an appendage, however graceful, and did not take her work seriously.

Having admitted my subjectivity, there is still much that can be said about Gyusel as an artist. She is not innovative by the standards of contemporary art in the West, nor is she a mature artist. Her changes in technique over the past ten years reveal not the endlessly varying perspectives of an artist who is sure of herself but the restless search of one who has not truly found her own way.

Her work consists almost entirely of portraits and some still lifes. Sitnikov's influence is strongest in the paintings completed during the years when she was his student, before she followed Andrei into exile. The portraits between 1965 and 1969, done mainly in pastels, are more abstract and reflect Gyusel's interest in disproportion as a means of depicting the human figure, particularly the female form.

Despite the immature quality of many of them, a few capture the inner life of their subject so completely that they reveal the value of Gyusel's search and her potential as a mature artist. The majority of her portraits are of women—one of her best pieces of work is an early painting of her sister—but she shows particular sensitivity in depicting some of her male subjects. Andrei's stubborn integrity, as well as his determination not to let the bastards get him down, is depicted with as much clarity in her portraits as in his own writing. A portrait of another young man of quite different temperament reveals the anguish of an artist who wants to struggle against the Soviet system but lacks the moral stamina.

When Gyusel began painting again after Andrei's trial, it seemed to me that her portraits had gained strength. She had given up her exclusive use of pastels and was painting in stronger, brighter colors. It was her greatest hope that she would be able to use the years of Andrei's imprisonment to find herself as an artist and, implicitly, as a person.

"You lose something of yourself in being married to a terribly strong personality. I don't know which is more cutting—to feel that people are only interested in me as Andrei's wife, or that they like my paintings only because they like me. You want your art to be valued for its intrinsic qualities, not for what people think of you. I believe that the soul develops through suffering, and I hope to find a new strength on my own that will be reflected in my art."

Gyusel's painting is only one expression of the strong aesthetic sense that is her most basic quality; it sets her apart from her society as surely as Andrei's passion for historical truth has marked him a social outcast. "I feel it is a human being's right to demand beauty in everything," she says, "and his duty to create beauty in everything. Why should a person have to accept shoddiness and ugliness and sameness?"

The implications of Gyusel's statement hardly seem subversive to an American familiar with the ugliness his own country's technology has spread throughout the world, but the unplanned havoc of Western technology cannot be compared with the Soviet Union's all-encompassing enthronement of mediocrity. Aesthetic standards fall to much lower depths when the state sets itself up as the ultimate arbiter of individual taste. Nearly everything beautiful in Russia is a survival from before the revolution. Tourists notice the glittering golden domes of the Kremlin; the ordinary citizen's daily needs are met with a shoddiness and lack of attention to detail that pervades every area of life. Furniture is varnished so unevenly that glasses tilt when a housewife sets them on the table. Clothes come from factories sewn with thread that clashes with the color of the material. Children's birthday candle holders come in one color—muddy brown. I do not think Gyusel would necessarily be a painter if she lived in the West. In a society that offered more scope for artistic creativity in commercial life, as opposed to one's private work, she might be a fashion designer or an interior decorator or a designer of stage sets.

Russians often explain that the Soviet state, struggling to overcome czarist backwardness and the devastation of World War II, had neither the time nor the financial resources to pay attention to beauty or "good taste." But lack of money is not the only explanation; when aesthetics are politicized, the general standard of taste and public expectation can sink to the level of the most insensitive bureaucrat. Hence, in Moscow it is nearly impossible to buy cheap reproductions of Impressionists or old masters. Impressionist paintings, after all, were only allowed back on the museum walls after Stalin's death; they are still regarded as slightly *outré* in official circles. Why should the state spend its money to reproduce French painters instead of Lenin addressing the workers? Gyusel believes human beings have a "right" to demand beauty in everything. In the Soviet

Union, it is only acknowledged that a citizen has the right to demand beauty as defined by the state.

In this world, Gyusel nevertheless succeeds in imposing her own high standards on her surroundings. The piano, which takes up an inordinate amount of space in the room where Gyusel and Andrei must do all of their living and working, is kept not merely because it belonged to Andrei's father but because it is a beautiful old object. Neither Gyusel nor Andrei knows how to play it. Much care is lavished on small matters; I have seen Gyusel spend half an hour arranging flowers in what seemed to her the most graceful way.

My husband and I remember with particular gratitude the night of her twenty-ninth birthday, which we celebrated in her apartment with some other friends. The room was lit only by strangely shaped candles dripping wax into brandy glasses. Gyusel had produced an elegant dinner in the communal kitchen—beef stroganoff, potatoes mashed with spiced cream, several kinds of salads. Keeping the food warm was a tricky accomplishment managed with candles; in a communal apartment, one cannot inconvenience the neighbors by occupying the burners on top of the stove with simmering food. We sat eating and drinking for a long time around the desk covered with Gyusel's best tablecloth. We drank toasts to Andrei's freedom and Gyusel's beauty, and I silently toasted an inner freedom that mean-spirited neighbors and KGB searches could not touch.

Circumstances never pressure Gyusel into abandoning her standards of taste and hospitality. One old friend recalls a visit to the Amalriks' apartment several years ago when Gyusel and Andrei were down to their last five rubles. Andrei gave Gyusel the five-ruble note, telling her to go out and buy something at the store (meaning food for the guest). She returned with a small flower vase and no change. Andrei looked at it, shook his head and gave the vase to the guest. "You see what kind of a wife I have," he said. "Obviously, this is for you." Gyusel said there had been no food worth serving a guest in the store.

Some foreigners have a tendency to overdramatize the Amalriks' life. Gyusel was particularly angry when a young Englishwoman who had been doing research at the Lenin Library for several months came to her apartment and praised her as a "hero" for being able to live in such surroundings. "Why a 'hero'?" she later said to me. "I try to live as a person, in my own style. I have no use for heroics and fanaticism. It is not my way. We take what life gives us, and if it's the worst, you try to turn it into the best. That's sense, not heroism."

One correspondent who knew the Amalriks quite well suggested in print that they have no children because Andrei's position vis-à-vis the Soviet authorities makes it impossible for Andrei and Gyusel to allow themselves the experience of parenthood. A dramatic and perhaps logical but nevertheless inaccurate explanation. Gyusel and Andrei have wanted children very much and intended to have them, but she has had several miscarriages. It would be completely out of character for them to avoid having a child because of the uncertain life they are forced to lead; their entire credo is based on living by their own standards despite outside pressures.

Gyusel would make a good mother, I think. She has a rare quality of conveying respect for people of all ages. She once showed me drawings by the five-year-old daughter of a friend who had visited her for informal art lessons. They were quite remarkable for a child of that age, and Gyusel was delighted. "She already sees the world as an artist sees it," she said excitedly. "I only hope school won't squeeze those instincts out of her." Her ability to deal with young people was particularly apparent in the way she treated teen-age acquaintances, who liked to visit her because she talked to them as equals. I hope Gyusel's wish for a child will be granted someday.

Despite her annoyance at being called a hero, there are many times when Gyusel wonders whether the life she and Andrei live is worth the sacrifice. Their destinies are, after all, largely defined by Andrei's insistence on telling the truth as he sees it at any cost.

A visiting American historian asked Gyusel what she would hope for after Andrei was released from prison. She said, "I would like to be able to live as normal people do. I want to do my work, and I want Andrei to carry on the scholarly work that was his real interest—old Russian history. I would like privacy and peace."

"Will that ever be possible for you here?" the American asked.

"No," she said sadly.

Gyusel says she often thinks about what life would be like somewhere other than in the Soviet Union. In his open letter to Anatoly Kuznetsov, Andrei wrote:

. . . in all that you have written and said while you have been abroad—at any rate as far as I have heard—there are two things that seem to me incorrect and which I therefore want to object to with all frankness.

You speak all the time of freedom, but of external freedom, the freedom around us, and you say nothing of the inner freedom, that is, the freedom according to which the authorities can do much to a man but by which they are powerless to deprive him of his moral values.

But clearly such freedom and the responsibility attributed to it is a necessary prerequisite of external freedom. Perhaps in certain countries the freedom to express his thoughts is as freely available to a man as the air he breathes. But where this does not exist, such freedom, I think, can only come about as a result of a stubborn upholding of his inner freedom.

Gyusel has often argued with Andrei, saying, "You have this inner freedom, yes, and I have my inner freedom. But we are dying physically. We have this freedom—it's the freedom for you to be sent back to camp again and again, and for me to spend the rest of my life waiting for you. You and I will not always be young. You need physical strength to uphold any freedom, internal or external."

Gyusel is haunted by the vision of life as a never-ending cycle of imprisonment and persecution. Andrei has a congenital heart defect; she fears his body may not be as resistant as his mind to the hardships of life in a labor camp, especially since the meningitis attack.

The idea that they might, in theory, be able to leave the Soviet Union some day is not as farfetched as it sounds. The Soviet authorities have shown some willingness to permit emigration of people they regard as social parasites or "Colorado beetles." (The latter phrase was applied to Solzhenitsyn by Mikhail Sholokhov, Nobel Prize-winning author of *Quiet Flows the Don*, who is now one of the hardest-line conservatives among Soviet writers.) Dissenting intellectual Valery Tarsis was allowed to leave the Soviet Union in 1964. Solzhenitsyn might have been permitted to travel to Sweden to accept the Nobel Prize in 1970, but he feared the Soviet authorities would not allow him to return.

Gyusel knows Andrei would never consent to leave Russia if he could not come back. "I say to him, 'Why couldn't we have our inner freedom somewhere else, where you could work as a historian, as you started out to do, without constant interference?' He says, and I know he is right, 'What inner freedom do you have if you run away in the face of trouble?' He can say this, even though he probably would have been happier to have been born somewhere else. . . ."

Gyusel herself has no illusion that the Western world is a perfect place in which to develop one's inner freedom. "Where is it possible to live without interference?" she asked a visiting American columnist at a small dinner I had arranged. "In your New York? I think not. The conditions of life there must make inner peace very hard to obtain. I think of our cabin in the country, where Andrei would write and I would paint and we grew our own vegetables. We were completely at peace, even though we were expecting Andrei's arrest. Now that seems like a dream too."

Yet Gyusel possesses a deep hunger to see the rest of the world. "When I was a child I used to dream that I would travel everywhere and see everything. That was one of the things that made me different from the rest of my family. We have such dreams as children in this country, until we grow up and realize our dreams are impossible. But I still dream, sometimes. Maybe it is a kind of inner freedom not to lose your dreams even when they seem impossible."

Sometimes I tried to describe my favorite scenes in the world for her—Ghiberti's golden doors to the baptistery in Florence, the brooding face of Michelangelo looking down on his unfinished Pieta in the cathedral across the square, the tawny light over the Arno at sunset. We have a book consisting entirely of photographs of Michelangelo's sculpture; I was glad Gyusel had a chance to see the pictures, because my Russian lacks some of the sensitive shades of meaning needed to describe great works of art.

By an odd coincidence, Andrei once tried to donate the royalties from a book his father had written to aid the restoration of Florence after the 1966 flood. (His attempt was unsuccessful; the Soviet authorities will never voluntarily exchange Soviet rubles for hard foreign currency.)

Gyusel and Andrei are the kind of people who care about any catastrophe, natural or man-made, that diminishes the human spirit. If Gyusel ever has a chance to read this chapter, I hope she will realize that her apartment and the stones of Florence have something in common: One leaves them with a heightened sense of the dignity and potential glory of being a human being.

VI

Yosif and Marina

The Jews, the Jews, only Jews encircle us
Even Khrushchev, glory to God,
Used to run to the synagogue.
The Jews, the Jews. . . .

—Songwriter unknown

I MET YOSIF AND MARINA for the first time in a crowd of dancing, singing young people who were celebrating the Jewish holiday of Simchath Torah in front of Moscow's main snyagogue. Yosif told me his eighteen-year-old daughter and twenty-four-year-old son had "dragged their stuffy parents out of the house" to take a look at the celebration. A plump, cheerful couple in their early fifties, Yosif and Marina were watching the youthful exuberance with pleasure and some surprise. "I never would have believed so many Jews would come out and identify themselves this way," Yosif commented under his breath.

In Jewish tradition, Simchath Torah commemorates the giving of the Ten Commandments to Moses and the completion of a year's reading of the Torah, the first five books of the Bible. In the Soviet Union, it has become a holiday of youthful self-expression for some Gentiles as well as Jews. More than 10,000 people were gathered outside the synagogue on the rainy autumn evening in 1969 when I met Yosif and Marina. They were drinking, dancing and chanting predictable songs of the Jewish diaspora like "Hava Nagila," as well as contemporary verses satirizing the hardy Russian anti-Semitism that has outlasted the czars.

The song about "Jews encircling us" parodies the proverbial anti-Semite who sees Jews conspiring everywhere. (Like much of what Russians consider political satire, it was written during the years when cultural restrictions were eased under Khrushchev.) The verses make fun of anti-Semitism at all levels of Soviet life, suggesting that Jews are even surrounding Russians in outer space (one Soviet cosmonaut is half Jewish) and that Soviet leaders secretly eat matzo in their private offices. Yosif became uneasy when he heard the words, although his wife, son and daughter were laughing. "You young people don't remember how things have been," he said, shaking his head. "And Marina, you at least should know better. A real anti-Semite might take that song seriously." She replied, "I don't see any real anti-Semites at this exact moment. There's nothing in our marriage license that gives you the right to tell me when I can laugh." Looking sheepish, Yosif laughed himself. "But I'm laughing at us, not at the song," he said.

An open celebration of Simchath Torah would have been unthinkable during the Stalin years, when expressions of Jewish culture—both religious and secular—were ruthlessly suppressed. It was during this period that the Russian word for "cosmopolitan" took on a pejorative political meaning and became synonymous both with "Jew" and "anti-Soviet." (The Russian for a cosmopolitan person is a cognate—*kosmopolit*. If someone was accused of being a cosmopolitan in the Soviet press during the Stalin era, it usually meant he had been or was about to be shot. The word is still used pejoratively by the press, although it now signifies a political attack and not a physical execution.)

Dancing in the street on the eve of Simchath Torah was allowed for the first time by Khrushchev, and his successors continue to permit the celebration. Non-Jewish young people take part in the holiday simply because it is one of the few spontaneous gatherings the authorities allow. "This is a very good place to meet girls," Yosif's son David pointed out. Yosif was surprised at the presence of some Gentiles in the crowd, despite the fact that his son and daughter had told him what to expect.

We knew many Jews in Moscow, partly because they are heavily represented in the college-educated segment of the population most interested in meeting foreigners. Some of them were completely assimilated into Soviet life and displayed little consciousness of or interest in their Jewishness; at the other end of the spectrum, we knew Jews who had applied to emigrate to Israel. Most of those we knew who had applied for exit visas left in the spring of 1971, when the authorities relaxed their emigration policies in an effort to get rid of the leaders of the Jewish movement. They do not belong in this book, because they are no longer Soviet citizens. Yosif and Marina fell somewhere between the assimilationists and those who wanted to leave. They are not the only Jews described in these chapters, but they are the only ones who regarded Jewishness as an important part of their lives.

Yosif and Marina were born in Kiev, the capital of the Ukraine. Their escape from the fate of most Ukrainian Jews under the Nazi occupation profoundly influences their reactions to many seemingly unrelated aspects of life in the Soviet Union today. They are very ordinary people, incapable of dramatizing their lives to themselves or others; their story sounds dramatic only to one who has never experienced the terror and tragedy that were the usual stuff of life for Soviet Jews of their generation.

Yosif is a slight man whose left leg was crippled by a childhood attack of polio. His bespectacled, somewhat academic air led me to suspect he was a teacher or scholar; at various times in his life, he has worked as a cook, a bookkeeper and a designer of holiday greeting cards. He was trained as an electrical engineer in his youth and is now the assistant manager of an electrical parts factory in Moscow. The other jobs were part of the strange life he and Marina were forced to lead between the beginning of the war and Stalin's death in 1953.

Yosif denies that he displayed any special astuteness in escaping the Nazis in 1941. "It didn't take any unusual brains to figure out that Hitler would attack Russia. After the nonaggression pact, I felt it was only a matter of time until he moved east.

At the time, most of the people in the Ukraine didn't believe all the propaganda about eternal friendship between the German and Soviet peoples. But our Ukrainian neighbors, at least some of them, felt the Germans couldn't be much worse than the Russians. They were wrong, of course. But as a Jew, I didn't think that even for a moment. I knew Hitler meant death for me, personally."

Marina met Yosif in the fall of 1940, and it took him several months to convince her to leave with him. "He kept telling me the Germans would attack Russia and probably occupy all of the Ukraine," Marina remembers. "He said the Russians might be beaten at first but they would never let the Germans take Moscow. We would be safe if we went that far to the east. I don't know whether I really believed him, because I was only thinking of the heartbreak of leaving my family. We were a typical, very close Jewish family. I could never convince my mother and father to come with us—their entire life was in Kiev. But I loved Yosif, and I made the decision to go with him. He told me he would not stay with me and die in Kiev just to make my family happy. So I left with him in January, 1941.* It was my great good fortune, although I did not know it then. Yosif is wrong when he says it didn't take any brains to figure out what was going to happen. We didn't have access to accurate information about Hitler. Where were we going to find it, in the Soviet papers? We only had rumors about the Nazi policy on Jews. A neighbor of ours had an aunt who lived in Poland, and the aunt had written a letter about what Hitler was doing to the German Jews. The letter got through the censor because it was sent long before the signing of the Russian-German pact. But that was the only sort of third-hand information we had. It's not surprising that most people didn't take it seriously. Who could imagine the mass murders and concentration camps? My husband could!"

---

* Kiev was occupied on September 19, 1941, and liberated by Soviet troops in November, 1943.

Marina's entire family and all but one of Yosif's relatives died at Babi Yar, the ravine outside Kiev where more than 35,000 Jews were shot in thirty-six hours. It is estimated that 100,000 Jews eventually died there. Today only a small stone marks the site, and the inscription does not mention that the majority of victims were Jews. The authorities have never been willing to acknowledge that Jews suffered more than any other Soviet citizens under the Nazi occupation. For twenty years after the war, officials refused to put even a small marker at Babi Yar, prompting the poet Yevgeny Yevtushenko to write in 1961: "No monument stands over Babi Yar." His poem stunned a generation of Russians who had become accustomed to official silence about the fate of Jews during the war and a younger generation who did not know what had happened.

After leaving Kiev, Yosif and Marina thought he would be able to find an engineering job in Moscow. Instead they were required to spend most of the war in Siberia in a special settle- ment with other refugees from the western Ukraine, the Baltic republics and various Eastern European countries. Stalin did not trust refugees either from foreign countries or from the border regions of the Soviet Union; he was afraid they would engage in espionage and sabotage among the populace if they were allowed to live in areas near the military front. At the same time—through the wondrous doublethink of the period— Soviet citizens who remained on occupied territory were widely distrusted because they had not retreated east with the Soviet Army. It was thought that they must have collaborated with the occupiers in some fashion and, as Boris Alekseivich re- counted, many of them were sent to Soviet prison camps as soon as the Nazi occupiers were driven out. Yosif and Marina felt they were suspect because they had left Kiev at a time when propaganda was proclaiming Soviet-German friendship. Given the paranoia of those years, they were fortunate to have been "resettled" in Siberia instead of being sent to a camp.

"We could have proven our patriotism more thoroughly by waiting until the Germans were marching into Kiev," Yosif said, "or better yet, by dying there." He refuses to talk about the years in Siberia. Marina explained, "We never could understand it. We were grateful to Russia for having saved our lives. Yosif would have served in the army if his left leg had not been shorter than his right; since he only walks with crutches or a cane, active duty would have been impossible. But how stupid not to put his knowledge to use in a factory, where he could have helped the war production effort. They needed trained people desperately because the able-bodied men were all at the front. We cried when the news reached us that the Germans had been stopped at Stalingrad. It was true that some people from the border republics collaborated with the Germans, but how could anyone have thought a Jew would do that? We ran away to escape them." In 1944, when the Russian-German front had moved far west of Moscow and Allied troops had landed in Normandy, Yosif and Marina were allowed to leave Siberia and return to the capital.

After the war, Marina wanted to go back to the Ukraine, but Yosif would not hear of it. The most bitter anti-Semitism in prerevolutionary Russia had been there, and Yosif did not think Communist power had changed anything. The extermination of Ukrainian Jews was carried out with a speed and thoroughness equaled only in Latvia, Lithuania and Poland, also traditional centers of anti-Semitism. Marina and Yosif have never returned to Kiev or to the ravine where their families died. They feel anti-Semitism is still stronger in the Ukraine than in the rest of Russia, although they know the absence of a marker at Babi Yar for so many years was dictated by central as well as Ukrainian government policies. There is considerable evidence that discrimination against Jews in higher education and certain types of employment is strongest there. The situation in universities is another case of central government policies reinforcing traditional local prejudice. Soviet education authorities are concerned about the underrepresentation of students from rural areas; they are making efforts to admit "marginal" applicants whose performance on entrance examinations may have been

hindered by a generally poor cultural and educational background. The rationale is similar to that of preferential admissions for black students in some American universities. But
preferential treatment for rural students means the exclusion of
some who would normally have been admitted on the basis of
their performance. In some Ukrainian universities, a disproportionate number of those excluded seem to be Jews—and unofficial "Jewish quotas" had always been a widespread practice.

"It is painful to think that there is so little regret for the
past," Marina said. "In the Ukraine, there was still hatred after
the war for the Jews who had survived. We heard some people
even blamed the Jews for starting the war in the first place.
Yosif thought our children would have a better chance to grow
up free of hatred in Moscow. Although things are far from
perfect here, I think he was right. We have never wanted to go
back to think about ghosts. I never want to see Babi Yar until
they raise a real monument over it."

Yosif and Marina were not able to lead what might be considered a normal life until Stalin's death. The policies of the
regime became more openly anti-Semitic after the war than
they had been during the 1930's. Virtually all Jewish cultural institutions were closed, leading Yiddish-language writers
were secretly tried and executed, and the "doctors' plot," in
which prominent Jewish doctors were accused of having caused
the death of one government official and conspired against others, was concocted at the top levels of the government and
secret police. Only Stalin's death saved the doctors from execution. Several of Yosif's and Marina's Jewish friends were sent to
camps for offenses ranging from alleged violations of currency
laws to collaboration with the Germans. A year after their son
David was born, Yosif and Marina left Moscow for a small town
on the Volga River—their version of "going to the *dacha*." "It
wasn't just Jews who did this," Yosif pointed out, "but all kinds
of people who had reason to think they might get into trouble.
We kept on the move constantly, living in six towns between
1947 and 1954." In *Hope Against Hope*, Nadezhda Mandelstam

attributes her survival—and, consequently, the preservation of her husband's poems—to the fact that she never stayed too long in one place during the years after Mandelstam's death in 1938.

While they were away from Moscow, Yosif and Marina both worked at a variety of odd jobs. She was a medical attendant in a nursery school. He was a cook in small-town restaurants; to earn extra money, he sometimes found a child or two whose parents were willing to pay a few rubles for private drawing lessons. (Yosif had a natural aptitude for art and he had also been trained as a draftsman in engineering school.)

Yosif's and Marina's experiences during and after the war explained their most striking trait: a deep reverence for life, a feeling that their own lives were gifts preserved in the midst of cosmic evil. "I never question why things happened as they did," said Marina, a gay woman with deep-blue eyes and light-brown hair that was only beginning to gray. "I think of our lives as a present, and when I think about what is wrong in this country—as I often do—I am still grateful for every minute of the last twenty-five years. Life is better than death."

Marina was more talkative by nature than Yosif and more open about past and present difficulties in the Soviet Union. "You know that Russians don't talk very much about the Stalin years," she said. "Well, Yosif is a Jew on top of being a Soviet citizen. He lived through two separate catastrophes, and he always bore the main burden of worry—first in persuading me to leave Kiev ahead of the Nazis, then in seeing that we had food in our mouths for eight years after the war. He always said we would live longer than Stalin. He never forgets how much better life is now than it was then. I don't forget either, but I still can't keep my mouth shut about things that are wrong now—at least not unless Yosif is around to keep me quiet. He says I talk too much."

After Stalin died, Yosif and Marina returned to Moscow and a happier life. Their daughter Nadezhda was a year old. "She was an accident—we thought an unhappy one because we were still on the run from town to town," Marina said. "But how glad we were to have her when our lives took a turn for the better." Yosif has been working steadily since 1955 in the profession for which he was trained. He was promoted to a supervisory job in 1960 and has been an assistant manager of his electrical parts plant since 1966. Marina is a Ukrainian-Russian translator specializing in scientific and technical material. She received several awards for her work at one publishing house. The couple's combined salary totals about 350 rubles a month, and Marina only works part-time now. She does most of her translations at home.

The family lives in a two-room apartment with its own kitchen and bath—a comfortable dwelling place by Soviet standards. They lived in a communal apartment until four years ago, when their turn came on the waiting list. David and Nadezhda, like other young people, have little hope of finding their own place until they marry and can add their names to the waiting list. They sleep in one room, their beds divided by a curtain. Yosif and Marina sleep in the other room, which is also used as a living and dining area. The apartment is spotless, filled with small knickknacks and household articles painstakingly acquired over the years. A set of patterned wine glasses was a prized possession; matching dishes and glasses are among the many consumer goods that seem ordinary elsewhere but are difficult to obtain in the Soviet Union.

The lavishness of Yosif and Marina's hospitality was often embarrassing. Our favorite foods were always on the table— gefilte fish for Tony, potato pancakes or chopped liver for me. We knew Marina had usually spent hours shopping for the ingredients. Liver, for example, is difficult to find and often costs several rubles a pound in farm markets. Farm markets sell produce that collective farmers grow on small private plots permitted by the state. The fruit, vegetables and poultry are of higher quality—and a higher price—than the ordinary collective farm produce sold in state stores.

Our friends always tried to offer us something special, although we constantly told them not to fuss; Yosif once spotted bottles of red Cinzano on the shelf of a wine store before the May Day holiday and waited in line three hours to make the purchase. The appearance of any imported Western product immediately attracts large crowds of shoppers.

The saddest aspect of our friendship was that we were never able to entertain them in our home. Yosif felt it was safe for us to come to them but not for them to visit us, mainly because of the KGB guard posts. We offered to drive them past the guard huts in our car, as we did other friends, but Yosif was too uneasy to try it. We attempted to compensate for our inability to return their hospitality by bringing occasional gifts—eye shadow for Marina, an English pipe for Yosif, a jazz or Broadway musical record that made everyone in the family happy. They owned a German record player that was at least thirty years old, which they had bought in a commission store. (The commission stores are another semiprivate, government-sanctioned operation. People take old objects to the stores and they are resold. The former owner receives a percentage of the profit.) Yosif thought the tone was better than that of Soviet-manufactured hi-fi sets. David and Nadezhda were saving their money to present their parents with the newest Soviet stereo model for their thirtieth wedding anniversary. With all of the additional equipment they felt was necessary, it would cost about 400 rubles. Nadezhda asked for my opinion, and I told her that the best Soviet record players did not have as true a tone as Western ones, but that they were a great improvement over the older Soviet models and over the thirty-year-old German set.

Yosif and Marina's hospitality was unfailing, even when I felt duty-bound to warn them at times when the KGB was paying particular attention to our activities. It would have been unfair to endanger any Russian by coming to his house when we thought we might be followed without discussing the possible consequences in advance. "There are places where you have to draw a line about being careful," Yosif once said in a rare comment on political realities. "You are our friends, and no one can tell me who I see in my own home. A man's thoughts and his friends are his own."

Yosif and Marina lived quietly, concerned mainly with each other and their children. He sometimes had to work extra hours when the factory was under pressure to overfulfill its state production plan, but his day ordinarily began at nine and ended at five. The family did not own a car—only a tiny minority of Soviet citizens do because they are expensive and waiting lists are even longer than the ones for apartments—but their home was only ten minutes from a subway stop. Marina reported to her office only once a week to obtain new material for translation. The couple shared chores like cooking and shopping; Yosif helped his wife in the house far more than most Russian men do. "Jewish men make good husbands," Marina said. I laughed, and when she asked why, I said because this was such a universal cliché. "That's because Jews are universal," she replied.

They were generally bored by the available entertainment and ventured into theaters and concert halls only when an occasional touring foreign company was making an appearance. Marina loved the ballet but considered most of the Bolshoi productions stiff and old-fashioned, despite the company's splendid individual dancers. She was thrilled when she managed to obtain a ticket to see the Alvin Ailey American Dance Theater when it toured the Soviet Union in 1970 under the U.S.-Soviet cultural exchange agreement. Most modern Soviet films they dismissed as "boring propaganda." They tried not to miss the occasional foreign films shown in Moscow, always with dubbing rather than subtitles. They particularly enjoyed *My Fair Lady* and *The Apartment*, shown respectively in 1969 and 1970. Movies from the West are shown so seldom to the general public that people remember them by the year. Unlike Galya, they did not have access to foreign film showings for the Soviet cultural elite.

The entire family listened regularly to news and entertainment programs carried by the VOA. They were interested both in news of the outside world and of the Soviet Union—especially reports concerning Soviet Jews. The broadcasts kept them fairly well informed about what was going on in the world, although they often asked us for explanations of the short news items. They learned Tony had been roughed up by KGB thugs from a news broadcast that quoted a New York *Times* story about several correspondents. We had broken off contact with them because we were fearful of involving them in an incident like the one with the friend who allegedly signed a statement calling for Tony's expulsion from the country. Marina phoned me from a pay booth to ask if everything was all right. The call was safe, since I recognized her voice and she did not have to identify herself.

Yosif and Marina's main concern was the way Soviet society would treat their children in the future. Their daughter was studying to be an English teacher (every middle-class Soviet parent seems to have the same idea about the advantages of having his children learn English). Their son was already working as a professional photographer for newspapers and magazines and making extra money by moonlighting at weddings and anniversary parties. Although Yosif and Marina were quite satisfied with the way their own lives had turned out, they were not at all sure the Soviet system offered the kinds of opportunities they wanted for their children. "We have seen progress in our own lives," Marina said. "We have better housing, better clothes, better food than we did ten years ago, not to mention the period after the war. We also feel more free—we are no longer terrified of a knock on the door at night that would send us away to a camp. But that isn't enough for our children. You like to give your children something much better than you had, and I don't know if that's really possible here. Things were so bad twenty years ago, and they have improved so much, that I don't think the comparative improvement can be as great in the next twenty years. Our children know how the Soviet standard of living compares with America and Europe; there is enough foreign merchandise on the black market for them to have some idea. They want cars and attractive clothes and nice apartments of their own. You can't blame them for that—they're young. They don't care what things were like twenty-five years ago, they are interested in now."

Yosif and Marina try to go out occasionally in the evening so that their children can entertain friends alone. "It's terrible for them, having no privacy," Yosif said, "and it's terrible for us too. I know grown children do not live with their parents in America, and that would be much better here. The children feel we invade their private lives, but they don't realize how much we would sometimes like to be alone without them. That their parents would like to make love without anyone else being able to hear them never occurs to young people."

Marina and Yosif are sympathetic to their children's complaints about aspects of life that are less tangible than the housing shortage. Nadezhda heard that foreign-language students in the United States and Europe are able to participate in exchange programs by living with a family in another country. She would like to do the same thing but knows it would never be permitted. Yosif says David comes home angry "three nights out of five" because the photographs he regards as his best work have little chance of being published. He likes to take candid shots, but nearly all pictures used by Soviet newspapers and magazines are posed. He did a series of one woman's face in repose, anger and laughter. An editor told him the pictures were outstanding but could not be used because they did not portray the woman performing a socially useful function. "Young people just don't have enough opportunity to develop themselves professionally if they have ideas of their own," Marina said. "The old people sit on new ideas here in an organized way—it's not just the expectable disagreement between the young and the old. David took some nude pictures that I didn't especially care for, but why not publish them if someone wants to look at them? Despite their problems, though, my children cannot imagine a different life. They are Soviet citizens; their life is here. They would not think of applying to go to Israel. Most of their friends are Russian; I think it's unlikely that they will marry Jews. If they did, it would be by sheer accident."

Yosif and Marina remain uneasy about their children's future as Jews in the Soviet Union—a feeling that is not merely a product of their past experiences.

If they lived in the United States or Western Europe, they would probably be assimilated Jews with a deep respect for their cultural heritage but only a mild interest in practicing their religion. They would not speak Yiddish or Hebrew but the language of the country in which they lived, though their son would learn a few words of Hebrew for his Bar Mitzvah. If they belonged to a synagogue, it would be reformed. They would celebrate both Christmas and Chanukah, to the delight of their children and the disgruntlement of their rabbi. They would not urge their son or daughter to marry Jews, although they might be secretly pleased to see their children married under the traditional canopy. Always mindful of the tragedy that befell European Jewry under Hitler, they would strongly support Israel—but they would not choose to live there themselves. They would find no conflict between being good Jews and being good citizens of their country.

With the exception of the last sentence, this description fits Yosif's and Marina's lives in the Soviet Union. But there are conflicts between being a Jew and being a Soviet citizen; Soviet policy on what some officials still call "the Jewish question" is fraught not only with traditional Russian anti-Semitism, but with modern anti-Zionism as well.

Jews are classified as a separate nationality on the internal passports issued to all Soviet citizens, as are Georgians, Ukrainians, Uzbeks and many other people who would simply be regarded as members of ethnic groups in the United States. The exact number of Jews in the Soviet Union is a matter of some dispute. According to the official 1970 census, the number dropped from to 2,151,000 from the 1960 figure of 2,268,000. Many activist Jews in the Soviet Union, as well as Israeli officials with their own propaganda axes to grind, had predicted that the census would show a Russian Jewish population of more than 3,000,000. It was assumed that many more Jews would declare themselves as such on the census as the fears of Stalinist anti-Semitism receded and because of the pride engendered in many Soviet Jews by Israel's military performance during the Six-Day War. The assumption may have been incorrect on several counts. The natural rate of population increase among Jews is low, because most Soviet Jews live in urban areas where the housing shortage discourages large families. While the Six-Day War did make some Russians proud to be Jews for the first time, it also triggered a break in diplomatic relations between Israel and the Soviet Union and an anti-Zionist campaign in the press. "For every Jew who was proud," Marina said, "there must have been one who was scared and tried to declare himself as being of another nationality. You can do that sometimes if your last name isn't obviously Jewish and you speak only Russian. There's something else you have to remember too. The rate of intermarriage between Jews and Gentiles is now quite high; I know that from my own experience and that of my friends. A child of intermarriage can pick the nationality of either parent, and I don't know how many such children would freely choose to be identified as Jews on their passports." Soviet officials may have doctored the census figures for their own purposes, possibly to minimize the effects of worldwide publicity about Russian Jews who want to emigrate to Israel. The true figure probably falls somewhere between the official Soviet one and the 3,000,000 usually cited by Jewish sources in the West.

In contrast to Jews, Georgians, Ukrainians and members of other nationality groups can send their children to schools in their own language and in their own republics. There are no Yiddish-language schools. Hebrew is not even offered as an elective language in high schools, as it is, for example, in New York City. The only attempt to give Jews a region of their own to live in was a farce. The Autonomous Oblast (region) of Birobidzhan was established in the 1920's as an alleged center of Jewish culture in a desolate area of the Soviet Far East. At last count, the population was about 18 percent Jewish. The vast majority of Jews have always lived in western Russia; they were not likely to move to a backward rural area with a population under 170,000. Other Soviet nationality groups live in republics where their people have lived for centuries.

The lack of Yiddish-language schools and a Jewish republic is not in itself the truest indication of the government's attitude. Soviet officials are correct in their contention that most Jews in the world no longer speak Yiddish as their first language and that many, especially the young, do not even speak it as a second language. Yosif and Marina speak perfect Ukrainian and Russian but have forgotten the limited Yiddish they once knew. They were not interested in passing it on to their children. "It's much more useful for them to learn English," Yosif said. Jews like Yosif and Marina are also totally unconcerned about the lack of a separate Jewish republic. "Are you kidding?" Yosif said. "Jews lived in the Pale for years. Who would choose to live in a new ghetto today? It doesn't make any sense." His viewpoint was echoed by many Jews I met. What does concern a growing number of Soviet Jews, however, is the fact that organized cultural and religious life is virtually outlawed.

Yosif and Marina are assimilated because their parents believed in assimilation as the ultimate solution to anti-Semitism. But as survivors of Hitler and Stalin, they no longer have complete faith in it. "Anyone who lived through what we did, and still thinks you can forget about being a Jew, is crazy," Marina said. "We would have liked our children to learn something about Jewish culture in a more organized way that we were able to provide at home. But that is impossible in the Soviet Union."

Official organizations for the study of Jewish history, culture or religion are prohibited. The handful of open synagogues in Soviet cities are not permitted to conduct classes for young people. Moscow, with a population of several hundred thousand Jews, has only three working synagogues. It is, of course, impossible to tell how many Soviet Jews are agnostics, how many are erratic high holiday observers and how many would like to practice their religion regularly. Yosif and Marina keep the high holidays quietly in their home; they go to the synagogue at Passover time for matzo. The authorities allow the central synagogue to bake matzo once a year and distribute it to Jews who ask for it.

Although Jews are influential in the creative and performing arts, secular Jewish culture has not recovered from the blows it received during the Stalin years. Jewish writers like Isaac Babel and Mandelstam who were disgraced or executed during the 1930's have been officially rehabilitated, but virtually none of their work is in print. They are still too controversial, not because of the manner of their deaths but because their writing confronted the wounds of Soviet society too directly. That is why they died.

Jewish history is distorted by all of the Soviet media. It has often been said that we live in a post-Auschwitz world, and this has destroyed the previous respectability of veiled anti-Semitism. As far as their knowledge of what happened to Jews under Hitler is concerned, most Russians still live in a pre-Auschwitz world. The Nazi policy of genocide against Jews is never mentioned in school history textbooks. Soviet high school students learn only that Hitler "wanted to make slaves of the Slavic peoples." Thus, *Pravda* could publish an article in the spring of 1970 suggesting that Ukrainian Zionists were accomplices to the Nazis in their murders at Babi Yar. Official sources often hint that Jews with ties to Israel want to silence other Russian Jews who want to remain in their native land.

The official anti-Zionist campaign reached its height while we were in Moscow, as groups of activist Jews persisted in a movement demanding the right of emigration to Israel. The campaign took on many aspects—a barrage of newspaper articles, press conferences of Jews testifying to their joy in being Soviet citizens, verbal and physical intimidation of foreign correspondents who had contacts with Jewish leaders. One anti-Zionist press conference of prominent Jews staged by the gov-

ernment drew a blunt response from Marina: "It makes me
want to throw up." Yosif and Marina were particularly sad-
dened by the appearance at the press conference of Arkady
Raikin, who has been the most popular comedian in the Soviet
Union for many years. "They probably told him no more trips
abroad, ever, if he didn't sign that statement," Yosif said. His
comment was merely conjecture, but reliable sources in Moscow reported that Maya Plisetskaya had been threatened with
just that if she did not sign the same statement. Her name
appeared on the document, but she was not present at the conference.

Some aspects of the campaign backfired comically. A meeting of rabbis and other "safe Jews" was organized at the Moscow synagogue for the benefit of Soviet journalists. The few
Soviet rabbis always give public support to government policies
on Jews and Israel. The limited religious functions they are
allowed to fulfill could be restricted still further at any time by
the authorities. Some pro-emigration Jews tipped the foreign
correspondents to what was going on, and the authorities were
unwilling to make a scene by refusing to admit them to a conference ostensibly designed to educate the press. Unfortunately
for the conference organizers, some "unsavory" Jews had managed to crash the affair. One walked up to the foreign journalists and said, "Those rabbis don't speak for me. I have been
wanting to go to Israel for twenty years now and they won't let
me out." He was asked by an official to step out into the hall,
and the correspondents were treated to the sight of his being
hauled away by the police. We had a dinner date with Yosif
and Marina the next night, and they had laughed at the account of the affair carried by the VOA that morning.

Yosif and Marina were frightened by the possible connections between the anti-Zionist campaign and traditional anti-
Semitism. " 'Hate Israel' means 'Hate Jews' to ordinary people,"
Marina said. They were particularly upset at the trials of Jews
in the Leningrad hijack case and were deeply relieved when the
death sentences were commuted after protests by governments

throughout the world. "They [the authorities] didn't do it out of the kindness of their hearts," Yosif said. "They did it because they never expected the rest of the world to care so much about a few Jews." They were adamantly opposed to the tactics of the militant Jewish Defense League in verbally and physically harassing Soviet diplomats in the United States. "They're a bunch of fools who don't have any idea what it's like to live here," Yosif said. "Every time they throw a bomb at an Aeroflot office, they draw attention away from the way the Soviet government treats Jews and toward their own violent tactics. It gives the Russians something legitimate to scream about, to confuse the issue."

Yosif and Marina illustrate the difficulty of estimating how many Jews might want to leave the Soviet Union if emigration were free. They have no intention of applying to leave for Israel, although a few friends had done so. Their children had no desire to leave, and Yosif and Marina would never cut themselves off from their family. I asked Marina whether they would leave if they knew they could return to visit their children. "It's hard to say," she answered. "If this were the kind of country with free international travel, where people could just come and go as they pleased, maybe it wouldn't be the kind of country anyone would want to leave permanently."

The Soviets allowed more than 12,000 Jews to leave in 1971— a significant increase in emigration and a deliberate policy aimed at getting rid of the leaders of the Jewish movement. After we returned to the United States, many friends asked us why the Soviet government is determined to keep citizens who want to leave. "Why don't they just let them go?" asked one college professor. "What would they lose?" In the case of the Jews, they would lose a significant number of highly educated professionals. However, that is not the main reason for their reluctance to let Jews leave. Emigration is *not* regarded as a right under Soviet law—a fact that many Westerners find bewildering. When we tried to explain the elaborate rules that prevent most Russians from going abroad even on vacation, many of our American friends did not believe us. Until recently, Jews were treated no differently from other Soviet citizens in regard to emigration—it was simply not allowed. In letting thousands of Jews leave, the government has made a major exception to its past policies. The authorities must wonder what they will say to the next group of people who demand the right to emigrate or simply to travel abroad as tourists. "They're also afraid that other national minorities will get ideas about protesting from the success the Jews have had in getting publicity," Marina said. Her comment was astute, and the point of view is shared by many knowledgeable observers of the Soviet Union.

Soviet officials hinted that they might allow as many as 35,000 Jews to emigrate in 1972. The decision may have been prompted by a dual desire to get rid of malcontents within the Soviet borders and to embarrass an unprepared Israel with a flood of unexpected immigrants. However, the partial success of the emigration drive confirms Marina's opinion that Russian Jews are no longer terrified; in Stalin's day, any emigration movement by any nationality group would have been stopped with bullets. Marina is also correct to link the problems of Jews with those of other nationalities. Discrimination in the Soviet Union today is practiced by Russians against most minorities— especially the Asians—and by various minorities against each other. The Soviet Jews have been more successful than other minorities in bringing their grievances to the attention of the world, but their situation is not as unique as many Westerners believe. The Soviet Union is not a "melting pot" for anyone.

I asked Marina if she felt her family had experienced any direct anti-Semitism in the "good years" since Stalin's death. She replied:

"I cannot answer you with a simple yes or no. Once when David was in sixth grade, he asked me to put a scarf on my head and wear my skirt longer when I came to talk to his teacher for a school parents' meeting. He told me he wanted me to look more like a Russian. I make all my own clothes because the clothes in Russian stores have so little style. I try not to look sixty when I'm only in my forties. I said to David, 'What is this, have the other children been telling you your mother looks so young?' He finally told me a teacher had said the Jews always manage to get the best of everything, and he didn't want his friends to think we thought we were better than anyone else.

"Sometimes it works the other way. Once I was standing in the front hall at intermission at the Bolshoi. Yosif wasn't with me. A man came up and started talking to me. He asked where I was from originally, and I said Kiev. Then he said, 'But you're not Ukrainian, are you?' I said, 'No, I'm Jewish.' He said he had known it from the minute he saw me, because I was one of the best-looking women in the room. 'Anyone who stands out, you know he's a Jew,' the man said. I'm sure he was Jewish too.

"So we stand out, we always stand out whether we want to or not. I don't know if that answers your question, but it's the only answer I have."

VII

Oskar Rabin

OSKAR RABIN IS A FORTY-FOUR-YEAR-OLD ARTIST who describes himself as a craftsman with "strong nerves—like ropes." He needs them, because his canvases express an ironic vision of life that is unacceptable to the authorities who dictate official culture in the Soviet Union. His art reflects with great sensitivity the contrasts of modern Russian life: not merely the obvious ones between his country's prerevolutionary traditions and the drive to construct an industrial society, but deeper paradoxes involving cant and reality, meaning and sterility, humble human experience and great, sometimes inhuman, causes.

Oskar is an unofficial painter, which means he is not a member of the Soviet Union of Artists. Unlike Gyusel Amalrik, he is a mature artist whose life centers around his work. His paintings cannot be publicly exhibited in his own country, although he has had one-man shows in San Francisco and London and his work has been exhibited with that of other unofficial artists in several European cities. Although unofficial art in the Soviet Union takes in a broad spectrum of styles, its most distinctive quality is quite simple: It does not conform to the aesthetic dictates of the party. Unofficial art is a "gray area" of Soviet cultural life. It cannot be publicly shown, reproduced or written about (except in derogatory fashion), but the artists are free to paint privately and sell their work to anyone. They are alternately attacked in the press and ignored for long periods of time. Regulations make it difficult—but not impossible—for a foreigner to take unofficial paintings out of the Soviet Union. The exhibits of modern Russian art abroad testify to the fact that there are ways of getting around the rules.

The unofficial painters prefer to be called modern artists, because they do not recognize any valid distinction between "official" and "unofficial," "Soviet" or "anti-Soviet" art.

"I am a Soviet citizen," Oskar says. "I was born and live in the Soviet Union, and in this sense my art is Soviet. Just as the work of American artists belongs to American art. Everyone knows about Soviet, American and French paintings, but no one has ever heard about anti-American, anti-French or anti-Soviet paintings. Nevertheless, there are people who use the term 'anti-Soviet.' What for? To intimidate, to curse, to praise? I consider such people spiritually bankrupt and frightened for their entire lives by Stalin's time. Good and bad paintings, good and bad music, good and bad literature do not exist for such people. The label 'anti-Soviet'—and it is a political label—excludes any other approaches to art."

A tall, wiry man with a slight stoop, an almost entirely bald head and a red mustache, Oskar conveys the integrity of his art in his personal manner. His slow, warm smile brings a surprising change to a face that appears austere in repose. It is not a melancholy face, but it is lined with an awareness of pain not entirely accounted for in the spare life history he generally offers foreign visitors. Oskar is not taciturn when he is talking about subjects that matter to him, but he always considers his words carefully before he speaks—whether the subject is painting, dogs or Solzhenitsyn. His wit can be extremely cutting when directed at people and ideas he despises; he does not use it carelessly. He seldom makes small talk and is comfortable with silences; if he is thinking something through, he may stare into space or look at a visitor for several minutes without saying anything. Friends never feel the thread of communication has been broken.

Despite the gentleness and even humility of his manner, Oskar is a tough man who is not intimidated by political attacks that sent some of the other painters we knew into a state of intense nervous apprehension. His kind of toughness is usually noticeable in the few Russians who had the fortitude to survive life in prison camps with unbroken minds and spirits. The key to Oskar's "strong nerves" was something I was not able to discover during the two years in which we knew each other, but the quality was unmistakable. Said one of his friends: "You would understand why he is so strong if you had seen the way he and Valya [Oskar's wife] lived during the years when painting didn't bring in any money. They lived in a terrible old house, the kind with no decent heating or indoor plumbing, and both of them went on painting even when it didn't bring in enough kopecks for potatoes. [The ruble is divided into 100 kopecks.] At the same time, Oskar took on other jobs so they could eat. He bore most of the burden during those years, and you would never hear him say anything about it today."

One example of Oskar's toughness was his insistence on walking past the police guard post himself when he came to see us.

We made the usual offer to pick Oskar up in our car and drive him inside the compound. "It isn't necessary," he said firmly. "I'll come in by myself. I don't mind showing them my passport." Oskar's attitude was that he was a Soviet citizen, there was no law against Soviet citizens visiting foreigners, so there was no reason for him to sneak around. He is one of the minority of Russians who believe in exercising their rights under Soviet law rather than cowering before unwritten laws that restrict individual liberties far more than statutes.

Rabin the man cannot be separated from Rabin the painter. To understand both, it is necessary to know something of the tortured history of art since the revolution and its relationship to the condition of the modern Soviet artist.

Oskar's story has its origins in the seemingly dead period during the 1930's, when the most brilliant people in all branches of the creative arts had either emigrated, committed suicide, been murdered in one fashion or another or simply retreated into their private, silent worlds. It begins with his father-in-law, Yevgeny Leonidovich Kropivnitsky.

Kropivnitsky was one of a small number of men and women who preserved the Russian artistic heritage from the early part of the twentieth century throughout the Stalin era, when any open hint of interest in unofficial art would have been considered treason. The first three decades of the twentieth century produced a brilliant Russian avant-garde art that profoundly influenced and was influenced by art in the West. The mere names of Chagall, Kandinsky, Malevich, Tatlin, Lissitzky, Popova, Larionov and Goncharova testify to the importance Russians assumed in the evolution of the most significant artistic movements of their era: cubism, futurism, suprematism, surrealism, constructivism.*

The artistic excitement of the years immediately following the revolution is often forgotten because it was crushed so swiftly. Many Russian intellectuals in all fields believed the revolution would free dynamic forces in both the creative and performing arts that were seething beneath the surface of the czarist autocracy. Chagall, for example, actually held a minor cultural commissar's post under the Bolshevik government before he left Russia for the last time in 1922.

The realization that there would be no artistic revolution unless it served the purposes of the political revolution began growing before Lenin's death, although the iron grip of Socialist realism did not fully descend on every area of the arts until Stalin had assumed total power. Because of the Soviet government's attitude toward the early avant-garde Russian artists, an entire chapter of modern art history has been ignored by Western specialists until quite recently. It is as if the French government had made a decision in 1930 to lock up the paintings of every major artist from Matisse through Baque. Lyubov Popova, for example, is not as great a cubist as Braque or Picasso, but she is far more important than many cubists who are

---

* I will not attempt to describe in any detail the history of Russian art during the early 1900's. The best single source on this subject is Camilla Gray's *The Great Experiment: Russian Art, 1863–1922* (London, Thames & Hudson; New York, Harry N. Abrams, 1962).

well-known in the West. Yet her work is known only to a small group of collectors and art historians. Countless paintings by the Russian artists of Popova's generation are locked in the cellars of museums in Moscow and Leningrad. Some were saved from destruction in the 1930's by people who kept them in their homes at great risk. Now there is no question of the paintings being destroyed; they are preserved by museum staffs against the day when the government might allow them to be publicly shown again. A lucky Westerner with good art credentials can sometimes gain access to the cellars to view the paintings.

Oskar's father-in-law and mother-in-law were both painters themselves, but their work was seen by no one but their family and their closest friends during the long years of Stalin's rule. Yet they knew about the inheritance that had been denied by the Stalin regime and they preserved the knowledge for the next generation of artists—Oskar Rabin's generation. The Kropivnitskys were teachers in the truest sense, living conduits of knowledge that was officially dead.

Oskar met the elder Kropivnitsky when he was a teen-ager; he later married Kropivnitsky's daughter Valentina, who is also an artist. Oskar and Valentina are still married to each other—a record of unusual marital longevity in the Moscow art world—and they have a twenty-year-old son and twenty-three-year-old daughter.

Kropivnitsky, whom Oskar often speaks of as "my old master," obviously never tried to instill one style of painting in his students. Valentina's art, which consists entirely of a rich fantasy world of old Russian landscapes peopled by gentle beasts with half-human forms (or perhaps gentle humans with half-animal forms), is completely different from Oskar's painting. Neither of the Rabins' work resembles that of Valentina's brother Lev, who is also a painter.

There were other men like Kropivnitsky, and they were responsible for helping to train most of the important unofficial artists in the Soviet Union today. The best artists of Oskar's generation all know and respect each other's work; many of them studied together informally in small groups during the late 1940's and early 1950's. The danger of such activity does not seem to have been too great at that point, as long as the groups were small, and the artists' work gained momentum after Stalin's death.

Oskar's evolution into a full-fledged artist resembles the histories of other unofficial painters: an early interest in art, some type of formal and informal training, odd jobs to support himself while his art continued to mature and while the cultural atmosphere loosened enough to permit the development of unofficial art. He says, "Between the ages of six and ten I wanted to be a poet, an architect, the inventor of a perpetual motion machine. I played the violin for three years. When I was ten years old I started painting and have been painting all my life."

He attended a special music school and then an art school before the war; like most secondary schools, Oskar's was closed for the duration. He was thirteen when the war began—he would probably have seen combat had he been a year or two older, but by 1944 the military situation had improved enough so that the Red Army did not need sixteen-year-old soldiers. His mother died during the war; his father died when he was a small boy.

One of the gaps in Oskar's biography is his wartime experience, where there was chaos in ordinary social institutions and the agencies that might have cared for an orphaned teen-ager had probably ceased to function normally. We were talking about the war once with another man in his forties who said, "I never think about it at all anymore." Oskar said distantly, "I think about it often, very often." He did not elaborate when his Russian friend said, "Do you really?" in a surprised tone.

After the war, having already met Kropivnitsky, Oskar went to Riga, the capital of Latvia, to enroll in the Academy of Fine Arts there. His mother was a Latvian Jew, although he was born and grew up in Moscow. He spent three years in Riga and then returned to study at an art institute in Moscow. "At the

institutes where I studied I learned that boredom can discourage one from painting," he said. "Fortunately, that did not happen to me. I became a friend of the old artist Kropivnitsky. We
used to paint from nature together, arguing about art, poetry,
music and life. That was the best method of teaching."

Having learned about the discouraging nature of boredom,
Oskar continued to study with Kropivnitsky for several years.
He worked at a wide variety of jobs and painted in his spare
time. He was employed by the railroads for many years—as an
office clerk, a messenger, a loader and finally as a foreman who
supervised the loading of freight cars. "These were odd jobs
for a man who had no profession," he noted. Railroad scenes
recur in his paintings of the late 1950's and early 1960's, reflecting the fact that he always derives his artistic symbols from
objects that are a part of his immediate surroundings.

Oskar has also illustrated books for many years, and he still
does some graphic work despite the fact that he has been able
to support himself mainly by his own unofficial painting since
the mid-1960's. Although they do not belong to the Artists'
Union, nearly all of the unofficial artists do some work commis-
sioned by official sources. Many illustrate books, especially
children's fairy tales; others decorate buildings, pavilions for
special exhibitions, or New Year's trees known as *yolkas*. None
of the good unofficial artists do any official painting; they work
on occasional projects to help support themselves in areas
which they feel do not impinge on their real creative work. The
fact that they receive commissions for such odd jobs, despite
their exclusion from the Artists' Union, is another example of
the gray area unofficial art occupies in Soviet culture.

Oskar and Valentina Rabin live a quiet life in a four-room
cooperative apartment, amid dozens of prefabricated buildings
that make up modern Moscow.* The neighborhood emerged in

---

* The main difference between a cooperative apartment and ordinary state
housing is that a co-op requires a down payment, often of several thousand
rubles. Monthly payments are also higher—7 to 12 rubles' monthly rent for an
ordinary apartment, 25 to 35 for co-op payments. In return, the buyer of a

its present form during the late 1960's; it alternates between the five-story buildings that were characteristic of the Khrushchev era and the higher apartment buildings that have been constructed during the past five years. (Khrushchev did not approve of taller buildings. In order to save money, no elevators were put in any of the five-story buildings—a situation that grieves people with apartments on the fifth floor.)

The Rabins' apartment is conveniently located, only a five-minute walk from a metro stop and food stores. The residential area is now established enough for stores and public services to have begun to catch up with housing construction; the lag in developing commercial and service enterprises is chronic and infuriating to residents of new Moscow suburbs. Nevertheless, the landscape still looks raw, as if the construction cranes had pulled out only yesterday. Outside of its historic center, Moscow is one endless complex of apartments; there are no private houses and few unusual buildings of any kind to break the monotony. This monotony and a feeling of rawness approaching bleakness are often apparent in Oskar's paintings of the urban scene.

While we were in Moscow, the Rabins lived with their daughter and Valentina's mother, who was seriously ill and needed continuous care. Valya's father was alive, but he could not provide his wife with the nursing she needed in their home. As Galya pointed out to me, Russians in all walks of life are reluctant to let the state look after their aging parents. Old customs are still given enormous importance; one artist we knew was literally starving because he had not sold a painting in several weeks and had spent his last several hundred rubles on a proper burial for his mother. (The cost of dying is minimal if a body is turned over to the state, but most Russians would not dream of

---

co-op can obtain his new apartment far more quickly than he could by waiting on the regular state list. He also has the permanent right to live in the apartment, although the word "ownership" is not used because it smacks of capitalism. A growing percentage of the new apartment construction in Moscow is co-op.

doing that. The prices of privately financed funerals in the Soviet Union would make another book for Jessica Mitford.) We
seldom saw the Rabins' son in their apartment; he had begun
his two-year tour of duty in the Soviet Army while we were in
Moscow.

The studio is the first full-size room in the apartment, just
beyond a cramped kitchen and an entrance hall half blocked by
a refrigerator. Oskar works and displays his paintings there; the
studio receives the best natural light of any room. It is bare of
furniture except for a bookcase and several chairs. Valentina
wheels a small table into the room for guests she likes and serves
tea, sausage, bread and sometimes mushrooms she has gathered
in the country and pickled. The studio is filled with objects that
are important motifs in Oskar's paintings—icons of the Virgin,
a violin, vases of flowers, sometimes a dead fish.

The rooms beyond the studio are reserved for family living,
and visitors are seldom invited past the door that leads out of it.
Once I sat in one of the "family" rooms with Oskar and re-
viewed his answers to some complicated questions I had asked
about his art. The room was part study, part bedroom, and
Oskar seemed to talk more freely in it than in the studio, perhaps because the family room was free of the usual groups of
visitors.

On another occasion, Valentina invited me into the back
room to discuss a personal matter she did not want to talk
about in front of others. Away from the studio, she expanded
even more visibly than Oskar. Both Russians and foreigners
often made the mistake of thinking her a cold and lifeless
woman because she rarely said anything, whether she was in a
small group or at a large party. I believed her silence, which
enveloped her so thoroughly that she did often seem unreacha-
ble, was connected with the fantasy world that is the vital element of her art. Many of her best drawings were so much a part
of her inner life that she absolutely refused to sell them. To me
there was something dear and admirable—albeit not entirely
comprehensible—about an artist who was incapable of selling

or publicizing her best work. Once she did a self-portrait I particularly wanted, and I was despondent when she shook her head with a stubborn look that meant this was another one of the drawings she would not sell. She saw how disappointed I was and agreed to do a copy.

When Oskar receives a visitor in his studio for the first time, he displays his and Valentina's work as well as that of any other unofficial artists whose paintings happen to be around. His studio is both used and abused by other unofficial artists, most of whom know that Oskar attracts many more potential customers than they do.

Oskar keeps one painting from each year to provide his visitors with examples of the changes in his style, but most of his best canvases from the early 1960's are now abroad. During that period regulations were less strict, and foreign citizens were often allowed to take unofficial paintings out of the Soviet Union. During any given period of time, Oskar usually has five or six new canvases to display. He works regularly each day and his painting is not interrupted by the heavy drinking, assorted emotional problems and depression over political attacks that have impaired the work of some of Moscow's best unofficial artists. This may be a result of his "nerves like ropes" or simply because he has a steadier personality than many of the others. The difficulties faced by unofficial artists in Moscow are not all connected with the political climate. Many of them possess erratic qualities that would adversely affect their work anywhere; in this respect, they are no different from artists in other parts of the world. Such personal factors do tend to assume greater importance amid the official hostility that is a nerve-racking constant in their lives. "The strong ones like Oskar become stronger," said another painter, "and the weak ones like me become weaker."

The paintings a visitor sees on Oskar's easel always correspond to his own unpretentious description of his art: "In painting I first of all enjoy the process itself, the mixing and spreading of paints—their brilliance and dullness, their thin and thick layers, their smells. But even more important, I want to express sadness, happiness, hatred, wrath, thoughts about life and about people. I want to capture life in my paintings and express it with my personal feelings.

"To accomplish this, I use the ordinary objects that surround me as symbols; their meaning in the painting is different from their meaning in real life. They may be houses, violins, money, photographs, newspapers, flowers, laundry on clotheslines, night windows, icons, bottles of vodka, herring and many other objects. The choice depends upon my mood in each particular case, on what surrounds me, on what I see and hear."

Observers have noted the absence of human figures in most of Rabin's painting, yet humanity is implicit in his choice of symbols that reflect both the pain and small joys of existence. Some of his objects symbolize humanity and others inhumanity; the human soul is strongly present in the canvases that lack human bodies. But Oskar Rabin is a solitary man, and the vision of life revealed in his paintings may be both the cause and effect of his solitary nature.

As a man and a painter, Oskar is deeply concerned with the importance of the ordinary. I remember one afternoon of conversation in which we first discussed at length the problems of shipping my dog to America when I left the Soviet Union. (Our dog, Sasha, liked to visit the Rabins because Valya fed him sugar lumps.) Oskar outlined several reasons why he thought the dog would be more traumatized by being left behind than by making a plane trip (good reasons I later used to convince my husband we should take the dog with us).

We then shifted to a discussion of Nadezhda Mandelstam's book, which had just been published in the West. Oskar had read the book in *samizdat* several years ago. He felt that one of its greatest strengths was its recognition that what happened under Stalin was not a passing aberration—the product of one man's insanity—but a national sickness that permitted the Stalinist terror to develop and may appear in mutant forms for generations to come.

Oskar seemed to give careful consideration to both the dog and Madam Mandelstam. I was reminded of her statement in *Hope Against Hope* about her feelings after Mandelstam's first arrest in 1934: "To think that we could have had an ordinary family life with its bickering, broken hearts and divorce suits! There are people in the world so crazy as not to realize that this is normal human existence of the kind that everybody should aim at. What we wouldn't have given for such ordinary heart-breaks!"

Before the Rabins moved into their new apartment in the mid-1960's, Oskar's painting featured the tumbledown pre-revolutionary wooden *izbas* (cottages) that are fast disappearing from Moscow. Now his paintings reflect its endless dun-colored apartments. Oskar's humble symbols are startling in juxtaposition to the urban background. A large violin—symbol from his boyhood—stands out starkly against apartment buildings tilting crazily upon one another. Reflections are another recurrent theme—the city is spread out below a church reflected in a cloud. Or a softer, less harsh city appears in a dream reflection of the real city's angular grayness. Always the life of the spirit contrasts with the realities of modern Soviet society.

During the summer, Oskar and Valentina live in a small village about seventy miles from Moscow. Then his subjects change; he returns to the city in the autumn with paintings of country *izbas* and flowers. When he came back from the village after the summer of 1970, we bought one painting of a vase with pussy willows sitting on a windowsill. To the left of the vase is a glass of the kind Russians prefer to cups when they drink tea. A chunk of squeezed lemon rests on the bottom. Beyond the window is a grave surrounded by a small fence, like countless graves in Russian cemeteries. The picture is bathed in a soft, rosy light that never appears in Oskar's urban paintings. He paints what he sees. What more could the authorities ask of a painter, if Socialist realism were truly realistic?

Socialist realism is a phrase credited to Maxim Gorky; Soviet cultural authorities apply its tenets to all of the creative and performing arts. In official Soviet ideology, Socialist realism is regarded as the only permissible style of art. It is based on two general principles: that a work of art must be comprehensible and meaningful to the masses and that it must contribute to building Communism.

Realism is a word that loses its meaning in such an ideological context. If a painter chooses to depict a shabby apartment or a drunk, he is being a "critical realist" rather than a Socialist realist, and the authorities frown on critical realism. In the Soviet Union, realism refers to reality as Soviet ideologues think it should be—not to a reality that an individual artist might perceive.

Socialist realism does, of course, have a certain flexibility. An old Georgian painter was able to get a rather abstract landscape past the local Communist cultural czar by portraying in one corner a gathering that could be interpreted as a wholesome political meeting. Without the meeting, the painting would not do.

Under Khrushchev, Solzhenitsyn's novel *One Day in the Life of Ivan Denisovich* was considered to be in accord with the highest principles of Socialist realism—at least by those who wished to ingratiate themselves with Khrushchev. Under the present leadership, Solzhenitsyn's work is regarded as a defamation of Socialist reality.

Some of Oskar's paintings can be interpreted as having political, as opposed to aesthetic, implications that could hardly meet with the approval of the Soviet authorities. We own one painting, done mainly in somber blue-black tones, with an old Russian icon of the Virgin Mary superimposed on a newspaper with the headline UNITY AND CLEARNESS OF PURPOSE. The unmistakable message is disharmony between the old and the new; it is a message the authorities do not care to hear. In another painting completed in 1969, a pair of heavy boots lies on a shredded newspaper, dated 1968, with headlines about the Soviet invasion of Czechoslovakia—an event that created despair among all liberal members of the intelligentsia.

Despite the everyday nature of Oskar's symbols, there is a surrealistic element in his combination of the comic, the ordinary and the downright tragic. My husband once remarked that Chagall might have painted some of the subjects Rabin chooses had Chagall been locked into a gray Soviet world for the last forty years. Whether or not the speculation is correct, there is a relationship between Rabin's work and a tradition of Central European Jewish painting—a connection several critics have noted. However, this relationship depends almost entirely on a common ironic attitude toward life. Rabin's symbols are Russian, his symbols of Old Russia are Christian. Even more Russian is the literary quality of some paintings, like the ones I have described, which attaches strong social overtones to them. The overtones (and undertones) may not always be entirely conscious, but they arise out of a strong intellectual as well as aesthetic vision.

One of Oskar's close friends once wrote a moving description of his art that was also a defense against criticism of the "literary" quality of his painting. (Attacks on the "literary" quality of painting by official Soviet critics are political attacks concerning subject matter rather than style.) This description is a better one than I or any foreign critic could provide and is worth quoting extensively:

He does not paint the Russia of a wide Gorky Street in Moscow, of a beautiful Nevsky Prospekt in Leningrad, or of Bratsk, where the majestic dam of the Bratsk hydropower station is being erected. No, he paints the Russia of remote villages, covered deep with winter snow; he paints with love and kindness. . . .

He strives to paint from nature, straining in through his consciousness. He knows rural life well, since he spends about three months at a village on the Oka River each year, and if there is a rural landscape in his painting it is prompted by the artist's memory. It is interesting that the theme of the church reflected in water runs through a number of his paintings—a church that does not exist in the landscape itself. Where does it come from? The artist perhaps did not find it in the world and the people surrounding him. He may have re-created the church and reflected it in the water as a sign of kindness and humanism.

When he lived in the suburbs of Moscow in a small settlement called Lianozovo, there were barracks in his paintings, meagre one-story buildings that sometimes were also reflected in the water, along with the church that never existed. . . . After he moved to Moscow, new prefab buildings appeared on his canvases. Rabin tries to render reality. Of course he does not cover reality in all of its complicated and multiform nature, but can one demand that even of a great artist? Once Rabin was called the Solzhenitsyn of painting. In any case, what Rabin cares to paint he does perfectly and with deep sincerity. Sometimes certain people accuse his art of having a literary character. That may be true, but literary character has always been a feature of Russian painting. . . . Oskar Rabin develops its traditions.

The sort of attack referred to by Oskar's friend is typified by a piece that appeared in the magazine *Moscow Artist* a year after his 1966 exhibition at the Grosvenor Gallery in London:

In his works, O. Rabin distorts the image of our society. His works reflect individual, ugly phenomena that have long since ceased to exist and do not characterize Soviet reality. They defame the achievements of the Soviet people, their daily life and culture. . . .

In his painting, "The Second Blind Alley of Jesus Christ," Rabin laments the fact that in the capital of our homeland, Moscow, there are no streets named after saints. He preaches about the shabbiness of Soviet people's apartments without seeing anything but an oil lamp and a bottle of vodka there.

(The oil lamps Rabin often paints are quite beautiful to the eye of a beholder who is not a Socialist realist.)

Oskar's only wry comment is, "What a shame they don't accompany the text with reproductions so that people could see these evil paintings for themselves." His position as a target of official attacks on "modernist" art is not unique. Many of the other unofficial artists of his generation, as well as younger painters, have been similarly attacked. The official critics may single out Oskar more than other painters because his art is largely representational; although he uses both disproportion and distortion, he is not an abstractionist. The official critics dismiss the more abstract artists with the "any-five-year-old-could-do-that-with-finger-paints" line. Oskar's art poses a thornier problem for them, because he deals with objects and ideas they can understand. They laugh at the abstract designs of Oskar's friends but find it necessary to attack the image of shabby apartments and vodka bottles.

Oskar is one of the few artists who possess the desire and the courage to reply to such attacks. Some feel their work speaks for itself and that to answer political criticism is contrary to the nature of an artist. Others are simply afraid they would make more trouble for themselves by speaking out. Oskar stands by his belief that political critics of art are "spiritually bankrupt and frightened for their entire lives by Stalin's time."

Despite the firmness of his stand, Oskar has been attempting to join the Artists' Union for several years. Why? "Because I am a Soviet citizen and an artist." His statement is so simple that its meaning may not be readily apparent to those unacquainted with the political nuances of Soviet life. Oskar Rabin believes there is no reason why he should be prevented from joining the union in his chosen profession. He would never change his style of painting; he is, in effect, asking the system to change and accept him as he is—highly unlikely, but that does not change Oskar's position. His attitude toward the Artists' Union is related to his stubbornness about entering the foreigners' ghetto without trying to bypass the guards.

Oskar does not need to join the union for financial reasons, although the automatic government commissions that union members receive would have been a great help when he was struggling to support his family years ago. His paintings generally sell for 150 to 300 rubles—a price range common among the best unofficial artists in Moscow—and he does not need the Artists' Union to produce customers. Only a handful of nonunion artists in Moscow and Leningrad—perhaps no more than twenty—are able to live, as Oskar does, mainly on the proceeds from their own paintings. They are artists who have gained recognition both within a small intellectual community in their own country and through exhibits abroad.

Foreigners, including diplomats and correspondents who live in Moscow and knowledgeable tourists who come to Russia with the specific intention of acquiring paintings, provide the majority of customers for unofficial artists. Russians who buy their work are usually scientists who see a link between freedom of expression in art and the greater freedom they desire in their professional lives. They are not afraid to hang modern paintings on their walls, because they know they are unlikely to be chastised for such a minor offense against Communist propriety as long as scientists are so important to their country's development. It is no accident that some scientists have begun to speak out forcefully in favor of a more open society with more respect for individual rights.

The size of the unofficial art community in the Soviet Union is impossible to gauge accurately. It is concentrated almost entirely in Moscow and Leningrad, with some members in the Georgian capital of Tbilisi and the Baltic cities of Vilnius, Riga and Tallinn. There are certainly hundreds of artists who consider painting their real work but spend most of their time at some official job, sometimes totally unconnected with art. How many of them would measure up to the highest critical standards applied to artists in the West is difficult to say. My guess is that only a small percentage would, mainly because of the isolation in which they work. The best unofficial artists, however, are very good indeed and do not suffer by comparison.

Even more important, I have met a number of young men and women who were beginning the road taken by older artists —studying with experienced painters, painting in their spare time, working toward the day when they too will be able to devote virtually all of their time to art. They tend to be more aggressive than their elders about making foreign contacts and acquiring art information from abroad. "In general, the younger they are, the less afraid they are," Oskar says. "Also, it is much easier today to learn about what is going on in the rest of the art world than it was when I started painting. This is very important for the stimulation of an artist's creativity. You see what is being done somewhere else, and it produces an entirely new response in your own work." One example of what Oskar was talking about was the ability to obtain art catalogs and magazines from abroad. Sometimes they are "lost" in the Soviet mails, but in other cases they arrive with no problem. Twenty years ago, it would have been impossible to receive such publications. There is still censorship of international mail to and from the Soviet Union, but it is selective. (The best description of the system appears in a book by the Soviet biochemist Zhores A. Medvedev, *The Medvedev Papers*, New York, Macmillan, 1970.)

Exhibits abroad are put together from the collections of foreigners who have managed to take unofficial paintings out of the Soviet Union. There is no specific law against this, but paintings are usually confiscated anyway if customs officers catch a foreigner in the act. Ordinarily, a foreigner who wants to export any painting or artifact must obtain certification from an official agency that the work is not a state treasure. The rule was designed to prevent icon-smuggling and was never meant to apply to contemporary art. Usually the official agencies will refuse to provide certificates for unofficial art—on the grounds that it *isn't* art. Then customs can confiscate paintings either on the technical excuse that they lack certificates or on the basis that they are "anti-Soviet." One correspondent's wife who foolishly tried to obtain certification to take a Rabin out of the country was told flatly, "We will never approve the export of a painting by Oskar Rabin." Nevertheless, many paintings still do find their way to the West. Customs does not have the manpower to search everyone leaving the country, and many foreigners simply take oil paintings off their stretchers, roll them up like newspapers and carry them out inside their suitcases.

The worst that can happen if someone is caught is he loses a 150-to 300-ruble investment. In some cases, official connivance and bribery must be responsible for the successful export of large numbers of paintings. In 1970, an exhibition in Switzerland featured hundreds of paintings by all of the best unofficial artists, including many recent works. They could not have been taken out piecemeal by tourists with suitcases. It seems reasonable to assume that the foreigners organizing the exhibit did some business with the Soviet authorities.

The Moscow art world is as full of jealousy and backbiting as the art world of any major capital, although the nastiness is on a somewhat more limited social and monetary scale. Some serious artists have criticized Oskar for his use of symbols like newspapers, which have political overtones. "He's catering to what the foreigners want," said one disdainfully. Oskar's entire history as an artist contradicts that criticism. He always derives his inspiration from whatever is of immediate interest to him; the change from rural scenes in summer to urban ones in winter attests to this. And many foreigners prefer to buy paintings without any political implications.

One witchy woman, a foreign citizen who has lived in Moscow for many years and was deeply involved in exporting unofficial art during the early 1960's, said, "Well, of course one has to wait in line to buy a Rabin but that hardly means he is a good artist." He was not one of the artists she patronized during the period when she was a link between the Moscow and New York art worlds. There is a kernel of truth in the remark—not in its reference to Rabin but insofar as it applies to the general Moscow art market.

Many foreign residents in Moscow who buy unofficial paintings do not really know or care much about art; they would never think of buying a painting anywhere else and do so in Moscow only because it seems terribly daring. "A better souvenir than a samovar," one artist remarked tartly. But few of the artists are particular about who buys their paintings. Each painting purchased by a foreigner may someday find its way into the hands of an art collector in the West. This increases the artist's prestige not only abroad but among Russians who care about such matters. It is one way of preserving this generation's artistic heritage.

There are some unofficial artists of dubious talent who deliberately prey on the sympathies of stupid foreigners. Many of them specialize in junky collages—the weirder the better. They use hard-sell tactics, phoning foreigners and moaning about their sad financial condition. Most of them are simply out to make a ruble (or, better yet, a dollar, if they can coax illegal hard currency out of the buyer). Some of them may well have KGB connections. Since the unofficial art world is a well-known point of contact between Russians and foreigners, it is perfect ground for KGB information-gathering and attempts to lure people into compromising situations. Professional KGB men seldom harass artists in the presence of foreigners. Once they made the mistake of walking in on an artist who was showing his paintings to two diplomats. They accused the painter of selling his work without paying his taxes, and he responded by quoting a decree by Lenin himself, forever exempting works of art from taxation. They were so flustered they admitted they had come from KGB headquarters—something unheard of in the annals of relationships between foreigners and the secret police.

Oskar and several other unofficial artists received a respectable commercial start in the early 1960's from a unique figure in the Moscow art world, a Greek named George D. Kostaki. Kostaki's father lost large landholdings in Central Asia after the revolution. He himself has lived in the Soviet Union since he was a small child; he married a Russian but preserved his Greek citizenship. He is passionately devoted to Russian art; one of his main missions in life seems to have been the preservation of the brilliant art from the early portion of this century. In his apartment he has an astonishing collection of paintings and drawings—walls covered with Chagalls, Kandinskys, Popovas, Goncharovas, Tatlin sketches—and extensive contacts with art dealers abroad. He doubtless would never have been able to acquire and keep such a collection had he been a Soviet citizen.

Kostaki does not collect modern unofficial art on a large scale but in the early 1960's he did buy some paintings by Rabin, Dimitri Plavinsky and a number of other promising, hungry artists. Needless to say, having a painting bought and displayed by Kostaki serves to introduce an artist's work to influential foreigners and Russians.

Several Russians have gathered collections devoted exclusively to current unofficial art, but as Soviet citizens they do not enjoy Kostaki's virtual immunity from official persecution. And much as Soviet officialdom fears the memory of art and literature it has suppressed in the past, it fears challenges to the Party's cultural hegemony in the present even more. A Rabin is more frightening to the authorities than a Chagall, even though neither can be displayed in Soviet museums.

Oskar does not take part in the backbiting that characterizes the unofficial art world in Moscow. He is generous in his praise of other artists' work, unlike some painters who never miss a chance to run down their colleagues to prospective customers. It is also well known that he is generous with his money when friends are having financial difficulties. An occasional silence is the only indication that he does not care for a particular artist; he considers the unofficial art world too beleaguered from the outside to accommodate internal bloodletting.

I ask Oskar why he thought the authorities allowed the unofficial art trade to continue unimpeded except for occasional attacks in the press and some KGB surveillance.

"What 'authorities' do you mean?" he replied. "Two or three art critics and a few journalists have written about my paintings unfavorably in the press. I cannot consider their opinions the opinions of Brezhnev or Kosygin. Once Premier Khrushchev did not like Neizvestny's sculpture, but Khrushchev is no longer premier and Neizvestny is still creating his statues." He was referring to the celebrated "Manege Affair" in 1962, in which Khrushchev stormed out of an exhibit at Moscow's Manege gallery that included abstract painting by several artists and sculpture by Ernst Neizvestny. He called abstract art "dog shit" on that occasion and held a lengthy dialogue on the subject with Neizvestny in equally earthy language.

"It's too bad that in our circumstances it is impossible to exhibit paintings independently of the Artists' Union," Oskar added in reply to my question. "I realize that the exhibit halls belong to the union and that the union has the right to exhibit artists it likes. But it is possible to exhibit paintings in parks, on the streets and boulevards. This is done in many countries. There is room enough for everyone. But our people are not used to this idea, and artists are afraid that it would be regarded as a political demonstration.

"The question about selling paintings should be addressed not to me but to those whom you call the authorities. But I don't advise you to ask such questions. Imagine asking President Nixon what he thinks of various American artists who sell their paintings. . . ."

In February, 1970, a *feuilleton* in the newspaper *Evening Moscow* attacked a Soviet collector of unofficial art. Oskar wrote a reply to the paper in defense of the collector, who was his friend. He began his letter with a quotation from Mandelstam, whose writing he knows well and loves. He addressed the quote to *Evening Moscow*'s satirist: "I would forbid such writers to have children. All of them are sold to a pockmarked devil for four generations ahead."*

He went on to speak of unofficial art exhibits that the righteous satirist said had been promptly quashed as a result of public indignation. "The exhibitions are closed . . . by 'public'

* The quote is from Mandelstam's "Fourth Prose," written in the late 1920's and never published in the Soviet Union. The full quote from one translation reads: "I would forbid these writers to marry and have children. After all, children must carry on for us, must say to the end for us what is most important to say. But their fathers have sold out to the pockmarked devil for three generations to come." Oskar may have read a slightly different version of the quote in a *samizdat* copy, or he may simply have omitted some words without using ellipses.

demand. 'Public' is an indefinite term. Does it mean people? It might mean two people. Only it turns out that certain people close exhibits in order to deny other people a chance to see them, god forbid. . . .

"If a satire writer were given a gun, he would shoot. True, first in the air. And then at moving targets.

"There was a time, in the 1930's and 1940's, when questions of Russian art were decided by satirists with guns in their hands. And they decided the question: There would be neither art nor literature, only satire.

"In the 1960's the first green sprouts appeared during the thaw, but the satire writers were right there eating them up. Now they don't shoot; they only make appointments for conversations."

Such a conversation took place between the author of the *Evening Moscow* satire and the art collector before the attack appeared.

In his letter, Rabin noted that the collector mentioned Chagall's name as he was leaving the newspaper office.

"Chagall? Marc? Who is that?" asked the satirist.

"But he is known to the whole world . . ." began the disbelieving collector.

"I haven't read your Chagall," the satirist said, cutting off the interview.

Rabin concluded his letter to the editors: "Now I am through. I am not paid money for my satirical stories. I am an artist."

The letter shows a good deal about what kind of man Oskar Rabin is and why his paintings sometimes have a literary character. Needless to say, the letter was never published, but Rabin himself was invited for a conversation with one of the editors. He was told his letter could not be printed because, in the first place, he had sent in a carbon copy rather than the original. It was also suggested that the letter could have no merit as satire because Rabin was an artist, not a satirist. Last but not least, the letter would not be published because *Eve-*

ning Moscow did not agree with Rabin's point of view (a peculiarly honest statement for the editor to have made).

Oskar Rabin is a man of integrity, artistic maturity and guts. He knows his rights and defends them—quietly, persistently and firmly. A rather pathetic official artist, whose work was touted abroad as a symbol of cultural thaw during the Khrushchev years and who has hewed more and more closely to the Party line since 1965, told me, "I really respect Rabin, although I know he does not respect me. I wish he did."

VIII

Anatoly Yakovlevich

ANATOLY YAKOVLEVICH FRAMES PICTURES and carves wood. He loves his work. He was one of the few government-employed workers I met in Russia who took immense and unabashed pride in his craftsmanship.

The picture-framing studio where Anatoly worked was owned by the state, but he did not regard the state as his boss. "I work for myself and my own satisfaction," he said. "Not all of the time, but on the pictures that are important to me. My frames make a beautiful object look even more beautiful, and I do them from start to finish. It is my work, not a director's, not a clerk's. If that's egotism—well, I'm an egotist. My wife says so, so it must be so."

Anatoly belonged to a legion of picture framers, tailors, seamstresses, hairdressers, doctors and accomplished men and women in countless white- and blue-collar jobs who make up a parallel private economy within the framework of a Socialist system. Yosif's son, David, who took photographs at weddings and anniversary parties in his spare time, was another supplier of the parallel economy's many services. The private economy functions because workers spend part of their time on government business and part of it on their own. Anatoly devoted part of his day to filling government orders for picture frames and the other portion to producing better frames for private clients. On the frames for private customers, he carved his initials in tiny Cyrillic block letters. The frames he made for the government were properly smooth and anonymous.

Anatoly's studio framed pictures for public institutions and for ordinary citizens at a government-set price. A man who walked in off the street and was only willing to pay the state price would probably have to wait several months for his frame. Private customers paid more and received both faster service and higher-quality workmanship. When there were no large government orders to fill, Anatoly would occasionally squeeze in private clients ahead of people who had been waiting for months on the regular list. He generally framed pictures for his "special" customers outside of regular working hours. Anatoly's private work was technically illegal, but it is a way of life in Moscow and other large Russian cities.

For a dental patient, the private economy means a porcelain cap instead of a flashing stainless steel one. It means a waist and shoulder line that fit to a woman who needs a new dress. It can mean a painless abortion with anesthetic in a gynecologist's home instead of the usual procedure without anesthetic at a state clinic. For Anatoly's customers, it means a picture frame slowly and lovingly fashioned with the best materials he can cadge from a variety of sources. (The customer never inquires about the source.) "I don't do my work just for money," he says. "If someone brings in a portrait and wants a frame like ten thousand other frames, I tell him to go to someone else. I work with people who want my special skill at finding the right frame to go with the right picture. I wouldn't get any joy out of my work otherwise."

Of course, the private economy greatly reduces the efficiency of the government economy. Somewhere an ordinary customer waits endlessly while Anatoly patiently glues together frames for his private clients. The same situation prevails in thousands of shops and offices. Access to the private economy is one measure of class distinction in the Soviet Union; educated professionals like Galya can afford it, while ordinary blue-collar workers cannot. In the cities, though, even ordinary workers sometimes stretch their budgets to buy goods and services from men like Anatoly (as they sell their own skills, if they have any). The private economy is, by general agreement, the only source of decent service and workmanship in the Soviet Union. It also helps establish some relationship between supply and demand in a society where much of the government-ordered business has no relation to what people want or need. The authorities do not make life difficult for citizens who engage in a little private business that grows out of their regular government jobs. "If they did," said one of Anatoly's customers, "half of Moscow would be in jail." Also, government officials use the private sector as often as anyone else. Crackdowns occur only when an entrepreneur goes into business on a grand scale. If Anatoly set up a workshop employing twenty carpenters, he would probably be in trouble with the law.

He was recommended to us by an acquaintance who was a member of the Soviet Artists' Union, probably in hopes that we would buy a painting from him if he provided a framer. (We never did, because his work was far inferior to that of the unofficial artists.) We needed Anatoly's services to replace a rickety fifteen-year-old frame on a favorite Modigliani reproduction.

We had no hope of getting our print framed through ordinary channels, because 1970 was the centenary celebration of Lenin's birth. Every studio was packed with pictures of Lenin, which had to be framed on time for official exhibits and ceremonies. For weeks Anatoly and his colleagues had been working overtime to get the portraits framed on schedule. They were not paid for the overtime; it was supposed to be the shop's "voluntary commitment" in honor of Lenin. "Voluntary commitments" to celebrate the centennial were organized by party functionaries in most factories, shops and offices. In one department store, salesgirls were asked to pledge that they would not keep the choicest merchandise under the counter to sell to their friends and relatives.

Each picture of Lenin meditating, writing, reading, sitting, standing or exhorting workers was framed in the candy-box gilt so beloved by the Soviet officials who manage such pageants. Anatoly was willing to put in overtime on something besides Lenin for foreign customers and his artist friend, who appar-

ently threw him considerable business. The Lenin frames required no skill anyway, Anatoly told us, because they were all
alike. He said he liked our particular Modigliani lady because
she had an exceptionally graceful shoulder line. He would find
us a new plain brown wooden frame and put it together for 20
rubles. Anatoly's regular state salary averaged about 150 rubles
a month but his private work added 50 to 100 rubles a week to
his income.

Anatoly apologized because he knew he would not be able to
find us a frame with a gold border like the old one. "I know in
the West a picture framer can order any kind of wood and mat
he wants, but here that isn't possible. There are only three or
four standard wood frames, and if I want something special for
a special picture, I have to search for months. I know all of the
people who work in museums. Sometimes they discard a frame
or a piece of a frame and I take it. You never know when it will
turn out to be useful.

"Once a woman from Leningrad came to me with a French
Impressionist painting that had been in her family since 1890.
She came from an old noble family. They had managed to save
the painting, both during the revolution and later from the
Germans. They were evacuated over the ice road, and they took
the painting out of the frame and carried it with them inside
her coat." (The ice road over Lake Lagoda was Leningrad's
only link with unoccupied Russia during the winter of 1941–42.
People were evacuated and food supplies were transported to
the starving city over the ice.)

"The painting was a Monet, I think—covered with flowers. I
must tell you I don't know much about art except what pleases
my own eye. This painting had a particularly interesting history. They had hidden it in a trunk throughout the 1930's, when
a lot of families that had held titles under the czar were being
expelled from Leningrad. A painting like that would certainly
have been proof that they were rich aristocrats before the revolution. Anyway, the old frame was lost when they got it out
during the siege and the lady never had the money to buy a

new one. She was living in a communal apartment, and she told me she kept the canvas under her bed between two layers of blankets for fifteen years.

"The family's fortunes changed for the better again. When the world turns upside down, a lot of the same people still wind up on top in the end. Her son grew up and became some kind of scientist—I think she said he was a chemist. He and his wife were given an apartment of their own with three rooms, and the mother moved in with them. The son had plenty of money, and he told his mother to bring that picture out again. That's when she came to me. Though I'm not an art expert, I saw how beautiful the painting was. I told the woman I would frame it, but only on the condition that she would wait as long as it took for me to find exactly the right frame. A painting that had gone through what this one had deserved the best work I could do. I think of the objects I work on as being almost living beings.

"I looked around for nine months without any luck. Then I finally came across an antique frame that was being discarded in a gallery in Moscow—I won't tell you which one—and begged the girl who worked there to let me have it. She did, for 100 rubles, only it was five centimeters too short on one side and ten centimeters on the other. I took some small pieces of wood and then I made a papier-mâché molding as close to the style of the original frame as I could get. I attached the papier-mâché to the wood pieces, gilded them with gold paint and glued them to the ends of the old frame. It was quite a job, but you could hardly tell the difference between the antique part and the new part. I charged that woman 250 rubles, and I can tell you I wasn't making much money from her. I had already paid 100 rubles for the frame, and I spent every night for two weeks trying to make the extra pieces fit properly. But it didn't matter. I had created something myself. My frame wasn't perfect, but it was as perfect as it could be with what I had to work with. That's all any man can do."

Anatoly said he did not enjoy much of his regular work. "Sure, it doesn't take any special talent to frame fifty portraits of Lenin the same way. The museums do their own framing, so I don't get to work on their collections. But every once in a while someone brings me a great old painting—like that woman from Leningrad—and I go crazy, because I'm so happy to have something good to work on. I can see in my head the way it ought to look, and I'll spend any amount of time to try and bring the image to life.

"I don't like to frame old Russian icons, though. Sometimes people bring them to me, and I usually advise against putting frames around them. The icons are already so ornate to begin with that frames spoil them. I'm getting some modern abstract paintings these days, and then I really have trouble. Where do I find frames for them? We don't have them hanging in galleries, because I guess the authorities think you should be able to see a face or a vegetable or something in a picture. So there aren't any suitable frames being discarded in museums. Although I usually work in wood, I try to find odd pieces of metal for the modern frames. The metal looks much better with modern paintings, but there isn't too much scrap metal in good condition lying around Moscow. And what there is, I've had to teach myself to work with because I wasn't trained to do anything with metal. The new paintings are a challenge, though, even more than the antiques. Once I made a frame of straw glued to a wood backing for one. That was a good idea, but it wouldn't go with every painting. That particular one belonged to a well-known scientist."

In his spare time, Anatoly carved small wooden figures, usually animals. He was particularly fond of horses. He had learned both woodcarving and picture framing from the father of a German girlfriend during the three years he was stationed in Berlin with the Russian occupation troops after the war. He was nineteen when the war ended.

"But that's a whole story in itself," he said one afternoon when he returned the Modigliani to us with its new frame. He was not afraid to come to our apartment because he had done some work for foreign embassies and many of the guards knew him. "I like to see what my paintings look like in their own homes," he explained. "I must admit I'm also curious about how foreigners live. I'd even open your cupboards if you weren't around, I'm so nosy."

I told him to open any cupboard he liked, and he inspected the pantry's imported canned goods and soft drinks, asking for an explanation of several items. "This is terrible," he said. "My wife would murder me. Anyway, if you want to know how I learned to frame pictures—it's true, I'm a master—you'll have to put up with the rest of my life story. Are you sure you want to hear it all?"

I assured Anatoly that I did, and we made a date to meet outside the foreigners' compound. Anatoly knew it would be unwise to speak freely in our apartment.

He was born in 1926 in Moscow, one of ten children and the youngest of seven sons. He and Galya were of the same generation, and his mother and father—like Galya's parents—had moved to Moscow from a small village after the revolution. His father was eager to fill one of the new factory jobs he was certain would be created by the Bolsheviks' efforts to industrialize Russia. Lacking any skills that would be useful in a factory, Anatoly's father worked as a trash collector for the first few years after he brought his family to live in the city. He entered a night school course and learned to read when he was thirty years old. He qualified for a job in a machine tool shop and later in an automobile factory, where he worked until the beginning of the war. "Eight of my brothers and sisters were already born when my mama and papa moved to Moscow," Anatoly said. "I was the second to the youngest. Papa had a great desire for all of his children to go to school—to know more than he did. After he learned to read, he was at us every day about the importance of books. He said they were even more important than our classes in school. Schools were one of the main reasons he persuaded Mama to move from the country. She never did learn to read, never really got used to the city. She was a peasant to the day of her death. She thought whatever happened had to be for the best, because God willed it. But Papa had dreams for us. I don't think he believed in God, although he would never have said so to Mama's face."

Anatoly and all his brothers and sisters finished seven grades of school—no small accomplishment at that point in Soviet history. Even today over half of the Soviet population above age ten has no education beyond seventh grade. (The figure is from the 1970 census. It is skewed somewhat unfairly, though, because it includes many old people who received no education before the revolution. About 65 percent of *working* adults have some education beyond seventh grade.) For Anatoly, there was no immediate possibility of education beyond the lower school. All of the children had to work and contribute to the family's support. A month before Hitler invaded Russia, he went to work in his father's automobile plant. In 1943 he was drafted by the army and fought with the Soviet troops all the way to Berlin. His father and six brothers were all killed in the war. Six uncles on both sides of the family also died. Of the two surviving uncles, one lost a leg and another an eye. Anatoly was wounded twice, but not seriously.

"How many times have I asked myself why I lived when the rest of my family died? You see the whole story of war in my family. My father comes to Moscow unable to read a word, but full of hope for his children. My mother is a peasant, but she learns how to stop having more children so the ones who are already alive will have a better chance. We all finish seven grades—some of us might have finished more eventually. Then the war—and nothing left. Six sons dead. Two sisters without husbands. Their own husbands were killed. Where would they find new ones in a world where so many of the men died? None of it makes any sense. Religion, Communism, all of the gods we dream up—young men go off to die anyway.

"My generation saw enough of war to last us forever. We say we don't even want to talk about it, but we always return to it. Our boots were falling to shreds at the front. A lot of my comrades died not from bullets but from frozen feet. You couldn't tell the dead from the wounded.

"I saw children with the look of old men and women in their eyes. I thought I could never hate anyone as completely as I hated the Germans when I saw those children wandering in the ruins of villages. Most of their parents were dead; the Nazis had destroyed the villages so as not to leave anything for the Red Army. Then when we came into Germany, and when it was their turn to suffer, I saw German children with the same look in their eyes. The Germans were animals, yes. They gassed people to death. I was there when we liberated one of their camps, and I will never forget the sight. But did those German children want war, any more than ours did? People never want war. Governments and generals want it. Anyone who wants war belongs in a mad house. And yet I saw some soldiers, even my own comrades, whose eyes glowed with the killing. They frightened me more than those half-dead children. I had a drink once with an American soldier who was there when the Americans liberated Dachau. He said an American general in your Civil War said, 'War is hell.' I say war is shit." (*Govno*, the Russian word for "shit," has much more profane connotations in Russian than in English. It is considered far worse to use the word in mixed company than to use most sexual obscenities.)

The three years Anatoly spent in Berlin profoundly affected his attitude toward the rest of the world. "The hate had already gone out of me by the time we got to Berlin," he said simply. "So then there was the American zone and the British zone and the French zone and our zone. Already, the clowns who run countries were carving up the wreck of the world. There were all kinds of rules about moving from one zone to another, but I didn't take them too seriously, especially during the first year after the end of the war.

"I knew some Americans. One of them was a flyer who had been stationed at a base with some Russians. He knew a few words of Russian; I learned a little English. Customs are different, but people basically want the same things. We all had two things on our mind then—girls and getting home. I think the Chinese must be the same way underneath. I don't know any Chinese. I suppose if I were a general I'd want to go to war with them just because I don't know them and don't like them. But, then, I'm not a general."

Anatoly said he was lucky to find a German girlfriend. "Most of the German girls wouldn't have anything to do with us—that was the bad thing about being a Russian soldier in Germany. They liked the Americans best of all because they were richer and could give them presents. We couldn't offer a girl a bottle of perfume or nylon stockings. Our own women didn't have nylons until old Stalin finally died and Khrushchev started spreading a little butter around to the people. But that's another matter. Anyway, my German girl was different. Guess it was just my charm, but she really liked me and I liked her. We never truly had any intention of marrying each other. I gave her protection —decent German women weren't very safe on the streets with all of the occupying troops there. But I was young—I didn't want to settle down. And anyway, you couldn't marry a foreigner in our country in those days. It would have been Siberia for me. The Americans were marrying German girls all the time, though, even when their officers didn't like it. I don't know why I didn't get into serious trouble for some of the things I did in Berlin. It never really occurred to me that I could have been plucked out of there and sent off to a camp, although I knew with my head—don't let anybody tell you he didn't know—that people were shot for less.

"My girl's father was one of the finest men I've ever known. He valued everything—the wood he worked with, nature, books. He was like my papa in the way he felt about books. He didn't have a lot of formal schooling, but he had read everything. He would tell me about books he didn't have and couldn't get, because people had burned a lot of books during the Nazi period. I spoke quite a bit of German by then, so we could talk easily. Now I don't remember a word, because I've never had any practice since I came home in '48. Anyway, he told me books had been burned in our country too under Stalin. I didn't believe that, young fool that I was. Of course we burned books. I feel about the book burners like I do about generals."

Anatoly never went into any lengthy discourses on capitalism or Communism, Stalin, Khrushchev or the present Soviet leaders. He was not particularly interested in politics unless they touched on his life in the form of something he regarded as idiocy, like the war or the military rules in Berlin that eventually forced him to break contact with his American drinking companions. His general attitude was that all governments were crooked, but some less so than others. Many of his beliefs contradicted each other. He said Stalin's death was "the greatest blessing we Russians could ever have hoped for." At the same time, he thought a political leader should be "a strong man who can make everyone else agree with his point of view." I told him I thought unanimity of opinion was a bad thing and that Stalin was the perfect example of a political leader who tried to make everyone else agree with him. "Well, I didn't mean a leader should kill people who don't agree with him," Anatoly said.

He would have made a good journalist; he was able to acquire more knowledge than most people from things he saw with his own eyes.

"I looked at the way the Germans worked in the rubble of their country," he said. "I was never surprised that they built back again, and no one can tell me it's because of American money in West Germany or Russian help in the GDR [German Democratic Republic]. The GDR has the highest standard of living of all the Socialist countries—a much higher standard than we have been able to achieve in Russia. Why? I think because the Germans work harder than we do. My girl's father, for example —he taught me over and over that you don't just make a frame look right on the outside but also on the inside, at the corners where you can't see it. With that attitude, German products won't fall apart. Look at the long lines for imported products from the GDR in our stores.

"Now I don't know any Japanese, because I wasn't there, but I know that they are also one of the most important economic powers in the world today. I have a feeling that work must be the key there, and not American money. I just don't believe the explanations in our newspapers, not after what I saw in Germany. It's ironic that Germany and Japan, both defeated in the war, should be the two most important economic powers in the world outside of the United States. I don't include Russia, because while we have the possibilities we haven't developed them.

"Personally, I believe the Germans work too hard, like machines. But there ought to be a middle way between being a machine and doing sloppy work of the kind that is common in Russia. Most Russians love their vodka more than their work. I love my vodka too, to be honest, but I can't drink it at the same time I'm trying to make two sides of a picture frame fit together. I believe in the Socialist system, but I think there should be more room for private initiative.

"I think I have a solution. I'm the best picture-framer in our shop. Let me do the work that requires a craftsman, and leave the Lenin portraits to the workers without any special skill. But I should be able to charge more for my work, and my private customers could become regular government customers. I wouldn't make as much money as I do now from my private work, but it would be more than my present government salary. The important thing is that I would be working all day at something important to me. Oh, I know, I know—the whole idea isn't very Communist. But we have a combination of Communism and private enterprise now, only the private enterprise is supposed to be illegal. Why not just make the whole thing legal, some kind of sensible combination of the best aspects of Socialism and capitalism?"

Anatoly's work was not his entire life. He was an avid movie and theater fan and, to my delight, had seen most of the films and plays I had attended in order to improve my Russian. We had a long discussion about the movie *Osvobozhdeniye* (*Liberation*), an epic about the war that was expected to run into six parts. Only three segments were released while I was in Moscow. Anatoly said he liked the film, despite his dislike of war, because it showed how bravely Russia had stood alone

against the Germans before the Allies opened a second front in
Europe. I criticized the film-making technique because it
showed huge sweeps of tanks and armies while seldom focusing
on an individual scene or soldier. It had a Cecil B. DeMille
quality that struck a particularly sour note with me because I
had just seen *Mash* and *Patton* during our summer vacation in
Europe. "I think it's a valid criticism that this movie doesn't
focus enough on what war does to individuals," Anatoly said.
"While I enjoyed the movie for some of its historical points, it
doesn't show how bloody and dirty war is. When you see tanks
advancing on a screen, war looks like fun. When you see an arm
blown off a soldier, it gives a truer picture. Maybe some day
we'll make such a movie in this country. I don't think any of our
movies focus enough on individuals, in war or peace."

Anatoly's favorite theater was the Taganka, which periodi-
cally ran into trouble with the authorities for presenting plays
that were more politically controversial and contemporary in
their staging than productions at other Moscow theaters. While
the Taganka productions would not be considered as avant-
garde by Western audiences as they are by the Moscow public,
they were the liveliest shows in town. The cast was young and
enthusiastic, the sets imaginative and the themes sometimes
politically interesting. Anatoly particularly liked the Taganka's
dramatization of *Anti-Miri* (*Anti-Worlds*), based on a collection of Voznesensky poems. Voznesensky occasionally appeared
on stage himself to recite his verse. A later production based on
another batch of his poems was canceled after one performance
because it displeased the Ministry of Culture. There was one
set of rumors that the play would be presented again with of-
fending portions deleted and another that the theater was about
to be closed completely. The Taganka remained open, but the
play was not staged again.

Anatoly said he especially enjoyed dramatizations of poems
because "the Russian language is at its best in poetry." He had
read all of the great classical novelists and poets and many
twentieth-century poets who were persecuted during the Stalin

era. His favorite was Anna Akhmatova, who was expelled from the Union of Writers during a wave of political and cultural purges in Leningrad after the war. The Soviets only began to publish Akhmatova again in censored form after Stalin's death, and she is still regarded as a doubtful figure in orthodox political circles. Anatoly also loved Pasternak's poetry.

"Russian is the best language in the world for praising God and cursing," he said. His own speech sometimes veered between the two. He respected language deeply but could be completely irreverent about it. Once I asked him if a word he had used was a noun or verb and he replied, "As Dostoevsky said, if it moves, it's a verb. Or maybe Dostoevsky didn't say it, but I did." With his seventh-grade certificate Anatoly was far better educated than Tanya, a second-year college student. His wide-ranging knowledge was a result of his passion for books. "I felt I owed that to my father," he said, "so that all of his efforts didn't come to nothing. I've tried to pass on the love of books to my own children."

Anatoly lived with his wife, a rosy-cheeked woman three times his size, in a two-room apartment in one of the new suburbs of Moscow. Half of the bedroom was partitioned off for a work area, and the entire flat was littered with wood shavings. Anatoly's carvings of horses in various postures dominated the living room.

He was professionally critical of his apartment building's construction, although he was happy to have his own kitchen and bathroom. "The people who say these new buildings will fall apart in twenty years are right," he said. "Everyone can hear everything his neighbors say to one another. I have a fight with my wife, and a neighbor listens in and gives me an opinion the next morning on who was at fault. I walked down the stairs just yesterday and an old woman stopped me and said, 'You weren't very good to your wife last night, Anatoly Yakovlevich. She is a fine woman.' In old houses, the balconies were strong; here you're afraid to sit on them for fear they'll collapse. My wife complains that the windowsills in the kitchen aren't wide enough for flowers or salt. If I had the materials, I could build a better apartment by myself."

Moscow's general city plan—a mixture of apartment construction and wooded areas—met with Anatoly's approval. "Ten minutes from my house is a forest where my wife and I go skiing in winter and a beach on the Moscow River that we use in summer. Ten minutes by bus in either direction is a metro stop. It takes me twenty minutes by metro to reach my studio in the center of the city, no matter what the weather." Anatoly felt strongly that more effort should have been made to preserve old buildings in the center of the city. He grew up just off Gorky Street in a nineteenth-century building that has since been destroyed to make room for offices. "They should have renovated the inside of that building with modern plumbing instead of tearing it down," he said. "Those apartments were better than anything being built today. People expected to take refuge in the metro when there were threats of bombing raids on Moscow, but we knew our cellar was sturdy enough to be a bomb shelter."

Anatoly admitted that some changes in the old city center have been for the better. "When I was a boy, most of Moscow still lived in wooden houses without indoor plumbing. They were falling down even then; they couldn't have been renovated. Better to replace them with new buildings even if they aren't pretty. Also, Moscow is much cleaner now.

"Layers of dirt have been removed from buildings. Someone who left Moscow thirty years ago would never recognize the city if it weren't for the Kremlin. Garbage collection is better. There isn't any question that Moscow is a better place to live in now than when I was growing up. I just wish a little more attention were paid to building things that are worth looking at and will last. We could do better. People who respect old things and good workmanship should have something to say about building a city."

Anatoly had two children—a nineteen-year-old son and a twenty-three-year-old daughter. His son was in the army. "He doesn't know what he wants to do when he gets out," Anatoly said. "He seems to have some talent for writing, but he says he won't become a writer because you can't get anything honest published. I think he's a rebel, and I suppose my talk has contributed to it. I've always told my children to think for themselves." His daughter was a pianist who had recently married another musician. She had just moved into a new apartment with a kitchen Anatoly envied. "Someone has been taking the women's complaints into account, because the windowsills in the new kitchens are much wider. There is room enough for both salt and flowers."

Unlike most Russian men, Anatoly sympathized with the difficult lot of Soviet women. "I hope my daughter will have an easier life than her mother. My wife illustrates children's books and she had to go back to work one month after the birth of each child. Fortunately, she could do some of her work at home, so she had it easier than most women. But I was never able to help when the children were young. I wasn't as good at my job as I am now, and I worked in a restaurant at night to make ends meet. Now I help with the work—I do the vacuuming, for instance, and if I don't help fix dinner I clean up afterward. I don't think women should be expected to do all the housecleaning just because they're women, and most Russian men are dogs about helping. I hope I won't be a grandfather too soon. My wife and I had our daughter the first year we were married, and it was very difficult. My daughter and her husband should have a chance to get to know each other and save some money before they have a child. Of course, they haven't asked for my opinion, but I suspect they agree with me."

Anatoly emphasized, "I believe life is better for my children than it was for me. Thank God, they've never known war or any serious deprivation.

"My secret dream is to have a house in the country where I would do my work and own a few horses. In our country at this time I know that my dream will never come true. Our family does have a small cottage 300 kilometers from Moscow, but you couldn't live there. On a warm summer weekend we take the plane to the nearest town and then a short bus ride to the cottage. We sit in the sun and pick berries. The countryside is still so isolated from the cities that I couldn't work there. No one wants picture frames in a small town. My Moscow customers aren't so faithful that they would come all that way. Even if I am the best framer in the city. I couldn't afford a *dacha* near Moscow—that's only for Party bigwigs, important writers, those kinds of people. And the state owns all the horses, so I can't very well raise them. I go riding once a week. And that's what I have to be content with. It's much more than my parents had, and I believe my children will have more than I do.

"It all depends, of course, on whether we are all smart enough to avoid another war. I approved very much of the treaty between the Soviet Union and West Germany, because I think it reduces the chance of another war. I am an optimist in this sense: I don't believe either the American or Soviet government wants to destroy humanity, and that is what another war would mean. I worry about China; I think we should stop shooting off our mouths and try to bring China in touch with the rest of the world. I hope America and Russia will start doing some things together, like exploring space. The day we landed a probe on Venus, I thought how ironic it is that we can manage to send a machine to another planet but we still can't manufacture enough cars for our people. And you on the moon, with your slums. We should be paying for the exploration of outer space together, so that each of us will have more money to build a better life for our people at home. That's what I'd do if I were running this country. Or yours. Don't you think I'd make a great American President?"

IX

Vera

VERA IS a thirty-one-year-old journalist. She works for a newspaper that faithfully reflects the current Party orthodoxy on political and cultural matters but tends to take a more liberal stance on social and economic issues. Its coverage emphasizes problems such as the high Soviet divorce rate, child care, the status of women, housing, consumer needs and education. Vera specializes in issues connected with the role of women in Soviet society. She has written about topics ranging from the reasons for the spiraling divorce rate—now the highest in the world—to the special problems of working mothers. Vera's personal and professional lives fit together more easily than those of most Russian women. Married to a research chemist, she is the mother of a five-year-old son. The social issues she deals with in her writing are an important part of her everyday life.

Vera was also a member of the Communist Party—the only Party member I knew well. It was not surprising that a foreigner would have known few Party members. In the first place, Party membership totals only 14,500,000 out of a population of more than 240,000,000. Upon my return to the United States I found many Americans under the misapprehension that belonging to the Party is like being a Republican or a Democrat. The Communist Party is an elite; the law of averages worked against a foreigner meeting many Party members. Those we did know usually had some official connection. The officials we dealt with in the Foreign Ministry were Party members, but it seems superfluous to note that they were not personal friends. Our closest friends could hardly have belonged to the Party, since they questioned the basic premises of the Soviet system. Most of the official intellectuals did not belong either; they made their peace with it and kept their distance. Not every journalist is a member; Vera said she had joined because "it's the best way to work for constructive changes within our system of government." She described herself as a "liberal" within the Party spectrum of opinion but said her thinking did not necessarily typify that of younger members. "There are reactionaries among the young as well as the old," she emphasized.

Vera's description of her background was sketchy, but it clearly placed her family in the Soviet upper class. Her father worked for the Foreign Ministry and her mother was a violinist. Vera never told me exactly what her father did, but the omission was not surprising. He may have been connected with the KGB, like many Soviet diplomats, or he may simply have been forbidden to disclose the nature of his work. When we met Foreign Ministry officials face-to-face in Moscow, it was seldom possible to determine precisely what they did for a living. Vera did say she had lived in Europe for several years when she was a child. She spoke some French and English but was unable to carry on a sustained conversation in either language.

In 1962 Vera was a third-year student at the Moscow Institute of Architecture. "I had shown some talent for art as a child and at one time wanted to be a painter," she explained. "But as I grew older, it became clear that my aptitude for painting was only that of an amateur. So I decided that my interest in art could be put to good use as an architect. But that wasn't the right profession for me either. It was obvious after three years at the institute that I really hated the detailed work that is such an important part of architecture. And I didn't want to design large office and apartment buildings. There isn't anything else for an architect to do in our country. I think I would have enjoyed designing a private home, as architects can do in the West. In any case, I decided to leave the institute and find something else to do with myself. My parents were disgusted with me. They said I ought to be old enough to know my own mind. I said I was old enough, and I knew I wouldn't make a good architect."

The Soviet system of higher education is based on the assumption that students will enter the professions for which they have been trained in universities and institutes. The university admissions process is tied to central economic planning; the number of architectural students is determined by the government's estimate of how many architects will be needed at a given point in time. But Vera's experience was not uncommon; many students do change direction while they are still in school or even after graduation. Andrei Voznesensky was also a student at the Institute of Architecture (several years ahead of Vera) when he opted for poetry instead of designing buildings. In his poem "Fire in the Architectural Institute" (about an actual fire that destroyed his diploma thesis), Voznesensky wrote:

> *O youth, phoenix, ninny,*
> *your dissertation is hot stuff,*
> *flirting its little red skirt now,*
> *flaunting its little red tongue ...*
>
> *Everything's gone up in smoke,*
> *and there's no end of people sighing.*
> *It's the end?*
> > *It's only the beginning.*
> *Let's go to the movies!*

"I didn't need a fire. I just left," Vera said. "I didn't know what to do with myself, so I started writing little stories at home about people and events that interested me." As a student, she had been struck by the shoddy construction of most new apartment buildings in Moscow. She wrote a short article about a particularly bad building and sent it to an editor at the newspaper where she now works. The editor did not accept the article for publication but invited Vera to come to the office for a talk. The result was that she went to work as a copy girl, performing the mundane chores for editors and reporters that copy boys and girls do on American newspapers—carrying stories back and forth between reporters and editors, sharpening pencils, getting coffee for everyone. She was given an opportunity to write unimportant stories and within two years was a full-fledged staff reporter. "I started out writing mostly about housing and transportation. Housing is obvious because of my background. As for transportation—well, they were just short a transportation writer."

Vera told me many Russians, like American journalists, wind up working for newspapers because they didn't seem to fit in anywhere else. "Misfits, no doubt about it," she would say, running her fingers through a wild mop of short black hair. I smiled inwardly, because I found it difficult to think of a Party member as a misfit in the Soviet Union, but Vera was serious. "I never fitted in anywhere until I came here." Conversations with other Soviet journalists confirmed Vera's statement that they have diverse backgrounds. I did meet a few journalists who had been pining to work for newspapers since they were teen-agers, but they were the exceptions rather than the rule. The education editor of *Izvestia*, an admirable woman who knew more about schools than most of the educators I met, said she had never wanted to be anything but a journalist. But she pointed out two members of her staff who were former teachers and said many of the reporters at *Izvestia* had been trained as scientists, engineers, agricultural specialists or economists.

Vera's desire to write about women's problems grew out of her own experiences as a wife and mother. She was married in 1965 and became pregnant a year later. "We hadn't planned on a baby so soon," she said. "We only had a one-room apartment and, as you know, it isn't so easy to get a larger one. Also, I didn't want to quit my job at that time. But I wasn't about to put a tiny baby in a state nursery. How would we manage? It's very difficult to find someone to help out with a small child."

Soviet women receive fifty-six days of paid maternity leave, and their jobs are held open for a year after the birth of a baby. When Vera's son Sasha was born, her mother loaned her a housekeeper who had been with the family for many years. The presence of such a housekeeper was another sign of the upper-class status of Vera's family; it is nearly impossible to find even part-time household help in Russian cities. Working in someone else's house is regarded as demeaning; most people would rather work at a government job even if it paid a lower salary. Like most Russians I knew, Vera never discussed the Soviet class system that had benefited her and her family. She often said she was luckier than many Russian women, but she never examined her "luck" in terms of class status—either her own or her parents'.

When Vera's baby was three months old, the housekeeper decided she was too old to look after such a small child and retired on a government pension. Vera was planning to return to work, but she had to take the rest of her year's leave because there was no one else to care for the baby. Her mother and mother-in-law both had jobs and were reluctant to take on the responsibility of caring for their grandson every day, but they decided to share the work after the boy was a year old. "My mother's musical schedule was light enough so that she could take Sasha two or three days a week," Vera said. "I would have lost my job at the paper if I hadn't gone back to work after a year. But I'm now glad it worked out that I had to stay home the first year. I would have missed a lot of precious experiences with my baby if I had gone back to work right away. That's why I think we have to revise the law that only gives a woman fifty-six days of paid leave. It's not enough." When Vera did return to work, everyone in the family agreed that a state nursery was unsuitable for such a small child. The boy was not enrolled in a state kindergarten until he was three and a half.

"I think there's a world of difference between sending a one-year-old baby away from home for an entire day and sending a three-year-old to the kindergarten," Vera said. "My son is lively and curious, and he wants to be with other children now. Even if I didn't work, it wouldn't be good for him to be home with me all day. But now he is mentally and physically ready for kinder-garten, and he certainly wasn't when he was only a year or two

old. I don't know what we would have done then if his grandparents hadn't been so good about helping us."

Vera and her husband were fortunate on several counts.
They had enough money so that they suffered no particular
financial hardship when Vera had to quit work for a year after
her baby was born. In households where the husband makes an
average salary, women work out of financial necessity. Family
economic needs are a more compelling force than ideological
pressure in putting four-fifths of all Soviet women to work outside their homes. The cheap housing and medical care of a
Socialist state do not make up for the fact that ordinary items
like television sets and refrigerators can cost a worker three or
four months' salary. To live with any degree of comfort, most
Soviet families need two salaries.

Vera was also fortunate because her parents and her in-laws
liked each other enough to cooperate in caring for Sasha when
she wanted to go back to work. "I can assure you, that isn't
always the case," she said.

Her working hours are flexible enough so that she and her
husband see more of their son than most Soviet parents. Her
normal working day runs from 10 A.M. to 7 P.M., and she ordinarily drops Sasha off at the kindergarten at about 9:30. Most
work schedules require parents to leave their children at kindergartens before 8 A.M. Vera's husband begins work at 8:30,
and he is usually able to pick up his son before 6. Vera can also
count on extra time off when important official holidays and
public events are coming up, because at those times Soviet
newspapers are required to devote most of their space to un-
diluted propaganda. Reporters have little to do when their entire paper is occupied by a Brezhnev speech or a eulogy of
Lenin. "I really didn't do any work for three weeks before and
two weeks after the Party Congress," Vera said.* We all had a
fine time—getting our hair done, having long lunches, shop-

* The Twenty-fourth Party Congress was held in the spring of 1971. Party
congresses bear something of the same relationship to the regular party apparatus as American political conventions do to the regular Democratic and Re-

ping. I came home after a half day and picked up Sasha in the
afternoon. I know how lucky I am to have a job that gives me a
certain amount of freedom. None of my problems was insurmountable after Sasha was born, but I was lucky. When I got
back to work, I wanted to write about the whole range of family problems in a country where most women have jobs. I don't
agree with all of these people who are shouting, 'Back to the
home for the women,' but I do think our society has to make
some better arrangements for working mothers with small children. That was about the time I joined the Party too. I think
women should have a stronger voice in the Party." Only 20
percent of Party members are women, mainly because Russian
women do not have much time left for political activity after
they have met the demands of their jobs and their families.

Coverage of women's issues in newspapers and magazines
provides an excellent example of how the official press works
when it is not functioning simply as an organ of political propaganda. Without giving away any secrets, Vera told me as
much as she felt she could about the operation of her newspaper.

Soviet papers—like books, magazines, canned food labels and
every other form of printed material—are subject to official
censorship. The existence of censorship does not, however,
mean that every statement in every newspaper represents the
official policy of the Soviet government. *Pravda*, the organ of
the Party Central Committee, and to a slightly lesser extent
Izvestia, the government newspaper, are forums for top-level
statements on foreign and domestic policy. To use a favorite
phrase of Stalin's, "it is not by accident" that articles appear in
Pravda and *Izvestia*. Columns by important political com-
mentators sometimes reflect the official government position on
important matters. In other cases, they are trial balloons designed to elicit foreign reactions. Even *Pravda* and *Izvestia*

---

publican organizations. Soviet Congress delegates have little power, though;
they ratify decisions that have already been made by the Central Committee.

sometimes carry veiled debates on issues that are still being discussed within the Party.

Below the level of *Izvestia* and *Pravda*, the press reflects a whole spectrum of opinion that the authorities regard as officially permissible. There is a wide variety of newspapers and nonglossy magazines, each of them aimed at and sponsored by a special constituency. Every important union has its own paper; there are publications aimed at teachers and school administrators, writers and actors, agricultural and industrial officials, children and parents. Most of the papers are dull by Western standards, but some are less dull than others. A passerby seldom sees Muscovites reading *Pravda* or *Izvestia*, but many people pick up *Evening Moscow* to find out the times of movies or read the Soviet equivalent of personal classified advertisements. It is true that every newspaper must toe the official line on certain subjects. No paper, for example, could get a favorable mention of Solzhenitsyn past the censor in the current political climate. His name would not be mentioned at all except in unusual cases, as in the carefully orchestrated press attack when he was awarded the 1970 Nobel Prize for Literature.

There is a "black book" of unmentionable names; its contents change from time to time. The existence of such a volume is taken for granted by Westerners in Moscow, and I once asked Vera if she had ever seen it. "Yes," she said in a troubled tone. "You might say it is a standard reference work for a Soviet journalist. This is something I regret very much. I don't think any subject is so dangerous that it should be unthinkable even to discuss printing something about it."

A knowledgeable reader of the Soviet press is able to pinpoint certain "black book" names by what is left out of stories. At a press conference convened by the Writers' Union, my husband asked if and when new editions of Mandelstam and Akhmatova could be expected. A union official replied that Akhmatova had already been published during the past ten years and that an edition of Mandelstam's collected verse might appear in the not-too-distant future. Literary officials have been promising to publish Mandelstam's collected poetry for fifteen years, and the nonappearance of such an edition has become something of an international literary joke. Although Mandelstam was officially rehabilitated, the necessary political approval for publication has never been obtained. The publication of writers who were killed or banned during the Stalin years is an important issue among Russian intellectuals. The official at the press conference would not specify a publication date, but afterward he told my husband, "Probably in 1973."

A purported transcript of the press conference was published in *Literaturnaya Gazeta*, the Writers' Union newspaper. It omitted the question about Mandelstam and Akhmatova. A later story put out by the English-language service of Tass, the official Soviet news agency, mentioned Akhmatova's name but not Mandelstam's. Clearly the ordinary Russian press has a longer blacklist to contend with than English Tass.

Outside the category of proscribed names and subjects, there is considerable latitude for discussion of public issues, particularly those of an economic and sociological nature. The more conservative newspapers and magazines constantly trumpet the successes of Soviet society. When they do make any criticisms, it is usually because they think they have unearthed bourgeois deviation from the path of True Communism. The more liberal papers focus on issues like education, the status of women and unmet consumer needs; they discuss failures as well as successes. *Literaturnaya Gazeta* and *Komsomolskaya Pravda* run dozens of articles each year pointing out consumer shortages and criticizing bureaucratic waste in government agencies. *Literaturnaya Gazeta*'s reporters did some enterprising research and came up with an estimate of how many extra textbooks could be printed if every government form did not have to be filled out in triplicate. It also scolded publishers for printing books with little regard for demand, noting that more than 45,000 pounds of unwanted and unpurchased books were sent to the scrap heap in 1969. "These are the kinds of articles all young journalists want to write," Vera said. "I think we should have fewer long speeches by leaders in the papers and more investigative reporting."

Ideas for articles are initiated by party authorities, editors, reporters, outside specialists and sometimes by readers. Letters-to-the-editor columns are extremely important in Soviet newspapers; they provide what is essentially the only public forum for complaints about the way various institutions are run. Letters in sensitive political categories, like Oskar Rabin's defense against the attack on modern artists and art collectors in *Vechernaya Moskva*, are not printed. But letters on the everyday aggravations of Soviet life are published, and they sometimes trigger full-scale newspaper campaigns. In the autumn of 1970, the Council of Ministers of the USSR placed a legal limit on the amount of homework teachers could assign children, ranging from one-half hour a day in first grade to four hours in high school. Excessive homework had long been a sore point with many parents; it was part of the rigid Stalinist educational system. Newspapers began to receive hundreds of letters from parents complaining that teachers were ignoring the 1970 directive or assigning more homework than before. Many of the letters expressed concern for the health of teen-agers who were expected to do eight or nine hours of homework a day.

Because they were receiving so many letters, the newspapers most oriented toward coverage of social problems began to run articles about the detrimental effects of too much homework on the general physical and emotional condition of children. The papers took the parents' side, and the articles sharply criticized teachers who ignored the new limit.

The expanded newspaper coverage of women's problems between 1969 and 1971 resulted from a combination of growing public and official concern. Vera told me her paper's interest in issues related to the status of women began to grow along with the volume of letters from readers.

In late 1969, the monthly magazine *Novy Mir* published a short novel titled *A Week Like Any Other* by a young woman writer named Natalya Baranskaya. The novel was published while Aleksandr Tvardovsky was still the magazine's editor in chief.

A Week Like Any Other was an unusual candid portrayal of the problems of a woman trying to bring up small children without any help from a grandmother or housekeeper, hold a full-time job, keep up with new developments in her scientific field and remain attractive to her husband. The heroine was a scientist named Olga who had two preschool-age children.

In a startlingly explicit passage by Soviet literary standards, Olga recalled her distress at learning she was pregnant a second time. She had scheduled an abortion (they are legal and are the most widely used method of birth control in the Soviet Union) but found she could not bear to go through with it after she had talked the matter over with her husband. With two children under age three, Olga had to quit work and her husband had to take a second job to make ends meet.

When the children were slightly older and enrolled in a nursery, Olga's main problem was insufficient time and energy to cope with all the demands of being a professional, a wife and a mother. One night she and her husband made love and forgot to set the alarm clock. (The meaning of the passage was unmistakable, although lovemaking was not mentioned explicitly. One of the censor's functions is enforcing official prudery about sex.) Olga overslept, and she described the resultant chaos the next day. She and her husband were both late for work. Because she was so rushed, she forgot to tell him about a compulsory political education meeting scheduled that evening for workers in her section. She was unable to reach him at work. When she arrived home, her husband was furious, her children whining and hungry because he had fed them canned food.

Olga was torn between concern for her family and her desire to use her talents in the profession for which she was trained. Her husband offered to take on a second job again if it would make her happier to quit work, but she felt her sense of independence and personal worth would be diminished by leaving her job.

In contrast to most literary offerings in Soviet periodicals, *A*

Week Like Any Other was controversial enough so that people got angry about it. Men and women fought over Olga's plight at parties. Although the piece was printed in *Novy Mir*, other publications received a flood of mail referring to it. The reaction made it clear that Baranskaya had touched on problems that Russian men and women take very seriously.

"I walked into the office the day after that issue of *Novy Mir* came out and I hadn't even read it yet," Vera recalled. "The first thing I heard was a lot of shouting—two men and one woman reporter. The men were saying Olga had brought all her troubles on herself—no one forced her to have the second baby. The woman was arguing, 'Nothing forced her but her own conscience. I suppose a woman gets pregnant all by herself. I thought we stopped believing in virgin births after the revolution.'

"It went that way all day. My editor said it was hopeless to think about getting anything done. By the time I got home, I had read the piece in the office and my husband, to my astonishment, had read it at his laboratory. Yuri [her husband] said one of his women colleagues had brought a copy of *Novy Mir* to the office and was fighting about Baranskaya's article with another woman, so he asked if he could borrow it to see what the fuss was about. I must say that my husband was sympathetic to the author's point of view. He helps me a great deal around the house, especially with Sasha, but he thinks most Russian men expect their women to do everything at home in addition to working.

"And Yuri doesn't believe in abortion, so he didn't take the attitude that no woman had to have a baby unless she wanted one. He is a chemist, and he has seen publications about Western birth control pills. He thinks it's terrible that in the last half of the twentieth century, Russia is relying on abortion as the main means of birth control."

For several months before I left Moscow, Vera was trying to get an article into print that mentioned the antiquated birth control methods used in the Soviet Union. She was unsuccessful, largely because of the official puritanism that keeps sex to a minimum in both the press and literature. (In no other area of Soviet life did I find a wider gap between public pretense and private behavior.) The general ban on sex in print restricts much-needed factual information as well as fictional eroticism and pornography. A debate about the desirability of sex education in schools is creeping into the newspapers, but it is heavily laden with euphemisms about "education for physical and mental health." There is simply no euphemism for contraceptive devices. Stalin's murders can be encompassed by the term "personality cult," but how can a writer find another word for condom or diaphragm? An American who has spent any length of time in Moscow can only giggle at attempts by right-wing groups to portray sex education and pornography as "Communist plots."

"The situation is known to everyone," Vera said. "Condoms made in the Soviet Union are so thick and clumsy that they destroy sexual pleasure. No one wants to use them. Diaphragms, if you can believe it, only come in two sizes. So they aren't exactly reliable. And our health authorities consider the birth control pill unsafe. A few gynecologists have access to birth control pills for their private patients—I use them—but they can only accommodate a tiny percentage of people. They should be available in state clinics. Now our women get pregnant all the time when they can't afford another child and go have an abortion. This our health officials consider perfectly safe. A majority of women who have abortions are married. Think what a bitter thing it is to kill the child of a man you love. But also think of what it does to a family with one child, living in a one-room apartment, to be faced with the prospect of another. I never want to be faced with the choice. I don't think it's enough for health authorities just to say 'the pill is dangerous' when they can't offer Soviet women anything better."

Vera said her senior editor agreed that a discussion of contraception and abortion was needed but that it was still "too sensitive" to print in the newspaper at the time. "I think my editor really wanted to write something about this but was told by someone higher up that it was impossible. Those of us on the staff who aren't important editors don't always know at what level decisions are made about stories. I only know that the answer came back 'no.' "

I asked Vera how decisions were made about coverage of broad topics like the status of women. She said many newspapers, including her own, followed a practice unknown in American journalism—an "editorial conference" that includes reporters, editors, some readers whose letters had indicated particular interest in or knowledge about the topic under discussion and appropriate professionals. Her paper's conference on women was attended by several social scientists, doctors and educators—especially those who worked in nurseries and kindergartens. There is no need for special Party representation at editorial conferences, since most senior editors are Party members. They continually consult with higher Party officials about the proper political line to follow in their coverage.

One decision made at the editorial conference was that the paper would conduct an investigation over a period of several months into conditions at nurseries and kindergartens. In fact, I met Vera at a nursery-kindergarten that was a stop on an officially organized tour of Moscow for Benetta B. Washington, former director of the Women's Job Corps and wife of the mayor of Washington, D.C. Vera was doing some fact-finding at the nursery because it was one of the few in Moscow that remained open during the summer months (something education officials neglected to mention to Mrs. Washington).

"This is really a great problem," Vera said. "An ordinary worker has one months' vacation. But most kindergartens and nurseries are only open until the end of May. A child under seven isn't eligible for camp, and besides, there aren't enough camps to take care of all the older children. Some mothers and fathers take their vacations in separate months to help solve the problem of what to do with a small child during the summer. So they never have a chance to get away together. This is very hard on a marriage."

I watched Vera's articles carefully for a reference to the problem she had outlined, but none ever appeared. Apparently a "no" answer had been received again. As time went on, I had a distinct feeling that she was feeding me ideas she wanted to see in print but could not get past the censor. Her observations were always useful to me; she noticed things that any foreigner would miss.

I acquired considerable information by reading Vera's articles and those of her colleagues. In Moscow, which has better educational facilities than any city in the Soviet Union, there are places in nurseries and kindergartens for only half of all children under age seven. But there are empty places in nurseries for the under-three age group. "The empty space is a reflection of the fact that most parents will do anything before they put a small baby in a state nursery," Vera said. "At the same time, there are long waiting lists at the kindergartens for children over three." Several stories in her paper suggested that the state ought to pay more attention to parental desires and concentrate on increasing places for older children instead of wasting space in the infant nurseries.

Vera's paper had been particularly forthright in discussing job discrimination against women in the Soviet Union. Officially, of course, there is none. The principle of equal pay for equal work is more solidly established than in most Western nations, but there is the usual gap between principle and practice. Although educated women have easier access to professions that are male bastions in the West, women are also disproportionately represented in the poorest-paying, least attractive jobs. Women professors, doctors, lawyers and scientists are all more numerous than in the West. But the most prestigious jobs in each field usually go to men. Seventy percent of Soviet doctors are women, but there are few women surgeons or hospital directors. On farms and in factories men occupy the majority of managerial jobs, while women perform the heaviest manual labor—everything from plowing to ditch-digging. Khrushchev once remarked at an agricultural conference: "We all know what an enormous role women play in all sectors of the building of Communism. But for some reason there are few women in this hall. Take a pair of binoculars and look around. It will be said that it is mainly administrative workers who are present here. It turns out that it is the men who do the administering and the women who do the work."

Vera's paper dealt in many articles with the need to increase female participation in farm and factory management. One article pointed out that the number of women doing unskilled jobs in heavy industry is twice the number of men.

The paper also suggested that women should be paid family allowances after the birth of a child so that they would not have to go back to work for several years unless they chose to. "Why, in a Socialist state, shouldn't we admit that it's socially useful to bring up children?" Vera asked. "Why should a woman have to go to work to support her family—unless she wants to—and turn her child over to a stranger who is paid to do the job the mother would like to do? I personally wouldn't want to stay at home for more than a year or two, but that doesn't apply to all women. We could have special classes for women scientists and doctors, so that they could keep up with new developments in their field and return to work after a few years without having lost touch with their profession. Why should a construction worker make several hundred rubles a month and a mother nothing for taking care of her children?"

Vera was not bothered by the fact that many of the Soviet Union's revolutionary fathers believed the upbringing of children should be taken over by the state. "They weren't realistic about everything," she said. "That idea has been pretty much discredited in our country. It just isn't in human nature to carry it out. I consider myself a good Communist, but it's not up to the Party to bring up my son."

Many of Vera's ideas on these subjects did make it into the paper, though not always above her by-line. She told me she had contributed to many articles on women that were signed by social scientists.

Examples of the divergent viewpoints represented in the Soviet press were contained in articles about women in more conservative newspapers. They always stressed that women were luckier in Russia than anywhere else in the world and asserted that the Soviet system makes it perfectly easy for women to work and raise a family.

An article in *Pravda* by Aleksandra V. Nuzhnida, who held the title Hero of Socialist Labor, suggested that women who do not work belong in a class with "loafers, parasites, drunkards and lovers of the easy life."

She wrote: "Now I want to talk about the reserve of worker strength, such as women, who have skills but sit at home. There is one I know. I will call her Nina. She has a secondary school education and took courses in bookkeeping. However, this strong, healthy woman has not worked in many years. . . . She sits in the courtyard with the old women, cracking sunflower seeds with her teeth and spitting out shells, chatting about the latest courtyard news. Sometimes she strolls around from store to store." Nuzhnida said she could not get the factory out of her mind—she polished metal rollers—even when she had to stay at a hospital while her daughter was sick. Once the child was better, "I flew on wings to the shop—believe me, my soul was singing."

In the conservative newspaper *Literaturnaya Rossiya*, a woman named Tamara Reskova wrote a sarcastic reply to Baranskaya's *A Week Like Any Other*. The article was headlined CERTAIN PEOPLE DON'T HAVE THICK SOUP BUT OTHERS WISH THEY HAD LARGE PEARLS.

"The black demon of Olga's life," Reskova wrote, "is her lack of spirituality. Having become a mother, she is concerned mainly that her children be clean, fed and healthy . . . the instincts of maternity are revealed in Olga above everything else in a biological love for her children. . . . But soon the time will come when her Kotka and Gulka will say to an ever-busy mother, 'Don't you feed us, talk to us.' "

Vera said she would not work for a newspaper like *Litera-*

turnaya Rossiya under any circumstances because its policies were much too conservative for her.

I never asked her directly how she could stand having so few of her ideas survive into print. The ones that did were diluted and disguised to get by the censor. However, she brought up the subject herself by asking what the difference was between censorship and the editing at my newspaper.

I answered her honestly. In my career as a reporter there have been only two occasions when an editor prevented me from writing something I believed to be true. In both instances, I thought the editors were wrong and had made their decisions on the basis of unreasoning personal prejudices. I told Vera the basic difference between editing and censorship was that editing is a personal matter and censorship is institutionalized. In a quarrel with an editor, one can generally appeal to another editor or, if the disagreement becomes too intolerable, there is always the option of changing jobs. Vera worked for one of the most liberal Soviet papers; she could not have taken her contraception idea to another publication and expect it to be accepted. Editorial decisions on most matters have nothing to do with the government, I told her, except in rare cases such as the New York *Times'* failure to publish its advance knowledge of the Bay of Pigs invasion. I left Moscow just before the legal storm broke over the publication of the Pentagon Papers; I would have enjoyed the chance to discuss that with Vera. After giving her my views on editing versus formal censorship, I asked her how she could stand knowing that everything she wrote was subject not only to the prejudices of individual editors but to an overall political line.

"I suppose you might as well ask how can I be a Russian," was her reply. "People like me conceive of our jobs as trying to get something past that might not have gotten past the censor if we weren't there. Some of my ideas survive; a Russian reader can tell even if a foreigner can't."

As an example, she pointed out something that I would never have noticed in *A Week Like Any Other*. In one scene, Olga tells her husband that they only talk to each other about money, never about ideas or world affairs. He reminds her that they have talked about the war in Vietnam and Czechoslovakia. Vera said the juxtaposition of Vietnam and Czechoslovakia in the same sentence was a sly way of making an equation between the two that would get past the censor. She laughed triumphantly when I said I would not have spotted the meaning by myself.

Like most Russians—with the exception of political dissidents—Vera did not question the government's right to act as censor. She simply wanted to broaden the boundaries of discussion within the framework of official censorship. The "black book" bothered her not because she thought every idea should be disseminated in print but because she was against automatic proscription of any subject. Her attitude was similar to Galya's belief that the government had the right to ban certain authors but it had made a mistake in outlawing Solzhenitsyn.

Vera said frankly that she had joined the Party partly because membership would improve her chances of becoming an editor when she was older. "Probably the majority of our staff members don't belong to the Party," she said, "but most of the editors do. I want to be an editor. I want to be able to say yes to an article on abortion and contraception."

I asked her how she would feel as an editor if the answer from her superiors was still no. "I'll face that when it happens," she said.

X

Dmitri

DMITRI IS KNOWN to his friends as a *samizdatchik*—one who regards the writing of underground short stories and novels as his most important work. In most other countries he would be considered an apolitical writer; his stories are concerned mainly with love and sex. Because politics impinges on every aspect of Soviet literature, Dmitri's writing is politically as well as aesthetically unorthodox in the Russian context. Many of his stories are of a highly erotic nature, which rules out passage by the censor. They also deal with life in a little-known Soviet counterculture, the chief feature of which is the belief that individuals are as important as the state.

The counterculture exists on many planes, some of which intersect and some of which do not. The active political dissidents operate on one level. Volodya Bukovsky, for example, began as a writer and moved to open dissent, becoming particularly active in publicizing the Soviets' use of psychiatric commitment against political dissidents. Dmitri moves in the literary-artistic circles of the counterculture; he writes under a pseudonym and does not make any public protests against the regime. He does not know men like Bukovsky personally, but he does know about their activities and he shares many of their views. The political dissidents are also aware of what happens on the literary and artistic plane of the counterculture.

Dimitri's world is less offensive to the authorities than Bukovsky's, if only because it seldom leads to open confrontation. His type of *samizdat* does pose a serious political problem for the regime, though, because it concentrates on the personal

229

rather than the social meaning of existence. His early writing is more comparable philosophically to the Beat Generation novels of the fifties than to any subsequent Western writing. He now holds a less nihilistic view of the world, but he still does not believe in progress; that alone is sufficient to make him un-printable in the Soviet Union. The authorities do not want young intellectuals to be exposed to thinking like Dmitri's; they want satisfied students like Tanya, who concentrate almost en-tirely on the positive aspects of life in their country.

Dmitri acknowledges that his work is probably apolitical enough to prevent him from sharing the fate of more political *samizdat* authors like Amalrik, Andrei Sinyavsky or Yuli Daniel. (Sinyavsky and Daniel were sent to prison camps in 1966 after a widely publicized trial that was a benchmark in the cultural repression of the post-Khrushchev era. Daniel was released in 1970, Sinyavsky in 1971.) Nevertheless, Dmitri does not want to take any chances by signing his name to his work. His stories bear two false initials as a signature. "I am afraid," he said. "I can't stop writing, but I don't want to go to prison for it. I wouldn't be able to defend myself as bravely as Sinyavsky and Daniel did. As for Solzhenitsyn, who signs his name to the most powerful words our country hears, I could never be in that class as a writer or a man. I know that about myself. The place where I make a stand is this: I will continue to write as best I know how, and I will allow my writing to be circulated in *samizdat*. If the choice were prison or stop my writing altogether, I think I would take prison. Every man must decide for himself how far he will go to defend his personal freedom." At thirty-one, Dmitri is almost totally alienated from Soviet society. His background is remarkably similar to Vera's in some respects, but he took a completely different path when he dropped out of Moscow State University in 1962.

Dmitri said his grandparents on both sides were nobles in St. Petersburg before the revolution. "I won't tell you what their titles were, because I'm afraid it might make me too identifia-ble. Don't you think there must still be some lists of the nobility before the revolution and their descendants? Anyway, it's not important. We aren't noble now." Both sets of grandparents emigrated to France in 1918, but his parents embraced the revolution. His mother was an actress and his father a film director who, Dmitri said, "made a lot of terrible movies glorifying Our Kind Father Yosif Vissarionovich [Stalin]. Also a lot of terrible war movies that are still playing on television." Dmitri's father died after a heart attack in 1956. "I'm sorry to say the Twentieth Party Congress wasn't responsible," he said. "He died before that. So I suppose it's lucky in a way—he died thinking his life had been worthwhile." Dmitri was bitter and cynical about his father and everyone else of that generation who bowed down before the cult of Stalin. "Never did one generation give the next so little to be proud of," he said. "Except in Nazi Germany. As far as I'm concerned, the honors are equal."

"But you won't fight the system openly, even now," I said.

"Yes, but at least I don't give it any cooperation," he replied. "You don't see me churning away books about all of the wonderful achievements of Socialist society. I could do it, you know. You can put your writing skills to almost any use. Our so-called writers proved that under Stalin."

Dmitri's mother lives on a large state pension—she was allotted extra money because of her husband's extraordinary services to the arts. She has a city apartment and a *dacha* in the Moscow suburbs. Unless the weather is unusually severe, she spends most of her time at the *dacha*. Dmitri lives in an apartment with Tamar, his mistress for the past ten years, and another couple. The flat has two rooms and a kitchen; the four friends agreed to share it after the other girl's mother died, leaving her in happy sole possession of the "living space." "Tamar and I had been camping out for years, moving in and out of other people's apartments whenever there was an empty bed available," Dmitri said. "We've been here three years, and it's the first real home we've had. If I believed in a god, I would say this apartment was a gift from him." Dmitri could not stay with his mother, since she thoroughly disapproves of the way he lives. But she gives him money regularly, and he does not turn it down. "I need it to live on," he said. "You can't make any money of *samizdat*. Besides, I like to think of my father turning over in his grave at having his pension support subversive literature."

Dmitri had a brilliant academic record in high school, and he easily passed the entrance examination for MGU, which has the stiffest admissions requirements of any university in the Soviet Union. (Moscow State University is popularly known by its initials, which stand for *Moskovsky Gosudarstvenny Universitet*.) He was studying Russian literature, and his amorphous alienation became more substantive during his first year at the university. "The first thing that disgusted me was the way Russian literature was studied in university classes," he remembers. "We read most of the classical authors—Lermontov, Gogol, Chekhov, Tolstoy, Pushkin, even those who had been in bad graces during the Stalin years like Dostoevsky. But no differing interpretations were allowed; the professor would tell us what the author was all about, as though he had just received the word from Mount Sinai. By the way, I have read the Bible, although I hadn't when I was a first-year student. Bibles aren't so easy to get, although there are a few copies hidden away in various cupboards. Nobody has had the endurance to type the whole Bible in *samizdat*, though. Anyway, back to my first year at the university. We would hear about Dostoevsky's religious 'errors,' along with other garbage about the classical writers only knowing part of the truth because Marxism-Leninism wasn't fully developed. Oh, the trash I had to listen to and take notes on for two years. But even worse—the twentieth century. The twentieth century brings us to the relationship between literature and the Soviet government, past and present. That had the professors really walking on a high wire."

During his first year at MGU, Dmitri met a girl whose influence increased his skepticism about the value of a Soviet university education. Her father had been an officer in the NKVD (the secret police under Stalin, now the KGB) and he shot himself after the Twentieth Congress. (Many participants in the Stalin regime, not only secret police officers, committed suicide after the revelations of the congress. Some were honestly shocked by the extent of the terror they had aided; others became mentally unbalanced by the attacks on policies they had thought unchallengeable and unchangeable.) She detested his memory with a depth of emotion that far exceeded Dmitri's feelings about his own father.

"This girl was my first serious involvement," Dmitri said. "Her feelings and ideas did have a profound effect on me. As the daughter of an NKVD officer, she had learned many things about Stalin's secret police that were only hinted at during the period after the Congress. Her father tried to conceal the real nature of his work from her, but she found things out by accident anyway. She said she used to wonder how he could come home and eat dinner after conducting an interrogation of an innocent man, maybe even being a witness to torture. She would say that Khrushchev's de-Stalinization was all very well, but why were there no public trials now of the people who had committed crimes under Stalin?

"She was a Russian literature student too, but she was interested mainly in the twentieth century. She had access to a fantastic collection of books that she said her father had obviously acquired from prisoners, since the family itself had no literary background. She had prerevolutionary editions of Blok and Mandelstam and Akhmatova—books no ordinary person could get his hands on. They were my taking-off point.

"From that time, I began to read as much twentieth-century prose and poetry as I could. *Samizdat* was just becoming an important force among young intellectuals. I read the poems Mandelstam wrote during his exile in the thirties. I read Akhmatova—poems that had never been published or the uncensored version of poems that had been published in censored form. I read *Dr. Zhivago* in *samizdat*, in two nights. That's all the time I had before I had to pass it on to the next person who was waiting to read it."

Samizdat as Russians know it today began during the period after the Twentieth Congress. It included both fiction and non-fiction that fell into three basic categories: camp memoirs and other attacks on the Stalinist system, officially banned works by writers who were killed or otherwise silenced during the thirties and literature by a new generation of writers who had come to maturity after Stalin's death. *Samizdat* has its deepest roots in the thirties, when some people risked their lives to preserve typed or handwritten manuscripts by authors who had perished in the terror. However, manuscripts were hidden, not circulated, in those days.

Samizdat today is typed and circulated from one friend to another. Thin paper for typing must be acquired in surreptitious fashion. There are only a few stores in Moscow where high-quality office and typing supplies are sold; the secret police are known to be on the lookout for people who buy an unusually large bulk of thin typing paper. The *samizdatchiki* and their friends often take turns buying paper so none of them will seem to be carrying away an unusually large amount. Nor is it easy for private citizens to acquire typewriters; there is the inevitable shortage accompanied by waiting lists, and government offices have first call on available supplies. Many *samizdat* manuscripts are typed on ancient machines, and the copies are not easily legible. Government offices often take precautions to prevent their typewriters from being stolen or used for nefarious purposes. At Vera's newspaper, every typewriter had to be locked away before the staff went home at night. "You see how afraid our government is of the free printed word," Dmitri said.

Samizdat is important not only in the counterculture but in the establishment intellectual community. The well-known official novelist Konstantin Simonov made a statement during a trip to Berlin that he had read Solzhenitsyn's newest novel, *August 1914*, and thought it should be published in the Soviet Union. He could only have read the book in *samizdat* form.

While *samizdat* can properly be described as an underground movement, it is not illegal. It falls into a gray area which Soviet law treats differently under different circumstances. It is illegal for a novel to be published without official approval, but it is perfectly legal to type a novel and hand it to a friend; the latter does not constitute "publication" in the Soviet legal sense. The content of much *samizdat* literature, on the other hand, is often defined as illegal by the Soviet authorities. The young man who was tried for possessing a copy of Andrei Amalrik's open letter to Anatoly Kuznetsov was convicted not because it was in *samizdat* form but because the prosecutor had defined the ideas in Amalrik's letter as "defamatory to the Soviet state." The authorities are interested mainly in stopping the circulation of *samizdat* works by living writers who deal with political issues. During the 1960's, the content of *samizdat* literature became increasingly political. "For me, politics can sometimes be part of my writing," Dmitri said. "For many other *samizdat* writers, literature is primarily a vehicle for expressing political ideas. There is a need for both types of writing, but my kind is not the most widely read."

When Dmitri began reading *samizdat* manuscripts circulating in university dormitories, he was interested mainly in the writing that had been suppressed since the thirties. Some of the poetry and prose that appeared in *samizdat* at that time had originally been preserved not in manuscript form but in the memories of widows, friends and admirers of dead writers. Russian literature is intertwined with a strong oral tradition—one reason Stalin was unable to destroy writing along with writers. Russians have an astonishing capacity for remembering and reciting volumes of poetry; some of my friends seemed to have stepped straight out of the land of the book people in Ray Bradbury's novel *Fahrenheit 451*.

One Easter Sunday at Boris Pasternak's grave, I sat beside a man who recited Pasternak's poetry on religious themes for two hours, giving up only when I was too cold and damp to stay in the same spot. He was a former art historian, partially crippled by battle injuries from the war. He took the train to Peredelkino regularly and made it his business to sweep the dead leaves off Pasternak's grave. I remember the tears in his eyes as he recited lines from the poem "Garden of Gethsemane":

> *We had rejected without resistance*
> *Dominion over all things and the power to work miracles,*
> *As though these had been His only on loan*
> *And now was as all mortals are, even as we.*

Dmitri also recited prose and poetry with a dramatic flair. As he read Mandelstam and Akhmatova and Pasternak, he tried to commit as much as he could to memory. "You never know when some policeman will take a book away, so you try to remember," he said. "It's a Russian custom older than the revolution."

Dmitri said he began writing short stories when he was twelve years old. "But I never had any intention of becoming a writer. That would have been a political profession, subject to constant censorship by Them. I didn't want anything to do with politics. My idea was to compromise with the system by becoming a scholar in some obscure literary field that no one was interested in. Then I could do honest research, at least on a narrow subject.

"After I really began reading during my first year at the university, this type of compromise no longer seemed possible. Honest research? The great writers I was reading could hardly be mentioned in our classrooms. What do you say about Mandelstam? 'Now, dear students, we turn to the greatest Russian poet of this century. He was murdered in 1938, of course.' To say such a thing is unthinkable. Not to say it is unthinkable. What if I just decided I wanted to be a scholar on Mandelstam? I'm sure every Soviet university would open its arms to me. . . .

"There was something else. In reading these writers, I felt their greatness and it renewed my own desire to be a writer, which I had deliberately suppressed. I didn't know if I could ever be a great writer, but I wanted to try. At the same time all of this was rumbling around in my head, *One Day* came out. I thought things might have changed enough so there was actually a possibility of publishing honest writing. So my motives for leaving the university were contradictory, in a sense. I thought honest scholarly work was impossible, but I also thought society was opening up enough so a writer might, just might, be able to do honest work himself. I was also just damn bored with the university.

"So I dropped out and did absolutely nothing for the next two years. I met Tamar at MGU—her father did something important in the Party in Georgia, and that's how she got into the university. She really didn't speak Russian well enough at the time she took the examination for her to have been admitted under the regular rules. Now she does, but she's been living in Moscow for nearly ten years. She says her written Russian was especially poor at the time she took the exam, so she could not possibly have passed it with high enough marks. So you see how free of graft and pull university admissions procedures were. Anyway, we both dropped out at the same time and decided to live together. Her father disowned her—said he no longer had a daughter. But her mother comes to see her, even now."

Dmitri and Tamar plunged into a world of dropouts consisting, according to his own description, of drinking, drugs (mostly hashish), sexual promiscuity and laziness. In the Soviet Union, men and unmarried women must have some type of official work papers or they are theoretically subject to exile under the parasite law. People in the dropout subculture get around the requirement by taking casual jobs that enable them to meet the letter of the law. Dmitri signed on as a personal secretary to a zoology professor who thought he had writing talent. The job involved about one hour of work a day, but it kept him in good standing with the authorities.

"I was a phony, a put-on of a rebellious young writer," he said. "I would sit down in a corner with my pen, in whatever apartment we happened to be staying, and say I was going to write. I'd kick anyone out of the apartment who was there, and they would be tolerant because I was supposed to be a serious writer. Then I'd start in on vodka or, if I didn't have enough money for that, wine. I'd go out to another friend's house to sleep it off, so no one would know I'd gotten drunk instead of working. Everyone did know, of course, including Tamar.

"She wasn't doing anything with herself either—we set lousy examples for each other. I should have been trying to publish then, because the controls were much less strict than they are now. But I wasn't producing enough to submit to anyone. We were smoking hashish—it wasn't very hard to get if you knew the right people. It didn't do me much physical harm; it was just another way of killing time, of wasting the days away. I was interested in having as many girls as possible, one after the other. Tamar was no angel either, but I could blush when I think of the junk I would tell her about how I couldn't possibly be a real writer until I had wider experience with women. Oh, god, what a fool I must have seemed to everyone but myself. We justified it all, saying we needed to free ourselves from the rigidity of MGU. We lived like pigs. We hardly ever washed our clothes, because we would be in one person's apartment one night and in another's the next."

The inhabitants of the counterculture Dmitri described would please Spiro Agnew no more than they do the Soviet authorities, except Agnew would call them left-wing degenerates and the Soviets call them bourgeois capitalist degenerates. After two years, Dmitri became sickened by the life he was leading. Undiscriminating sex, drugs, alcohol and too much free time had not blotted out his desire to write.

"It wasn't any one thing that changed me," he said, "and I haven't changed entirely. I still go through bouts of doing nothing but sleeping for a week. It's another form of escape, like the hashish and vodka used to be. But I pull myself out of it now. One day a good friend said to me, 'You know, if you lived in America or anywhere but here, I don't think anyone would put up with you. You live with no goal; you produce nothing. People put up with you here just because you're a rebel and they're happy to meet anyone who's against the system. But is

that enough for you?' The answer was no, it wasn't enough. I
wanted to write. Somewhere I had forgotten that. We got a
room in a communal apartment, and when I chased Tamar
away it was because I really did need to be alone to work. I
don't know how good a writer I am now, but I do know I am a
serious writer."

When I met Dmitri for the first time in 1969, it was obvious
that he had been working seriously for the past five years. He
had completed more than forty short stories and a first novel
about his youth that he described as "abominable." He was
halfway through a novel about the counterculture which he
described as "a great improvement over the first one." The first
novel is nihilistic; it disavows all official Soviet values, including the work ethic, but suggests nothing to replace them. I
never saw the second novel, but Dmitri said it concerned "the
need to go on trying to make sense of the world even when your
deepest belief is that the world makes no sense at all." The
short stories are mainly about sex and love—ranging from
erotic adolescent experiences to the question of whether a man
and a woman can be thoroughly committed to each other when
they have opened themselves sexually and emotionally to different people. The later stories also expound Dmitri's view of
the need for freedom within commitment and—an old Russian
theme—the struggle between carnal and spiritual drives. The
best story I read portrayed a writer trying to finish one para-
graph while his mistress paced restlessly around the room. The
writer could not decide whether he would lose his words or find
them if the woman left; they eventually came to him in the
middle of a bitter quarrel. "I'm searching for unity," the main
character said, "but is the soul contained in the flesh or the flesh
in the soul?" Not surprisingly, many of Dmitri's other stories
deal with conflicts between children and their fathers. He
knows it is no accident that his only serious involvements have
been with two girls who hated their fathers as he hated his.

"I hope to do a major novel on this subject some day," Dmitri
said. "I know conflicts between generations are normal and

usually very boring, but we have an abnormal situation in this country. Can you have a 'normal' level of conflict with a father who was a murderer? That may sound like a strong word to a foreigner, but what about my first girl whose father worked for the NKVD? Can I respect my father, who devoted his professional life to glorifying the head murderer?

"I don't know how they can make peace with my generation —that's for an older writer to deal with. I am concerned with how my generation can make peace with them, if peace can be made. My inclination is to believe there must be a clean break between the generations in our country, but human experience suggests that is impossible. How, then, does the younger generation make peace without corrupting itself in the process? This isn't the petty quarrel between generations in the West. Our older generation is covered with blood. How do we approach them without becoming diseased ourselves? I'm repeating myself, but this problem obsesses me."

One of Dmitri's problems is he has no proper external standard by which to judge his writing. *Samizdat* is completely cut off from official literary criticism in the Soviet Union, and Dmitri has no respect for official critics anyway. "Our literary criticism is all political," he says. One Russian reader of *samizdat* whose literary judgment I respect told me Dmitri's writing was "very promising but still immature. He uses Russian in beautiful and intricate ways, but there is still too much youthful self-absorption for him to have deep insights into human nature. I think that will change, though." My Russian friend said Dmitri was not as accomplished in his literary genre as Yosif Brodsky is in poetry. Brodsky, a protégé of Anna Akhmatova before her death in 1966, was exiled from Leningrad under the parasite law in 1964 but was allowed to return a year later. He is more widely available in *samizdat* than Dmitri and therefore more widely known among Russian intellectuals. He has also been published abroad, both in Russian and in translations.

The fact that Dmitri's writing generally refers to political

issues only within a highly personal framework does not increase interest in his work by the Russian *samizdat* audience or
in the West. Most of the *samizdat* that has made its way to the
West in recent years has been highly political. Western publishers, including Russian-language ones and ordinary publishing houses that translate Russian writers, are interested mainly
in works of political significance. Pasternak is a case in point.
Russians, including those who thought *Dr. Zhivago* was a fine
novel, revere Pasternak mainly as a poet. In the West, readers
who are not specialists in Russian affairs generally think of Pasternak only in connection with the controversial *Dr. Zhivago*.
The old man at Pasternak's grave was overjoyed to meet an
American who knew something about Pasternak's poetry as
well as *Dr. Zhivago*. "A writer who can be appreciated only for
political reasons is not really a writer," he said. "It doesn't matter whether his politics are good or bad."

Dmitri told me he felt the lack of opportunity for publication
was hindering his development as a writer. "It's possible I'm not
good enough for the people who do Russian-language publishing in the West," he said, "although I'm not sure of that. I do
know they can only select a limited number of *samizdat* manuscripts for publication. If it weren't for censorship, I would
certainly be published in Russia. This is a huge country with
room for all kinds of writers—the greatest, the near-great, and
merely interesting, the young, the old. There would be a place
for me. I sometimes find it hard to have the self-discipline to go
on working without publication. Can you understand that? I
have a history of poor self-discipline, it's true, but in this case
it's not just an excuse. It's part of what makes me go to sleep for
a week at a time. I know that my stories are circulating in
samizdat, that they are typed and passed on by people who
think they are worth reading. But still, it would be a different
and wonderful feeling to see a book. I feel ashamed of myself
for thinking this way; I know some others are completely indifferent to publication. But I am young, and I would like some
outside evidence that I am a writer. I feel ashamed again, just

saying that. When I feel this way, I try to remember Mandelstam's words, 'I divide all works of literature into those written with and without permission. The first are trash, the second—stolen air.' "

Dmitri is *not* an underground writer because he has no choice in the matter; he could certainly find an official publisher if he chose to tailor his writing to the ideological and aesthetic requirements of the censor. I am not familiar with the full range of official Soviet literature, but I have read most of the writers whom Russians of Dmitri's generation consider important, either in the original Russian or in translation. Of the younger officially published novelists, I can only think of one—Vasily Aksiyonov—who qualifies as a better writer than Dmitri by normal, nonpolitical standards of literary criticism. Aksiyonov is an example of another contemporary Soviet literary phenomenon—he is published both officially and in *samizdat*. He has often encountered serious difficulty in trying to publish his writing during the past five years, and some of his unpublished works appear in *samizdat*. The same is true of other writers who have had official ups and downs—Voznesensky, Yevtushenko, Bulat Okudzhava. When a censored work appears officially, the uncensored version will sometimes turn up in the inevitable typed manuscripts on thin paper. The combination of *samizdat* and official publication was more common in the early 1960's, though; the cultural repression after 1964 made official writers far more cautious about keeping their unpublished manuscripts, or the censored portions, to themselves.

Dmitri's attitude toward the official writers is, quite simply, that they are prostitutes. It is an attitude shared by all committed *samizdatchiki* and political dissidents. He does not assert that their work has no literary merit; he despises them because they cooperate with a system that discourages greatness and rewards mediocrity. "The essence of an artist is the uncompromising pursuit of his inner vision," Dmitri says. "How can you talk about any of these people as real artists, when they compromise their inner vision every day by submitting to the censor? The more talented they are, the more guilty for putting their talent at the disposal of such a system. A Kuznetsov is more honest than a Voznesensky or Yevtushenko. There are many forms of cowardice; running away from one's country isn't the only one.

"I don't believe there is any real likelihood of major political change in our country. I stopped believing in that possibility when the campaign against Solzhenitsyn began. Since then— certainly, some weeks are better than others. They tighten the screws and then loosen them a little, but the possibility that the censor would gradually lose his authority is gone. Why? Partly because of the activities of the official writers, some of whom are applauded as liberals because the West hasn't gotten over thinking this is still the Khrushchev era. They are liberal cowards. Suppose, just suppose, that every writer refused to cooperate with censorship and published only in *samizdat*. Suppose that writers simply stopped submitting their manuscripts for official publication. You've been here long enough to know that literature is important in Russia. What would the authorities do? Kill every writer? They didn't manage that even in Stalin's day. And where would they produce thousands of new writers? The problem is that most Russians, official writers included, are not even capable of imagining a world without censorship. There is the fatal mistake, drummed into Soviet citizens from birth, and nothing seems able to undo it."

The other reason Dmitri does not believe significant political changes are likely is the gap between the intelligentsia and ordinary workers and peasants. "*Samizdat* involves only the intellectuals," he said. "Ordinary people accept our system of government as the only possible way to live. They have no idea of any alternatives. So there are still food shortages more than fifty years after the revolution—they think the situation is the same in every country. If the supply of food and other goods get just a little better every year, I don't see any possibility for remaking the system. The only possibility for change I see is the disintegration of the Soviet state through conflicts with

China and the alienation of non-Russian nationality groups within the country.* But I don't really believe this will happen. I doubt there will be a war with China, and even if there is, it doesn't make sense to assume that it would destroy the Soviet government. There were people who thought the last war would free Soviet society, and it was followed by a period of intense repression until Stalin's death. Even after the terror of the thirties, people rallied to save mother Russia. Besides, I also think the government would use whatever force is necessary to put down any nationalist tendencies inside our borders. I feel despair for my country."

I asked him why, if he felt such despair, he went on writing.

"Because you have to work out some personal meaning in your life even if the world around you is mad. The alternative is killing yourself, which I don't have the stomach for, or living the way I did after I left the university. That life was a slow way of killing myself, nothing more."

Despite their despair, Dmitri and Tamar live relatively normal lives. His mother gives him 100 rubles a month from her ample pension, and Tamar earns 75 rubles as a part-time research assistant in a library. She works in a foreign-language section that is closed to anyone without a special permit and has been taking English lessons from a colleague because she wants to be able to read the foreign books. Dmitri works six or seven hours every day when he is not going through one of his "sleeping weeks." To make extra money, he occasionally tutors high school students for university entrance exams; he makes 25 rubles for an hour's session. (Parents who can afford private coaches for the exams often hire them to boost their children's chances of being admitted to a university. This is another aspect of the parallel economy.)

Dmitri and Tamar do not live like pigs anymore. Their one room is scrupulously clean, filled with some Georgian antiques

---

* Andrei Amalrik suggests this possibility in *Will the Soviet Union Survive Until 1984?* Dmitri may have read a *samizdat* copy.

and furniture Tamar's mother gave them. They always keep flowers in the house, no matter how short of money they may be. Because of the money from Dmitri's mother, they do not live in poverty. Many of the *samizdat* writers are too poor to afford milk and sausage, much less flowers. One thing Dmitri does with his money is help friends who are poorer than he is. "We give each other moral support," he said. "When they are going through their own 'sleeping weeks,' I try to pull them out of it. They do the same for me. When things get too bad, we give a party and try to laugh."

I heard my first Soviet *anekdot* (joke, usually with a political flavor) at a party given by Dmitri. The figures in the joke were never accurate and it is not politically outdated, but its bite was typical of underground political humor. Brezhnev and Mao Tsetung have a meeting to discuss Sino-Soviet disagreements. Mao says to Brezhnev, "Leonid Ilyich, you should begin to worry about us more because we are seven hundred million and you are only two hundred and forty million."

Says Brezhnev: "Do you remember the Six-Day War?"

"Of course, Leonid Ilyich."

"And how many Israelis were there?"

"One million, Leonid Ilyich."

"And how many Arabs?"

"Six hundred million, Leonid Ilyich."

"Well, in Russia we have three million Jews. So who should be afraid, Chairman Mao?"

Dmitri, who was not Jewish, pointed out to me that much Russian humor either resembles Yiddish folk humor or is concerned with Jews themselves, as in the Brezhnev-Mao joke. "That's probably because such a high proportion of the creative intellectuals, including the comedians, are Jews. Of course, there's also an old Russian tradition of anti-Semitic humor, if you want to call it that. Even some of the anti-Semitic jokes sound Jewish, though. All you'd have to do is switch the villain around and they'd make a perfect anti-Russian joke. We do it all the time."

Dmitri and Tamar had no plans to get married, because they never expected to have any children. Dmitri's feelings on the subject were the opposite of Gyusel Amalrik's. "We don't feel we have any right to bring children to life in a society like this," he said. "We are outcasts, by our own choice. But I wouldn't want to force this life on a child."

I asked Dmitri if he would emigrate if it were possible, given his belief that no change is likely and his inability to accommodate his work to the system. "No," he said firmly. "I'm becoming more political, almost against my will. I've been influenced by the example of people who have gone to prison for the right to say what they believe. I don't think change is likely, but deep inside me there is still a tiny hope. The novel I hope to do about fathers and sons—well, I hope I'll have the courage to sign my real name to it. That would be a step forward."

XI

Unfinished Conversations

ONE OF THE MOST COMMON and painful experiences for a foreigner in the Soviet Union is meeting a Russian he likes very much and realizing that no genuine friendship is possible. It can be as simple and final as sitting down next to a young mother on a park bench, talking for several hours and parting without exchanging last names or telephone numbers. Or the experience can be extremely complex, as in tenuous relationships with writers and other official intellectuals. They simultaneously offer and withhold friendship. They may invite you to their homes and even come to yours, but they conceal their most important thoughts about politics, art, love and life itself. The casual park-bench acquaintance and the intellectuals are both apprehensive about the possible consequences of opening their lives to a foreigner; they simply draw the line in different places. Russians possess powerful internal controls on friendships with people from other countries that are attributable only in part to fear of official disapproval. "Deep in our hearts, it isn't only worry about how 'they' might react," a writer told me. "We don't really trust you not to betray us. Betray us to whom, I couldn't say. This distrust is inside us; it doesn't come from the outside. It's older than Stalin, older than Communism, maybe even older than the czars."

There is an infinite sadness in such contacts. On a spring day, we took our dog for a run in Lenin Hills, a popular park near Moscow State University. We heard the sounds of an English church service coming from a radio and walked over to investigate. A man and two attractive young women, all of them English teachers, were listening to a BBC Easter broadcast. We walked and talked for several hours and gave them a ride home in our Chevrolet—their curiosity about the car obviously outweighing any nervousness about its conspicuous appearance. I told one of the women that I was particularly interested in Soviet schools because I had been an education reporter in America for several years. She took my phone number and said she was sure she could arrange an invitation for me to visit the special foreign-language high school where she taught. But she did not give me her phone number or address—a sure sign that a Russian has no intention of seeing you again, regardless of what he may be saying at the time.

The three teachers carefully had us drop them off at the entrance to their large apartment complex so we would not know exactly where they lived. We parted with promises to meet again soon, and my husband and I drove away with the certain knowledge that we would never see them again. We always hoped our predictions would prove wrong, but they seldom did.

Our experience with the teachers in the park was duplicated over and over in Moscow and other parts of the Soviet Union. But we were even more frustrated by relationships with Russians that ended abruptly just when it seemed to us that a genuine rapport had been established.

Isak Borisovich Piratsky

Isak Borisovich Piratsky (his real name) is the principal of a ten-grade school with more than 900 students between the ages of seven and seventeen. Our experience with him is a perfect example of a friendly contact with a Russian that was disrupted by forces we could not control.

Our trip to Piratsky's school, No. 607, was arranged by the press department of the Foreign Ministry after nearly six months of repeated requests to visit educational institutions. It is impossible to drop in at a school without authorization from

the press department, which in turn must make its own bureaucratic arrangements with the Ministry of Education. The appropriate officials selected School 607 for our visit; we had simply asked to visit any elementary and secondary school. Soviet
academic schools have ten grades, and they are usually housed
in the same building.

When we met Piratsky, we decided it had been worth the
wait and wrangling with the press department. Energetic and
ebullient at sixty-two, he looked at least ten years younger. As
we talked in his office, we were interrupted frequently by
knocks on the door from students and teachers who wanted him
to mediate the predictable daily hassles of a large school. A
short, bull-necked man, Piratsky was constantly in motion and
moved lightly on his feet despite his bulk. He told us he kept
physically fit by swimming regularly, summer and winter, in a
heated outdoor pool. Although he had been a school principal
for twenty-five years, he displayed none of the bureaucratic
torpor that usually affects officials who have held their positions for that length of time.

On one visit, he received us in his office with cakes and
oranges. He described something of his background as he sec-
tioned the oranges with a vigor more appropriate to carving a
tough piece of meat.

Piratsky was born in Byelorussia but spent most of his youth
in Leningrad. "I'm a life-long Communist. I was a teacher for
two years and then I went to work as a Komsomol organizer in
Leningrad. During the 1930's, I came to work in Moscow and
set up youth cadres that were sent throughout the country,
wherever they were needed. I was especially concerned with
the cadres involved in education. I worked for Bubnov." (He
was referring to Andrei Bubnov, the People's Commissar for
Education who was arrested in 1937 and reportedly executed in
1940. Bubnov was a respected old Bolshevik, a member of the
Party for many years before the revolution.)

Piratsky's offhand reference to Bubnov was unusual; most
Soviet officials who were around during the Stalin years tend to

avoid mentioning comrades who were purged. Piratsky was a blunt, self-confident man who obviously did not find it necessary to censor every memory. I wondered what he and Boris Alekseivich, who had also been a Komsomol organizer, would have had to say to each other. They started along the same path in the 1920's; it would have been interesting to know why one disappeared into the camps and the other escaped the fate that befell so many of his colleagues. But I could never have introduced them to each other. An unbreakable rule in relations between Russians and foreigners is that the foreigner never brings two Russians together unless he is certain they already know and trust each other.

To meet a civil servant who had lived through the Stalin years and remained human was a revelation to us; most bureaucrats of Piratsky's age with whom we came in contact seemed to have no passions left save one for self-preservation through mediocrity. Piratsky was something new in our experience: a dedicated Communist who would have been a first-rate administrator in any country, a man who had lived through the most shameful years of his country's history and neither condoned nor apologized for them, a professional who was, above everything else, devoted to developing happy and educated young people within the framework of Soviet society.

"I had been a director* for only two years in Moscow when the war broke out," he said. "I served in the Red Army until 1948—I was in the occupation troops in East Prussia. When I returned to Moscow, I took over this school. It was only for boys then. The problems were particularly difficult, because these boys had been running wild in the streets with no supervision throughout the war years. They were very tough; they were the products of a society disrupted by war. Most of them were above the normal age for being in school. I think we eventually succeeded with most of them through a combination of firm discipline and convincing them that we really cared

---

* A school principal is a *direktor* in Russia.

about their lives. One without the other is no good, then or now.

"But the situation is entirely different today. Today's children have not lived through revolution or war; they have been secure throughout their lives. Their minds are hungrier than those of earlier generations; they start school in first grade with much more information than children had twenty years ago. That's why I don't believe you can go on teaching the same way for a quarter of a century."

Piratsky said although he had been a principal himself for nearly twenty-five years, he believed that "people can stay in their jobs too long." He said school officials should be removed from their jobs "if they absolutely refuse to entertain any new ideas, or if they go along so grudgingly that no new idea can work where they are in charge."

When we visited School 607, Piratsky and his teachers were involved in a major departure from the traditional Soviet school program. In the autumn of 1970, a new curriculum was authorized for schools throughout the nation. Its basic aim was to teach children to think rather than simply to memorize. Piratsky's school had been a testing ground for the curriculum for seven years, from the earliest experimental stage through its approval for national use. A standard curriculum for use in all Soviet schools is laid down by the central Ministry of Education. There are variations between schools in different republics, but they are also taken into account in the central plan. Despite the centralization, Russian schools do vary greatly in quality—dependent, as in other countries, mainly on the caliber of each school's staff. This is a factor the central government cannot control, although it would like to. "We used to just stuff facts down children. We gave them the rules for getting a right answer. Now we try to teach them to understand how they arrive at an answer. It isn't easy to accomplish such a basic change in our approach to teaching.

"Many members of our staff were very much opposed to the new curriculum when we started working with it and, to be honest, some of them are still opposed. But a good many of them have come to see the advantages of thinking over pure memorization. We had one teacher who stood up at a meeting and vowed she would quit before she would work under the new program, but now she says she doesn't know why we didn't begin it earlier."

Unlike many other Soviet educators whom I had interviewed about the new curriculum, Piratsky spoke frankly about the problems connected with it. After a brief period of experimentation in the twenties, the Soviet educational system became one of the most authoritarian in the world. In discipline and teaching methods, the schools of the Stalin era resembled those of both czarist Russia and imperial Germany. The current curriculum reform is an attempt to modernize both teaching methods and subject matter. It is not a 180-degree turn from the old system, but it is a significant change by Soviet standards. "A great many teachers and directors are simply convinced that the children can't cope with the new material," Piratsky said. "For example, the introduction of certain elements of algebra and geometry in first and second grade has proved difficult. The idea that children can't absorb this sometimes becomes a reality simply because the professional educators think it is so. In Moscow alone, about 2,000 children are performing below the standard of work set for first grade. I believe this stems not from a child's inability to learn but from our difficulties in teaching them. For the new curriculum to work, a primary school teacher must be a truly educated person himself."

Like most school principals in the Soviet Union, Piratsky taught some classes himself each week. The practice is one that American schools would do well to adopt; it helps keep administrators in touch with everyday classroom problems. Piratsky strongly resembled the minority of dedicated teachers and principals I knew in America who never gave up the battle against apathy and mediocrity in large urban school bureaucracies.

A visit to Piratsky's school was a sharp contrast to the stuffy guided tours foreigners usually receive in Soviet institutions. In other schools, I had been whisked in and out of classrooms by the principal and watched nervous children recite lessons they had memorized to impress foreign guests. As we toured School 607, Piratsky introduced me to teachers but left me by myself to observe classes that particularly interested me. He encouraged me to direct some of my questions not to him but to the teachers, and he did not stick by my side while they answered.

At the end of our first visit, Piratsky invited us to return at any time. I told him as an education reporter in America I preferred to attend the same classes several days in a row so that the teacher and students would stop thinking about my presence. "I don't see why we couldn't do that here, with a teacher who agreed," he said. His casual invitation was another contrast to the usual prearranged visits; Soviet officials tend to sigh with visible and audible relief when foreign visitors walk out the door.

A few weeks later, we took Piratsky up on his invitation and brought along some photographs we had taken on our first visit. During that session, our conversation touched on a wide range of subjects.

Piratsky's salary was 300 rubles a month, partly because he took on an unusually heavy class load each week in addition to his administrative duties. An ordinary Soviet teacher with twenty years experience makes 200 rubles a month. The basic starting salary while we were in Moscow was 95 rubles; after ten years, it went up to 105 rubles. (The salary scale may have gone up slightly since that time.) The salary is for a twenty-four-hour teaching week in grades one through three and an eighteen-hour week in grades four through ten. Teachers who take on extra classes and nonteaching duties receive more money. While the overwhelming majority of teachers are women, principals tend to be men. Piratsky said one explanation was the relatively small salary differential between a principal and a teacher with twenty years of experience.

"Since women still have the primary responsibility for the

family—it's true, they do have a heavy burden—many don't feel the salary increase is worth the time a principal's job takes from their husbands and children.

"A principal is on call all the time, like a doctor. If a boy gets into trouble with the militia [police] the local militia post can say the principal wasn't looking out for his students. One night after a dance, we had an incident in which some boys got mixed up with a drunk who was carrying a sack of empty bottles. The boys grabbed the sack and took the bottles to the place where you get a refund for them. The police picked up both the kids and the drunk. We had a parents' meeting, conferences with the police—you get into all of these things if you're a principal.

"But a school can only do so much. We can't shield our boys and girls from whatever influences them on the street. We can't take the place of the home."

The discipline problems in a high school like Piratsky's would seem insignificant to an American principal. Sexual assaults, gunplay or knife fights in the halls of a Russian city school are virtually unknown. "Well, sometimes a boy will pinch a girl on her bottom," Piratsky said with a grin. "But that's about as far as it goes." Nor are Soviet schools plagued by the expensive vandalism that is a common occurrence in affluent suburban American high schools.

Piratsky said the low-keyed nature of discipline problems is due to the fact that most parents "have a deep respect for education. They will make a scene anywhere else, but not in a school. They back us up. Without question, our system of public education is one of the best things Soviet society has produced."

Piratsky offered me a second orange, which prompted my husband to ask why the Soviet Union could not manage to transport more fruits and vegetables from the warmer regions of the country to northern cities in winter. "Well, I remember when there wasn't an apple to be seen in Moscow, much less a lemon or an orange. Almost immediately after Stalin's death, a lot of fruit began coming into Moscow. I think our government wanted to make a gesture to show that life was going to be better. So now you have oranges in Moscow throughout much of the winter, even if the distribution problem isn't entirely solved. As a foreigner, you have no standard of comparison with the way things used to be."

Piratsky had not been in the West but he had traveled extensively in Eastern Europe. He was full of questions about the United States, especially about American schools. My husband's father, a teacher in the New York City public school system for forty years, was planning to visit us in the spring. "You must bring him here," Piratsky said. "I'm sure we would have a great deal to say to each other."

Piratsky was Jewish, and he questioned us about the activities of the Jewish Defense League. He said one of his swimming companions played with a Soviet orchestra that had just returned from America and their concert in New York had been disrupted by the JDL. (During that period, the JDL was interfering with performances of Soviet artists by throwing stink bombs, shouting obscenities and employing other equally genteel tactics.) "I don't understand this," Piratsky said. "No American artists would ever be treated this way in our country, whatever differences we might have with American policies on any subject. It's just hooliganism."

We did not know Piratsky well enough for a frank discussion of the problems of Soviet Jews, but we said emphatically that we disapproved of the JDL's tactics. We parted cordially, and Piratsky again repeated his invitation for us to return. "And please don't forget," he told my husband warmly, "I will be very happy to meet your father." We drove away, arguing about whether it would place Piratsky in an awkward position if we invited him to dinner.

In February, we phoned and asked if we could make another visit to the school. This was the period of Soviet retaliation against American residents of Moscow for JDL activities in the United States, as well as heavy harassment of correspondents who had contacts with activist Jews and political dissidents.

When we phoned Piratsky, he said we would have to make another formal request to the press department before coming to see him again.

We made the request and several weeks later, to our immense surprise, we were told an appointment had been arranged. A few days later, an official from the American section of the press department called and said Piratsky had "changed his mind." He could not allow us to visit his school again for fear that any information he gave us might be "misused or distorted."

The press department official told us, "You can call him yourself if you don't believe me." The incident followed an article in the newspaper *Trud* in which supposedly irate readers (most of them with Jewish last names) called for Tony's expulsion from the Soviet Union on grounds that he wrote distorted pro-Zionist stories about Soviet Jews.

We decided not to phone Piratsky again, but we did send him a copy of an article I had written on the new curriculum. It described his school in highly favorable terms, and we added a note saying we hoped he did not feel his earlier information had been "misused."

Piratsky had obviously been warned through some official or quasi-official channel that it was inadvisable to receive us at his school again. The KGB and the Soviet bureaucracy are particularly self-defeating when they prevent foreign correspondents from talking to men like Piratsky. We had been extremely impressed, both by his forthright personality and his school.

Soviet officials are responsible for forcing correspondents into a world in which the only Russians who will speak freely to them are political dissidents with nothing to lose. The policy is consistent: If a journalist writes about topics the authorities frown upon—like dissent or friction between nationalities—he will have little or no opportunity to meet Russians who project a favorable image of their society. The Soviets have no concept of how to publicize what correspondents can legitimately describe as the positive aspects of Soviet life. *They* supplied the sour ending to the story of Isaak Borisovich Piratsky and his fine school.

Nina

Nina, a sulky, greedy girl with a fair amount of sex appeal, was hardly a representative of the best Soviet society had to offer—however one defined "the best." She hung around the fringes of both the foreign colony and the intellectual-artistic world in Moscow, hoping to improve her social and economic standing. She used her acquaintances in each world to gain entrée into the other. She had contacts within the lowest, least interesting circles of the Soviet "creative intelligentsia," but she dangled them effectively before foreigners hungry for any taste of Russian life. Nina's acquaintances within the foreign ghetto were attractive bait for her arty Russian friends, because knowing someone who knew a foreigner afforded the possibility of material enticements from the capitalist world.

Nina was an Intourist guide who spoke fluent Russian, Latvian and Czech. Her contacts with foreigners were so lacking in the caution Soviet citizens usually exercise that it seemed highly likely she worked for the KGB as a sideline. However, her indiscretions could conceivably have been attributed solely to greed. She also had all the markings of a pathological liar; it was impossible to make a reasoned assessment of her character because her stories so often contradicted each other.

I bother to write about Nina only because she typified in many respects the Russians whom foreigners are most likely to meet. Her acquaintances are mainly among the journalists, because diplomats would have immediately suspected her of wanting to entrap them in a blackmail situation. Journalists are less blackmailable; some are bachelors and, in any case, foreign offices tend to lay out a stricter moral code of conduct for their employees than newspapers do. The fact that Nina had as many foreign acquaintances as she did testified eloquently to the desperation of foreigners for some contact—any contact—with

Russians. Long after I had discovered her dullness and dishonesty. I continued to see her out of journalistic curiosity. I stopped meeting her when she phoned me (she knew that the phone was tapped) and asked me to do something for her that was illegal.

Nina was a feline creature with something of the starved attractiveness of a Western fashion model. She had smoky gray-green eyes, which were her best feature, and long blond hair that had suffered from too much teasing. She would have preferred a curvier figure but was unable to gain weight. "Anyway," she said disdainfully, "I'd rather be as flat as a boy than look like a potato, the way most Russian girls do." Her thinness was appealing to the few Western bachelors who were adventurous enough to date Russian girls. Young women in Moscow are far more diet- and fashion-conscious than their mothers, but they still tend to be chunky by Western standards.

I met Nina for the first time in the apartment of a correspondent who had a sizable stable of Russian girlfriends. She was dressed in plaid bell-bottomed pants, obviously an acquisition from the West. I later learned that she possessed a large collection of clothes culled from her foreign contacts. She said she was frightened of the guards at their posts in the foreigners' compound, but she was not too frightened to walk from one man's apartment to another's.

I wanted to see Nina again. She was twenty-seven, and at that time I had few women friends in Moscow who were close to my own age. She did not give me her phone number or last name, but she eventually phoned and asked me to meet her. She wanted more than my companionship: Her first request was that I buy her a coat in a foreign-currency store. She offered to pay me four rubles for every dollar I spent on the coat; she had done her homework, because she knew exactly what sizes and colors were available. Soviet officials at the entrance to foreign-currency stores usually prevent Russians from entering, unless they have special identification showing they work for foreigners and are entitled to receive some payments in hard-currency coupons. When I was wearing my shabbiest dog-walking coat, I was sometimes stopped and asked what nationality I was. Since Nina's clothes were not typically Russian, she probably would have been able to get by the guard to look over the merchandise. She would not have been able to buy anything herself, though, because procedures for detecting Russians at the cash register are more thorough. It used to be relatively easy to evade the rules in the stores, but there was a crackdown on violators during our second year in Moscow. I told Nina I could not possibly agree to take four rubles for a dollar, since I had no desire to profiteer from my friendships with Russians. She seemed surprised; of course, she had not thought of me as a friend.

Nina had managed to pique my journalistic curiosity, though, and we agreed to meet again. At our next rendezvous, she was accompanied by a girlfriend "who just happened to be walking down the street." The other girl's desires were more modest than Nina's—she only wanted a dress from the foreign-currency store. When my reaction was less than enthusiastic, Nina said, "Oh, please don't worry about it. I just want to be your friend." In a sudden burst of confidence, she said that she had just quit her job with a publisher because her boss was making sexual advances to her and she found him too repellent to sleep with. Then she moved to the next stage of her campaign with me. Could I introduce her to any foreign bachelors, preferably an American or an Englishman? "Russian men are absolute pigs," she said firmly, as our Russian taxi driver stared straight ahead. "I could bring you an icon if you'd introduce me to someone."

I did introduce Nina to a bachelor (without taking the icon in return), and I warned him in advance that her sincerity was highly doubtful. She told me she was born in Riga of a Russian father and a mother who was half Latvian and half Russian. She said she had lived in Moscow only four years; she had obtained her permit to live in the city by marrying and divorcing a young man in a commercial deal. Such deals are common and illegal; they are based on the fact that anyone who marries a Moscow resident automatically receives a lifetime Moscow residence permit. A boy or girl from the provinces who does not have the right to live in Moscow pays several hundred rubles for the privilege of marrying a Muscovite. The marriage is followed by a speedy divorce, divorces by mutual consent being easily obtainable. The marriage racketeer keeps his matrimonial fee, the provincial boy or girl has the Moscow residence permit and everyone is happy. The Soviet press has carried exposés of marriage racketeers who were caught; they were usually married and divorced several times a year, escaping detection by registering each marriage in a different Moscow district. "I suppose some people even fall in love in these cases," Nina said. "That didn't happen to me. I was only married six months." She was desperate to leave Riga because it was "so boring." She said Riga was a much more beautiful city than Moscow (I agreed with her) but that she preferred the capital because "the rhythm of life is so much faster here." Her lively experiences in Moscow had included three abortions in four years. Unlike Vera, Nina did not attach any particular significance to abortion. "It's the easiest way to take care of the problem," she said.

I later learned Nina had told my bachelor friend quite a different version of her life story. She said her father had been the director of a science center in Novosibirsk concerned with developing guidance systems for missiles and satellites. With such a prominent father, she of course had no difficulty obtaining a permit to live in Moscow. She said she had never worked a day in her life until her father died two years ago. Although the story she told me may also have been laced with fabrications, I am sure it was closer to the truth than the one she told my friend. Her cultural and intellectual interests were extremely limited, which contradicted the story that she came from a well-educated family. Also, the daughter of an important scientist would have had a secure position in the world of the Soviet intelligentsia; Nina chased foreigners and third-rate Russian artists in a way that revealed her insecurity.

She was not articulate about anything except her desire for clothes; she was uncomfortable if conversations with foreigners turned to any serious discussions about the Soviet Union. She said she had never read Solzhenitsyn and was not interested in him. "Why think about all those things that happened so long ago? They don't concern me." (Such statements also suggested that she could not have been the daughter of a scientist. Novosibirsk and other science centers are well known as centers of intellectual ferment concerned with topics ranging from Solzhenitsyn to official restrictions on the international contacts of Soviet scientists. If she had lived in an intellectual-scientific community, she could not have been so indifferent to political and social issues.) Nina said she did not even care for establishment liberal poets like Yevtushenko and Voznesensky. She enjoyed ballet, but only classical productions. She did not like or understand modern dance. As a translator, she said she had no idea whether Russian was a beautiful language because she had used it all her life.

She admired my clothes and the furniture in my apartment in extravagant terms. To another acquaintance, she said, "In Russia, we aren't interested in apartments and clothes and things like that. We are a more spiritual people."

Nina took me to the studio of a mediocre official artist with whom she obviously had some type of arrangement to help snare foreign customers. She expressed disappointment when I said politely that his paintings were interesting but did not appeal enough to my personal taste for me to buy one. Perhaps she would have received a commission. And yet, she had a pathetic side that made it impossible to dislike her completely. When I complimented her on a new hairdo, she said, "If I were in the West, would anyone think I was pretty?" I said yes, and her face lit up with one of the rare genuine smiles she ever produced. She regarded her looks as her only asset and was disappointed when they did not prove a valuable enough commodity to assure her social standing in Moscow, which is to the rest of the Soviet Union in cruelty and competitiveness as New York is to the rest of the United States.

Nina badgered all of her foreign acquaintances ceaselessly, especially the men. Once she phoned a current lover and told him she owned two antique French plates that had been in the family since Napoleon's unsuccessful invasion of Russia. She wanted to give the man one plate as a token of her affection, "so that even when we're apart we'll be eating from the same dishes." At the same time, she was trying to persuade the man to buy her a maxicoat when he made a trip out to the West. When the man said no, the maxicoat was definitely out, she phoned me and made the same request. I refused and told her I never wanted to see her again. She phoned a second time and I hung up on her. During an entire year, I never learned her last name.

I felt guilty at first, because I had continued to see her out of journalistic interest even though I knew she was a greedy liar, however pathetic. A Russian friend who did not know Nina but said she knew many girls who fitted my description of her made me feel less guilty about my abrupt termination of our acquaintance. "This whole group of people preys on foreigners," she said. "I know the artist she took you to see, and he's the same way. They don't care about you; they'd never give you an honest answer about anything. You know Russians who are real people. Why waste your time here on people who would be worthless anywhere else in the world?"

Konstantin Aleksandrovich

Konstantin Aleksandrovich arrived at our apartment with a flourish and wagged a finger at Sasha, our trembling terrier who was barking at him from beneath the safety of a sofa. "I understand you have beauty salons for dogs in Europe and America," he said. "Here, I am the salon." His tone would have been appropriate to *"l'état, c'est moi."*

I immediately recognized Konstantin Aleksandrovich as a "dog person"—a classification that covers a multitude of eccentricities in any country. In his mid-forties, he sported a jaunty pair of sideburns that he said had been the same length for ten years. He had worn them when they were unfashionable, he said, but he had no intention of growing them any longer or thicker now that they were coming into vogue.

He was a senior official of the Moscow Hunting Dog Society, which includes terriers, spaniels, setters and a variety of Russian hunting breeds like the famed borzoi. Terriers were his specialty, and everyone in Moscow who owned a terrier seemed to know Konstantin Aleksandrovich. He gave haircuts to most of the registered terriers in Moscow, judged them at dog shows and was also involved in the introduction of new terrier breeds into the Soviet Union. He was a professional who resembled Anatoly Yakovlevich more than any other Russian I knew. Anatoly was a master with picture frames; Konstantin Aleksandrovich was a master with dogs.

Our dog, Sasha, was a Lakeland terrier; we had bought him in Finland and driven him in across the Finnish-Soviet border. A Lakeland, if one is ignorant about distinctions between terriers, is about the same size as a wire-haired fox terrier but somewhat slimmer and racier in appearance. Sasha grew shaggier and shaggier during our first winter in Moscow, but he needed the hair to protect him from the cold. A haircut began to seem imperative when the ice melted in April and it was impossible to see Sasha's eyes. I had no idea where to take him because, as Konstantin Aleksandrovich said, there were no beauty parlors for dogs in Moscow.

One day I saw a Russian woman walking down the street with a beautifully groomed fox terrier and I asked her where he got his haircut. She gave me the phone number of the Hunting Dog Society and said, "There's this wonderful man there named Konstantin Aleksandrovich."

Konstantin Aleksandrovich agreed to take on Sasha as a client, and an appointment for a haircut was speedily arranged. He came to our apartment to do the job, as he did to Russian homes. (I only saw him in his official capacity, so there was no reason to disguise his identity. Konstantin Aleksandrovich is his real name.) Despite the dog's nervousness, Konstantin wielded a steady hand with the clippers. When Sasha became obstreperous, he would call him Aleksandr in a stern voice. ("Sasha" is the Russian diminutive for "Aleksandr." Such diminutives have endless variations. Sasha was usually Sashinka—little Sasha—to Russian friends. On occasion, he was Sashulichka—little little Sasha. The same endearments are applied to children.)

As he turned the reluctant Sasha into a thing of beauty, Konstantin Aleksandrovich told me that dogs were a reliable index to the prosperity of Soviet society. The dog population of European Russia was virtually wiped out during the war; in territory that was occupied or besieged by the Germans, dogs either starved along with or were eaten by their masters. In Leningrad, no dogs and cats were left after the Nazi siege. "I always had a dog, even during the hardest years," Konstantin said. "I had a fox terrier with me when I was a soldier at the front."

When foreign tourists began to visit the Soviet Union in large numbers after Stalin's death, they often commented on the absence of pets. During the past five years, the number of dogs has risen dramatically, although it does not yet begin to approach the canine density in Western cities. More than 10,000 pedigreed dogs—an increase of over 70 percent since 1965—are registered with Moscow's two main dog clubs. The Decorative Dog Club is for poodles and other fancy breeds. The demand for dogs is much greater than the supply; people must sometimes place their names on waiting lists for several years before they receive a purebred puppy. A mongrel is easy to buy; a lively pet trade is carried on each Sunday in a square known as the bird market. "We can't build up the purebred stock fast enough for all of the people who want dogs," said Konstantin Aleksandrovich with the air of a man who had seen his idea's time arrive. "After the war we had to start all over again. We brought in dogs from other countries and are still doing that to broaden the selection of breeds. My dream is that the Soviet Union will become a member of the International Association of Kennel Clubs. Before that, we have to build suitable facilities for an international dog show. I'm really looking forward to that day, but I don't know when it will be. A ring for dog shows doesn't exactly have high priority on the construction lists."

The increase in Moscow dogs is directly related to the growing number of separate apartments. "Just try to keep a barking dog in a flat you share with five other families. The neighbors will all hate you," said one woman who was walking her fox terrier around the ring at a dog show where Konstantin Aleksandrovich was the head judge. "I got my dog as soon as I received my new apartment two years ago."

Konstantin Aleksandrovich said he lived in a relatively new apartment with his wife, Lyubov, and their two fox terriers. He was happy that Moscow was building new apartments in rings of suburbs with "green belts," because it provided better space for walking dogs than high-rise construction. He and his wife both worked, and he assured me that I should not worry about the dog when I returned to a full-time job in the United States because "terriers sleep all day." Lyubov, a slim blonde who was as energetic and dog-happy as her husband, played an important role in one of the minor catastrophes of our stay in Moscow —an attempt at mating Sasha.

Konstantin Aleksandrovich and I agreed that Sasha desperately needed a mate, since he had entered adolescence. But finding a mate for your dog is a long and arduous process if you are an American living in Moscow. Russians are not particularly eager to mate their dogs with foreigners. Pedigrees are taken seriously by the owners of registered dogs; a foreigner in the family tree can create problems when Soviet documents are needed to prove that the puppy is the purebred descendant of a champion. The obvious alternative, a passing mutt with a friendly disposition, is not feasible. Because the demand for dogs still greatly exceeds supply, there are virtually no strays. Russians take exceptionally good care of their pets, and a mating must be carefully prearranged.

Konstantin Aleksandrovich agreed to help in the search. He made a survey and discovered that there were no other Lakelands in Moscow. However, he thought a satisfactory mating might be achieved with a wire-haired fox. He spent several months and a good deal of care looking for the mate. One April night, Lyubov telephoned and said she thought the mating could take place the next day.

I was to meet the owners of the female fox terrier on the street; it was important that we size each other up before our dogs laid eyes on each other. They turned out to be an attractive pair of students and their dog was a great-granddaughter of one of Konstantin's fox terriers. We liked each other and proceeded to my apartment.

An important point on dog mating in Moscow: Since nearly everyone lives in apartments, there are no enclosed yards. Matings must take place indoors.

The female terrier, named Dasha, was set loose to explore our apartment while Sasha was locked in a bedroom. If Dasha had found the surroundings unpleasant, it would not have been a propitious omen for the mating. But everything was to her liking.

Enter Sasha.

"Ah," breathed Lyubov and Dasha's owners, "they would make beautiful puppies together." Lyubov had remained with us to supervise the mating, as April was Konstantin's busiest haircutting season and he had been delayed. Sasha, terrified at seeing several strange people, immediately crawled under the lowest available couch.

I suggested that we leave the room, fearing that Sasha and Dasha would never get acquainted if they were inhibited by human companions. Lyubov seemed upset. I did not understand why, because my Russian was weak on technical dog-mating terminology, Dasha's mistress spoke some English, but her English dog-mating vocabulary was as weak as my Russian. As soon as we left the room, Sasha came out from under the couch and began to wag his tail at Dasha. I was optimistic when they began rubbing noses, but Lyubov still looked doubtful. Then I realized the reason for her concern.

Sasha simply did not know what to do, although he was eager to try.

Lyubov explained that dogs often need human guidance in their first mating experience. Sasha began by doing all the right things but failed at the crucial juncture when it was necessary for a human to hold the female in the proper position. When we approached and tried to provide the necessary help, he ran away. He would make a poor subject for Masters and Johnson.

After two hours, Dasha became frustrated and impatient; she began to growl at Sasha whenever he approached. Sasha, his masculine pride wounded, retreated under the sofa for the last time. Dasha's owners, Lyubov and I were all more distraught than the dogs.

Konstantin Aleksandrovich arrived, surveyed the situation with a master's eye and said, "It's useless."

We all retired to the study for much-needed gin-and-tonics while Konstantin gave Sasha his spring haircut. He consoled the trembling dog in a soothing voice. "When you're older some day, this will all seem funny to you, Sasha. You'll be sitting around talking to your old friends and their tongues will be hanging out as you tell them, 'Ooh, la, la, you should have seen this gorgeous Russian madame they brought me and I—well, I wasn't even interested. But you should see what a beauty I turned down.' The other dogs will drool. Some day, Sasha, that's what you'll say."

The mismating was the last time I saw Konstantin Aleksandrovich before my husband and I left Moscow. Our conversations were not cut short by any outside interference; dogs are apparently an acceptable area of international cooperation. I was sad only because the unspoken barriers made it impossible to discuss anything but our mutual interest in dogs. I have a soft spot in my heart for Konstantin Aleksandrovich and his wife; my experiences with the "dog people" are among my warmest memories of Moscow.

The "Creative Intelligentsia"

At a premiere of a new work by the Soviet composer Rodion Shchedrin, we ran into a writer and his wife who had been at our house for dinner only a week before. We greeted each other cordially and began talking about the Shchedrin composition, which was something of a departure from the general run of contemporary Soviet music. Some Russian friends saw the writer and came over to say hello; he and his wife immediately turned their backs on us, declining to introduce us or include us in their conversation. The incident was typical of relationships between foreigners and Russians who are members of the "creative intelligentsia"—writers, musicians, actors, dancers, theatrical directors, a few scholars.

The limited nature of our friendships with official intellectuals was particularly frustrating, because they were the kind of people we would have come to know easily in any Western country. They were adventurous enough to see us occasionally in public restaurants or even in their homes, but they were so cautious about what they said that we left each meeting with a sense of intense frustration. Voznesensky or Yevtushenko might talk for hours, but we would realize at the end that they had said nothing we could not have learned from reading an official biographical sketch. In his introduction to Nadezhda Mandelstam's book, Russian literature professor Clarence Brown writes that "foreign visitors to the Soviet Union seldom realize how possible it is to meet people there without, in a sense, Meeting them. Very distinguished visitors have made this mistake. In fact, the more distinguished they are, alas, the more likely they are to be fooled, for the effort expended on them will be much greater. Nor does the effort cost very much. The role of Poet's Widow, Rebellious Young Poet, Disloyal Journalist, etc., etc., are all too practiced to fail often of their goal." Soviet officials do not regard most foreign journalists as distinguished visitors, so no effort was expended to fool us. I never had a capital-letter Meeting with a member of the creative intelligentsia; I could not have done a full-length profile of any of the poets or actors or other well-known personages we met. There were none of the tears I shared with Gyusel, or the laughter with Yosif and Marina or even the groping for understanding that took place with Galya.

Fear is omnipresent when official intellectuals associate with foreigners—fear that any association would reflect badly on the Russian if a foreign friend fell afoul of the authorities, fear that the outsider might indiscreetly repeat a confidence. Fear, also, that someone who lives in Russia and speaks Russian cannot be as easily deceived as a visitor, should a deception become necessary.

The fear was responsible for an endless string of broken dates, evasive conversations and minor insults like being ignored in public. The official intellectuals evaporated when we were subjected to heavy KGB harassment, leaving only the handful of Russian friends who really cared about us as people.

I phoned one actress whom I met just before we went away for Christmas vacation in 1970, and she sounded delighted to hear my voice. She invited me to her flat for lunch and offered me a spread of beef, chopped liver, *pirozhki* (meat pastries) and Hungarian wine. I wanted to discuss a personal matter with her and asked her outright if she felt we could speak freely in the apartment. She laughed and said, "If we couldn't, my husband and I would have been sent to Siberia long ago." A week later, Tony had further troubles with the KGB, and the account was broadcast back in Russian on the VOA. The report may also have gotten around Moscow via the grapevine, which in Russian is known as the OBS news service. (The initials stand for *odna baba skazala*, literally, "an old woman from the country said. . . .") When I phoned the actress again to confirm a prearranged appointment, her voice was cool and she said she had to go to the country for some time. I never saw her again.

Some foreigners in Moscow excused all of this behavior on grounds that "you can't judge a Russian if you're not a Russian." I often felt that they cared as little about the Russians as their Russian acquaintances cared about them; all some correspondents wanted from the official intellectuals was a tip on when the next interesting new ballet or play was scheduled for production. Friends make commitments to and demands on each other; to exclude Russians from normal standards was to classify them simply as freakish objects of curiosity. Just before I left Moscow, I told a young woman who wrote children's books, "I really would have liked to have been your friend." Her voice breaking, she replied, "If this were any other country, any other country, I would have done more for you. I would have introduced you to people—you would have liked my friends." These kinds of unfinished conversations are important not because of my disappointments but because they are part of the spiritual repression that is still such an important factor in Russian life. The list of topics we were unable to discuss with our friends among the official intellectuals seemed endless.

We could not, for example, have an honest conversation about Soviet literature with any of the writers we knew. One poet told us in his apartment that Solzhenitsyn is a highly overrated literary talent. "The only really good thing he ever wrote was 'Matryona's Home,' " the poet said.* We had absolutely no idea if he really thought Solzhenitsyn was a mediocre writer, if he was speaking for the benefit of a bug that might be in his apartment or if he was simply worried that we might repeat any favorable comment he made about Solzhenitsyn.

On another occasion, we listened to a discourse by another poet to the effect that complete artistic freedom does not exist in any country and the Soviet artist is really no worse off than anyone else. This particular meeting (with a small "m") had been arranged for the benefit of a visiting American poet. Having completed his speech on artistic freedom, the Russian turned to the American and admonished him in an ever-so-light

---

* "Matryona's Home" is a short story about a teacher's life in a house with an old peasant woman after he was released from a prison camp. It was first published in *Novy Mir*.

tone about a remark he had made when he was received earlier in the day by officials of the Soviet Writers' Union. The American, it seemed, had said something about a writer's ability to love his country and nevertheless disagree with some of his government's policies. He said many American writers who loved America were opposed to the war in Vietnam just as the Soviet poet X loved his country but had made a statement opposing the Soviet invasion of Czechoslovakia. "True, I was against sending our troops into Czechoslovakia," the poet told the bewildered American. "But it didn't do me so much good to have you remind them of it." To us, the significant fact was that the poet had, within the space of a few hours, received some static from the Writers' Union about the American's comments.

Censorship was another forbidden topic in conversations with writers. Conservatives who believed in heavy-handed censorship were never hesitant about stating their views, but liberal writers who were constantly struggling to get their words into print would never have jeopardized their chances by talking about their problems with an outsider. They may also have felt that Soviet censorship was a shameful matter to discuss in the presence of a foreigner.

When we met Anatoly Kuznetsov in London several months after his defection, he said, "But naturally they will never talk about censorship in front of you. But when Russian writers who trust each other get together, they speak of it constantly. You couldn't get away from it, it weighed on every writer every moment of his life." Reading the uncensored version of Kuznetsov's novel *Babi Yar* gave us new insight into the writers we knew in Moscow—an insight we could not have gained from talking to them. Among the many lines removed from the original Soviet version published in 1966:

There are always more people to burn books than to write them. You have your life ahead of you, Tolya, so just remember that this is the first sign of trouble—if books are banned, that means things are going wrong.

Other changes made in *Babi Yar* had nothing to do with politics. Scenes of Germans raping Jewish women were cut because they referred too explicitly to sex. Other sentences were chopped for no apparent reason other than the censor's personal taste. What explanation but caprice could there be for deleting a sentence that read, "He was a good-looking child with lovely eyes which looked at Dina as though she was his saviour"?

The Russian intellectuals we knew underestimated us in thinking that we could not understand their situation or, if we did understand, that we would betray their confidences. Vera, who was not as liberal in her political thinking as many of the intellectuals, was easier to talk to because she was more forthright. Her question about the difference between American-style newspaper editing and institutionalized censorship was one I would have liked to discuss with many Soviet writers.

One of the most common mistakes Westerners make is confusing outright political dissidents with the liberal establishment intellectuals. At an international music congress in Moscow, the American violinist Yehudi Menuhin made a speech in which he criticized strict political control of the arts. "We know what such mistakes can cost in terms of lively minds and independent spirits silenced or frozen into impotence by those whose vision is so short and imagination so limited that . . . they can only dominate by isolating all inquiring and questioning."

He praised the works of Solzhenitsyn, the composer Dmitri Shostakovich, cellist Mstislav Rostropovitch and Yevtushenko. "The size, power, depth and meaning of musical and poetic utterances, as those of a Shostakovich, a Solzhenitsyn, a Yevtushenko and many others, are an indication of the vision and greatness of men and women evolving in this vastest of lands."

Menuhin's speech was noteworthy because participants in international conferences held in Moscow usually go along with the polite fiction that Soviet artists are as free as artists anywhere to follow their creative impulses. However, the bracketing of a Yevtushenko and a Solzhenitsyn is absolutely wrong, both in terms of moral and literary stature.

Solzhenitsyn is not an official intellectual; he is officially regarded as a pariah because he has refused to tailor his writings to changing political moods. Yevtushenko is an official intellectual; his works are published, while Solzhenitsyn's are banned. He wrote anti-Stalinist poems during the Khrushchev years, when it was permissible to be anti-Stalinist in print, and now he writes on other topics. His views about Stalinism are presumably unchanged, but he can no longer express them in his public writing.

Members of the official intelligentsia almost never take a stand on political matters unless they feel their own professional interests are threatened. That is why most Moscow intellectuals were stunned by Rostropovich's brilliant public letter defending Solzhenitsyn's right to receive the Nobel prize. Rostropovich opened by saying it was "no secret" that Solzhenitsyn lived at his country home. He wrote that "every man must have the right to think independently without fear and express his opinions about what he knows, what he has personally thought about and experienced and not merely to express with slightly different variations the opinion which has been inculcated in him."

We asked one of our official friends what he thought of the letter. "Interesting," was his only comment. Another unfinished conversation.

One Finished Conversation

The scene was a cocktail party at the U.S. embassy in Moscow for a delegation of visiting American publishers. Vladimir N. Pavlov, a tight-lipped man who was Stalin's translator at Yalta and is now the head editor at Progress Publishers,* approached the president of Random House. How, Pavlov wanted to know, could any American publisher have accepted a book like Philip Roth's *Portnoy's Complaint.*

---

* Progress Publishers specializes in foreign-language books, mainly translations of Soviet writers.

"That book is pornography, absolute dirt," he said. "No Russian would ever want to read it." (It was not entirely clear from the exchange whether Pavlov himself had read the book.)

I broke into the conversation, since I was certain there would never be another opportunity for me to talk to one of Stalin's translators. "How can you be so positive that no Russian would ever want to read *Portnoy*?"

"I am positive became I am a Russian," Pavlov replied. "I have lived in Russia all my life. I know what the Russian people think and feel. Soviet citizens have clean minds and pure souls."

I tried to argue with him. "But I have lived in America most of my life, and I don't know what all Americans think and feel or what books they want to read."

"That is because of the class conflict in capitalist societies. You cannot possibly know what a member of the working class thinks."

"Even if I did know what people thought, I would still have no right to decide what books they should read."

"But I do have that right," Pavlov said curtly. "That is the difference between our system and yours."

CONCLUSION

Tony and i used to joke about what would happen if we invited all our Russian friends to the same party. Their reactions would probably have ranged from embarrassment to intense fear. Vera would have been appalled at being in the same room with Dmitri, because association with an unsavory *samizdatchik* might have blemished the clean record she needed for advancement in the world of official journalism. Dmitri would have been terrified that Vera would report him to her superior in the Party or even to the KGB. Boris Alekseivich would have been depressed by Tanya's ignorance. Tanya would have gawked at Gyusel Amalrik and Oskar Rabin as though they were creatures in a zoo. Only Anatoly Yakovlevich would have enjoyed himself; he doubtless would have offered his picture-framing services to everyone in the room. But most of our friends would have been afraid of each other and, consequently, of us.

Prison camps and insane asylums for political dissenters are not the only significant measures of repression and fear in a society. The Soviet Union is a country where a loyal citizen like Galya would never give me permission to use her real name in a profile. She was not certain what the consequences would be, but she thought they might range from an unpleasant reprimand by her department chairman to dismissal from her institute. She was convinced that being identified in a book written by a foreigner would ruin any chances she might have of a trip to France. (She was probably right.) The prevalence of such fears among politically orthodox Russians defines a repressive system as clearly as the treatment of dissenting minorities.

The Soviet Union is not a terror-ridden society, as it was during the Stalin years. Terror has evolved into repression as arbitrary arrests have been abandoned in favor of selective imprisonment. Boris Alekseivich was sent to a prison camp for doing nothing; the KGB no longer picks random victims. Ordinary citizens do not tremble in fear of a nighttime knock on the door that means the secret police have come to take them away. Official murder is not sanctioned; under Stalin, Vladimir Bukovsky and Andrei Amalrik would surely have been shot. During the Stalin years, men were imprisoned for an indefinite period; new sentences were handed out mechanically as old ones expired. Camp sentences today are issued for a specific term. This is one reason dissidents are more afraid of commitment to insane asylums, where the period of confinement is not specified by law.

If I were asked to describe the Soviet Union in one word, it would be "wasteful." It is a wasteful society both in human and economic terms, whether judged by its own professed standards or in comparison to other countries. The Russians I knew well had one thing in common: Their potentialities were either ignored or underutilized by the Soviet system. In most instances, Soviet society—not the individual—was responsible for the waste. Gyusel is not wasting her life; the ability to remain "life-glad" is so special in any contemporary society that casting out such a person is almost equivalent to exterminating an endangered species. A Soviet official would undoubtedly argue that the Amalriks have rejected the system and, therefore, the system is logical in rejecting them. The same argument would be applied to Rabin because he refuses to paint by the rules. But Russian society also wastes the talents of people who agree with its basic principles and play by all the rules, written and unwritten. Most of Vera's ideas for improving Soviet institutions were fully in accord with Party pronouncements but enough at variance with political and social realities so that they did not make it past the censor. She would be a far more effective journalist if she were not required to spend as much time concealing her real ideas as she does expressing them. Galya would be a better French professor if she had been able to visit France years ago, just as Tanya would become a better English teacher if she were permitted to participate in a student exchange today. In almost every instance, human waste intersects with political repression—whether the repression takes the form of censorship, restrictions on foreign travel or the general policy forbidding open criticism of the regime by its citizens.

When we returned from Moscow, friends invariably asked us. "What are the possibilities for change in the foreseeable future?" Americans usually mean two things by this question: "Will their standard of living improve?" and "Will the country become more democratic?" There is an unspoken assumption that an affirmative reply to the first part guarantees an affirmative reply to the second, as though more cars and refrigerators and baby foods will somehow persuade the Soviets to adopt the Bill of Rights.

Assuming the Russians do not become involved in a major war during the remainder of this century, their standard of living will almost certainly improve—although it will not catch up with the United States, Western Europe or even with the

Socialist countries of Eastern Europe.* If the present rate of housing construction is maintained, communal ·apartments like Galya's can be expected to disappear from large cities within ten to fifteen years. The ordinary Soviet citizen will still live in more cramped quarters than an American or a European, but he will no longer have to share his kitchen and bathroom with other families. More automobiles will be manufactured, and the growing class of university-educated professionals will have access to them. Vera and her scientist husband were on a waiting list for a Volga car and expected their turn to come in about four years. The day when an ordinary blue-collar worker can afford a car is still far away, but he can at least dream. "I don't think I'll ever own a car in my lifetime," Anatoly said, "but I believe my son will."

Government investment in the consumer sector of the economy is increasing, and Russians can see progress, however slow and slight that progress might seem to an outsider. We were able to see some improvements in the standard of living during our two years in Moscow. Flour and eggs were often absent from the shelves of ordinary stores when we arrived, but they were nearly always available by the time we left. In 1969 it was impossible to buy ready-made women's slacks; in 1971 they began to appear on shop racks in large quantities. Several people who were living in communal apartments when we first met them were able to move into separate flats within a year.

I do not see any necessary link between limited economic improvements and political democratization; on the contrary, it seems to me that a better-fed, better-clothed and better-housed people are less likely to question the policies of their government. Will a family that has just acquired its first private bath and kitchen worry about the imprisonment of Amalrik and

---

* By most standards of economic well-being, the Eastern European nations are better off than the Soviet Union. Russian tourists who have been allowed to visit Poland, Hungary, East Germany and Czechoslovakia usually return dazzled by the selection of consumer goods—one reason the Soviet government restricts travel to Socialist as well as capitalist countries.

Bukovsky? The Soviet Union is not immune to the "revolution of rising expectations," but it is a revolution narrowly circumscribed by the censorship that keeps most Russians ill informed about their own country and the rest of the world. A black child in a rat-infested tenement can turn on his television set and envy the seemingly bounteous life of white middle-class America; the opportunity to make comparisons inevitably produces questions about a system that allows such inequities. Ordinary Russians do not have an accurate picture of how ordinary Americans or Englishmen or Frenchmen live. If you show a Russian a photograph of an American factory parking lot and tell him the automobiles belong to the workers, he will probably conclude the picture is a fake. The more sophisticated Russians, who do know something about living conditions in other countries, do not necessarily expect their own country to measure up to the same standards. A one-room apartment is better than a communal apartment; most Russians do not blame the Soviet system because it has failed to provide ranch houses with paneled rec rooms.

Some dissidents do believe that the slow, limited improvement of living standards could work against the regime if it is unable to produce faster, more substantial gains. "People who are starving are thankful for even a morsel of food," a friend told me, "but once the most basic needs are met, a man begins to dream of other things that would never have occurred to him without that morsel of food." Discontent with the rate of material progress could lead to anger at a class system that fails to provide automobiles or a college education for blue-collar workers and their children. However, even the most hopeful dissenters admit that traditional Russian passivity in the face of authority could prove more powerful than rising expectations.

Some Russians, like Anatoly, would like their own houses. However, they are generally unable to grasp the concept of a system under which the individual, not the government, chooses the type of housing in which he will live. When he spoke of Party bigshots with *dachas*, Anatoly's tone was one of wry resignation rather than indignation. The old Russian attitude that government means "Them" ruling "Us" was not abolished by the revolution, nor has it disappeared in the generation since Stalin's death. This deep strain in Russian thought was summed up in Tanya's statement about emigration restrictions: "The state has the right to control its citizens." The corollary is expressed perfectly in a dialogue from *Fiddler on the Roof:*

"Rabbi, do you have a blessing for the Tsar?"
"May God bless and keep the Tsar—far away from us."

Westerners often assume that future generations of party leaders will be more pragmatic and receptive to proposals for change than the present generation. The top leaders are now in their mid-sixties, while the second ranks are in their fifties. Unless there is a major upheaval in the Party, the men who will move into important political positions during the next decade are already in their forties; they spent their formative years during the Stalin era. They may or may not favor individual reforms, but they are unlikely to promote fundamental changes in the system. There is not even any evidence that Party members in their thirties are more liberal than their elders. Vera told me that her ideas for modest social reforms were not shared by many of the more conservative Party members in her age group.

If my estimation of the powerful forces operating against change is correct, it would seem illogical for the Soviet government to react so strongly against any expression of dissenting opinion. "Why do they bother to arrest a few people whom no one pays any attention to anyway?" asked a visiting journalist. Most foreigners simply do not understand that intolerance of all minority opinion, however small or insignificant the minority, is a fundamental feature of the Soviet system. My husband wrote an article based on interviews with Jewish acquaintances suggesting that a majority of Soviet Jews disapproved of the Jewish Defense League's activities in the United

States. He was astonished when he received an official warning from the press department based on two paragraphs in which he noted that a minority of Jews felt the JDL was doing them a service by publicizing the plight of Soviet Jewry. We were talking about the incident with a Russian friend who said, "You still don't understand this place, after eighteen months. Everything has to be one hundred percent to please our leaders. How dare you write about the one or two or three percent who disagree?"

The second and equally important reason for the seemingly disproportionate official reaction to dissent is that the dissidents keep the possibility of change alive. Their existence does not make change likely; it does increase the possibilities slightly.

The Soviet dissenters are not an organization but a diverse collection of people who have at least one thing in common: the courage to speak or write publicly about what they regard as oppressive aspects of the regime. They range from reformers who believe that democratization is possible within the framework of a Communist system to more radical dissenters like Bukovsky, who ideally would like to see the formation of a multiparty parliamentary democracy.

Zhores Medvedev, a biochemist whose specialty is the genetics of aging, is one of the reformers who believes both in Communism and individual liberty. His main argument for reform is the relationship between political repression and waste. In his voluminous work *The Medvedev Papers*, he details official restrictions on the international contacts of Soviet scientists. He describes the almost insurmountable bureaucratic obstacles facing any Russian scientist who wants to travel abroad for extended study or research and the equally negative attitude of the authorities toward the idea of foreign scientists working in Soviet institutions. He notes that Charles Darwin could never have become the founder of modern biology if he had been a Soviet citizen, because he never would have received an exit visa for the long trips needed to gather information on the origin of species. Medvedev argues forcefully that his country cannot fulfill its own scientific or economic potential unless it ends the undemocratic restrictions that originated during the Stalin era:

> The Soviet Union is a great country with greater potentialities than the USA, let alone the countries of Europe. The scale of problems, so important for science, is at a maximum in our country. We have developed our own ideology, which has greatly increased the patriotic tendencies of the people and their national pride. These are all important moral factors which guarantee stability. So large and rich a country in conditions of greater democratization would invariably become not a source of a "brain drain" but a center of attraction.*

His patriotic but pointed criticism earned Medvedev a three-week stay in a mental hospital in the spring of 1971. He was released after protests from prominent Soviet and foreign scientists; few prominent Soviet figures are willing to risk their necks on behalf of more radical dissenters like Bukovsky.

The reformers and dissidents tend to agree that most of what is wrong with their country can be traced to an inability and unwillingness to purge itself of the Stalinist inheritance. I felt this to be especially true of the human waste I encountered. Boris Alekseivich is perhaps the most obvious example; his entire life was laid waste by his senseless arrest in 1935. His life has been wasted not only in the camps, but also during the years since his release in 1956. He emerged from his imprisonment with a sick body but an unbroken mind; I feel certain he would have been eager to aid in the rejuvenation of a Party determined to rid itself of the vestiges of Stalinism. Instead, he was given a document of "rehabilitation," a pension and the right to a life of anonymous silence. He watched as the partial de-Stalinization of the Khrushchev years was halted under the new Brezhnev-Kosygin leadership. The only figures in Soviet society whom Boris Alekseivich admires are men like Bukovsky.

* *The Medvedev Papers*, p. 160.

"I'm too old for all that now," he said. "But they [the dissidents] are the greatest waste of all. I was like them when I was young; I didn't know I was helping to found a system that would oppress them."

Without having met men like Bukovsky and Amalrik, it is difficult to comprehend fully the foolishness and tragedy of a society that can only deal with them by imprisonment. Volodya Bukovsky is a brilliant young man. Before he became an important figure in the dissident movement, he was a writer of *samizdat* short stories. The link between literature and political dissent is one reason the authorities react so strongly to unorthodox minority opinion; the printed word has immense moral force in a country where honest writers have risked death and continue to face imprisonment. Foreigners who penetrate the surface of Russian life are usually surprised by the moral significance Russians attribute to literature; writers and writing do not occupy a comparable place in any Western country. The names of Mandelstam, Akhmatova, Pasternak and Solzhenitsyn do not reappear in my conversations with Russians because I brought them up; my Russian friends awakened me to their importance.

Bukovsky, who is only thirty, has spent the better part of the past ten years in mental institutions or prison camps because of his dissident activities. He was first committed to a psychiatric hospital in 1963 for arranging an underground art exhibit and again in 1965 for organizing a demonstration against the arrests of Sinyavsky and Daniel. (This demonstration took place before the 1966 trial.) Two years later, he was sent to a prison camp for his role in another public protest on behalf of two dissident writers who had themselves been arrested after they took up the cause of Sinyavsky and Daniel. Released from camp in January, 1970, he was rearrested in April, 1971—this time under a severe statute dealing with "agitation or propaganda carried on for the purpose of subverting or weakening Soviet authority or of committing particular, especially dangerous crimes against the State. . . ."

His crime was the continuation of political protests, in letters and petitions to Soviet officials and in interviews with foreign journalists. He taught himself English from a dictionary while he was in camp because he wanted to be able to communicate with foreigners who did not speak Russian. He spoke out most forcefully against the confinement of political dissenters in insane asylums, describing the use of drugs which he said turned intelligent men into "human vegetables" and of a wet canvas roll into which inmates were put so that it shrank on them as it dried. As a result of his own "treatment" in a mental hospital, Bukovsky emerged from his second confinement with a chronic heart murmur and serious rheumatic ailments.

The last time we saw him was in March, 1971, a few weeks before his arrest. He had been sick for several weeks, and he was having so much difficulty breathing that he did not follow his usual practice of meeting us at the foot of the apartment stairs. He was afraid the climb back up might put him in bed again. As he made tea for us and a third American journalist, I had a premonition that we would not see him again.

My diary notes for the following day read:

"I am haunted by the way Volodya looked. I think of his fate with great sadness; it will surely be more imprisonment, until he dies of his heart trouble or really is an old man. At least he doesn't have a wife like Gyusel, who can look forward to a lifetime of waiting for her husband and writing letters to prison camps. I find myself crying today when I think about him. I shouldn't; better than almost anyone I know, he accepts the consequences of his actions. But damn—the waste of it all—the talent and energy and dedication. Where do they find the strength to wait for the inevitable with such good grace?"

Bukovsky always expected to be imprisoned again, and if he does not emerge a complete invalid, he will doubtless resume his activities and doubtless be rearrested. In the United States, he might be a defense lawyer specializing in civil liberties' cases or a Ralph Nader. "Or maybe he'd be in jail here, just like the Berrigan brothers," said an American newspaper editor who seemed to possess the odd conviction that anyone who was against Soviet repression must be in favor of repression in the United States. In any event, his analogy is inaccurate. A case can be made that the Berrigan brothers should never have gone to prison, but they were convicted for the specific act of burning draft records (assuming that John Mitchell and company will never be successful in selling the phantasmagoria of a plot to kidnap Henry Kissinger to a jury). Bukovsky and Amalrik are not in camp for burning Soviet draft records, throwing rocks through the windows of government buildings or disrupting traffic. They are imprisoned only because they have expressed ideas that contradict the official Soviet version of reality. It is a crime to ask the question, "Will the Soviet Union survive until 1984?"

Bukovsky believes it is vital to publicize every instance of political repression—the imprisonment of Amalrik for writing books, the commitment of an obscure religious dissenter to an insane asylum, job dismissals of Jews who have applied to emigrate to Israel. He wants the regime's acts to be known both inside and outside of the Soviet Union, so that there can never be a return to the silent terror of the Stalin years. That is why he gave many interviews to foreign journalists in Moscow. In an interview taped by William Cole, a former correspondent for the Columbia Broadcasting System, Bukovsky said:

"The essence of the struggle, in my view, is the struggle against fear—the fear which has gripped the people since the time of Stalin and which still has not left them, and thanks to which this system continues to exist—the system of dictatorship, of pressure, of oppression. It is into this struggle against fear that we put our greatest efforts, *and in that struggle great importance attaches to personal example*—the example which we give people.

"I personally did what I considered right, spoke out on those occasions when I wanted to, and I'm alive. I am now sitting here and not in prison. I'm alive, I can get about, I can live. For me and for many people that is very important—it shows that it is possible to fight, and that it is necessary."

I feel certain that Bukovsky still believes his own example has not been wasted, despite the fact that his heart condition could kill him in prison and that if he *does* survive, he will not be allowed to return from exile until he is in his early forties. At his trial, he said his only regret was that he had been unable to do more for the cause of human rights during his fifteen months of freedom.

The power of personal example may be what the Soviet authorities fear most. The dissidents "bear witness" to their personal philosophies in the early Christian sense. Some Soviet officials must ask themselves the question that Dmitri posed: What might happen if writers simply stopped submitting their manuscripts for official publication? Or if large numbers of scientists stopped cooperating with the system? The officials undoubtedly decide that neither possibility is likely, but a tiny flicker of uncertainty may remain. That is why they find it necessary to fight the dissidents, even though they are only a minority without access to any means of mass communication.

Volodya Bukovsky's grandmother always used to recite an old Russian folk rhyme as she walked past the Kremlin's Spassky Tower with her small grandson:

> *What proud man could lift the Bell*
> *Or move the Royal Cannon's weight,*
> *Or be slow to doff his cap*
> *At the Kremlin's holy gate!*

"I always tried to imagine that proud man," Bukovsky wrote in a short story. "There he was, standing at the Spassky Gate, hands on hips and looking up, with his head flung so far back that his cap almost fell off. And he looked so valiant!"